FREEDOM AND ORTHODOXY

FREEDOM AND ORTHODOXY

*Islam and Difference in the
Post-Andalusian Age*

Anouar Majid

STANFORD UNIVERSITY PRESS

STANFORD, CALIFORNIA

2004

Stanford University Press
Stanford, California

©2004 by the Board of Trustees of the
Leland Stanford Junior University.

Part of this book was previously published as
"Birth of an Arab Nation" in *Edebiyât* 17,
no. 1 (1996):115–26. Permission to reproduce
it here has been granted by the publisher,
Taylor and Francis, http://www.tandf.co.uk.

Printed in the United States of America
on acid-free, archival-quality paper

Library of Congress Cataloging-in-Publication Data

Majid, Anouar, 1960–
    Freedom and orthodoxy : Islam and difference in a
post-Andalusian age / Anouar Majid.
        p. cm.
    Includes bibliographical references and index.
    ISBN 0-8047-4980-9 (alk. paper) —
    ISBN 0-8047-4981-7 (pbk. : alk. paper)
    1. Orientalism.   2. East and West.   3. Islam—20th
century.   I. Title.
DS61.85 .M35 2004
306'.0917'67—DC22

                                        2003022051

Typeset by Tim Roberts in 10/13.5 Adobe Garamond

Original Printing 2004

Last figure below indicates year of this printing:
13   12   11   10   09   08   07   06   05   04

Contents

Preface

This book is an attempt to explore the rise and effects of European universalist and messianic ideologies after the defeat of Islam in Spain and how such ideologies have inspired the various forms of extremism that have erupted regularly in the course of modern history since 1492, or what might be better termed the *post-Andalusian* period. The focus will be on the reconfiguration of Islam in this new global order, both the ways Islam came to be perceived by Western imperial societies and the way Muslims have redefined themselves in the process of defending their identities. Building on the argument I advanced in *Unveiling Traditions: Postcolonial Islam in a Polycentric World* (2000), I want to argue, by examining crucial periods in a long span of history, that we are living under the dark cloud not of an ominous clash of civilizations, but of a world order racing headlong toward a global wasteland, an apocalyptic landscape that will ultimately engulf winners and losers alike. It is not the clash of civilizations that threatens world peace and harmony, but the failure of our *one and only* human civilization to capitalize on its tremendously rich cultural resources to establish a more humane global order. This civilization, made up of multiple and diverse components, succumbs to further injury when these components resort to violence and conquest to resolve differences, for if only the annihilation of Others, those who are intractably different, those who are attached to their ancestral ways, guarantees peace and security, then even total victory will turn out to be a catastrophic defeat for all. A monochrome world of clones is not the pinnacle of human achievement, but an index of our inability to transcend atavistic instincts in order to live up to our noblest ideals. Thus, the urgency of preserving the world's cultures and religions is not necessarily driven by religious faith, patriotic sentiments, or ethnic solidarity, but by the basic will to survive and, in the very best of circumstances, the hope to forge a new philosophy of rapprochement among and within nations. Only if we become aware of the impact of our deeply rooted narratives of self-righteousness and our own (barely discernible) convictions can we begin to address the world's global crisis. To be sure, our own fundamentalist attitudes may not be the reflection of ill will or malice and may very well be the expression of a noble quest for human solidarity and oneness. Still, paradoxically, it is this drive to save the world that is constantly endangering it.

I begin in 1492, the year when the world was called upon to adhere to the Euro-American vision of human salvation or risk ostracism, defeat, and even, in some cases, annihilation. To talk about a Euro-American (or, more broadly, Western) vision is not to imply that citizens of European and American societies are not passionately divided over policies and missions or that nations within the West are not at odds over issues of power and global peace. Indeed, as I am writing this (spring 2003), the West seems to be splitting into camps, leading to further polarizations and re-arrangements in the global political structure. There may be several explanations for these cracks in the Western body politic, but the perennial and dramatic U.S.-French contretemps (to take the two major players in this episode of discord) is not merely a contingent affair that stems from geopolitical maneuvering, but is the expression of an enduring clash of two powerful universal ideologies, for both nations, as I explain in the introductory chapter, inaugurated the most far-reaching revolutions in modern human history, each with its own separate concepts of liberty and justice, although both eventually found themselves mired in imperial ventures that did little to globalize the great ideals they espoused.[1]

I find it useful to keep this historical perspective in mind when trying to make sense of global events after 9/11 and during the crisis over Iraq. Much has been said about the motives of neoconservative hawks and the oil bonanza that would accrue to well-connected U.S. companies in the aftermath of the war, but such analyses, no matter how important, leave out the *longue durée* of American history and how U.S. intervention is also part of an impulse (one that has admittedly mutated over time) that goes back to the beginning of European settlement in America. After he was sworn in as president of the United States on 20 January 2001, George W. Bush saw himself as part of an unfolding American plan to bring light to the world. Except for the modern idiom of the text, his speech could have easily been made by a Puritan preacher or a Founding Father. For the new president, America's story is that "of a new world that became a friend and liberator of the old," while America's "democratic faith" is, in fact, "the inborn hope of our humanity, an ideal we carry but do not own, a trust we bear and pass along." As in the much older prophetic traditions, America is entrusted with the awesome burden of leading the world to freedom and confounding evil designs on the purity of its mission. Even during that relatively quiet moment in world history, a concern for security permeated the president's speech: Not only should America be strong to dissuade potential rivals from catching up with the country's military might (a prospect, given the vastly advanced arsenal of the United States, that has become, for the first time in history, virtually impossible to achieve in the foreseeable future), but it must also "confront weapons of mass destruction, so that a new century is spared new horrors." Two years later, as the world was bracing for a military confrontation in Iraq, and many were suspicious of the administration's designs, the American president delivered his annual State of the Union Address repeating his assertion that the role of his nation is simply to emancipate all humanity into freedom. "Americans," President Bush stated confidently, "are a free people, who know that freedom is the right of every person and the future of every nation. The liberty we prize is not America's gift to the world, it is God's gift to humanity." Indeed, the language of religious salvation, upon which the country was founded, and that of the Revolution, which brought the new secular nation into being, were merged into an indistinguishable ideology. "We Americans," Bush assured his fellow citizens and the rest of the world, "have faith in ourselves but not in ourselves alone. We do not claim to know all the ways of Providence, yet we can trust in them, placing our confidence in the loving God behind all of life, and all of history." A little more than two months later, after his forces had defeated the Ba'ath regime, the president thanked his troops on the aircraft carrier *Abraham Lincoln* and reminded them that theirs is a war for the security of their country and the freedom of the world's people. He then concluded by quoting the prophet Isaiah.[2]

Again, one could read all sorts of motives into Bush's message, as many critics later did when he launched a war against the bloodthirsty regime of Saddam Hussein in Iraq, but it would be rather simplistic to reduce this discourse of freedom to a mere smokescreen for an elaborate plot to profit from Iraqi oil.[3] To me, it appeared as the manifestation of a strain that is part of a larger and complex history, one that not only began with the American Revolution (to which the president alludes in his inaugural address), but goes back further in time to the early colonial set-

tlers and even to the Spanish conquistadors before them in other parts of
the Americas. What unites the Iberian conquests of the New World, the
British settlements in North America, and the American Revolution is not
only a quest for freedom, but also a messianic will to (re-)Christianize or
remake the world anew. (Hence, the agenda of reshaping the Middle East
is perfectly consistent with this enduring pattern.) These three moments
in history forged a fundamentalist view of the world, a multigenerational
social imaginary that I prefer to call post-Andalusianism—nowadays encoded in the economic system of capitalism—that is almost unbendingly
universal in outlook and that tolerates no alternatives in the management
of human affairs.

Yet the world is complex and made up of hundreds of different cultural heritages, each relying on a set of memories and myths that have
nothing to do with the European "discovery" of America, Europe's religious wars, the Puritans' dream of a Christian utopia, or the philosophies
of the Enlightenment. Aren't non-Western people entitled to build on
their heritages and live within systems that don't do violence to their
memories? Wouldn't they feel freer if they could worship their own gods
without being pressured to subscribe to what is often known as the "neoliberal" dogma? Indeed, I will argue that to encourage cultural independence could potentially reduce pressure on the world system by making it easier for people to live within their means. It is, in fact, the
Euro-American insistence on only one model, a one-size-fits-all approach
to human freedom, that ultimately breeds the extremisms that haunt the
world's imagination and threaten human civilization with unforeseen perils. If the West doesn't examine its own fundamentalism, as Hubert Védrine, France's former minister of foreign affairs suggested in February
2003, the future of cultural dialogue and the prospect for innovative Islamic thinking look even grimmer: Because the West's population is expected to be a mere 10 percent of the world's population by 2025 (down
from a third in 1900, the heyday of imperialism), the West will have no
option but to further militarize its borders against waves of desperate immigrants and refugees seeking survival, and intervening in dysfunctional
spots to protect the vast majority of poor nations' resources under its control. How will the West build better relations with the Chinese or Muslims, who, together, already encompass "70 percent of oil reserves and
nearly two-thirds of the global population"?[4] These are the questions that
animate this project and inform the context through which I make sense
of the crisis in Western-Muslim relations.

   This book, therefore, is not interested in short-term political conflicts or in defending one religion, culture, or nation at the expense of another. (Ethnic, economic, racial, religious, and political fundamentalisms are all premised on exclusionary outlooks that ultimately undermine the quest for an international *modus vivendi*.) Under the shadow of the West's supremacy, Islam—with its strong cultural heritage and large number of adherents (about of one-fifth of humanity) occupying significant portions of the globe—has become the absolute image of Otherness in the West's popular imagination not only because of many Muslims' chronic inability to work out the tensions between religious obligation and the pressures of a Western-dictated modernity, but also because much of the Euro-American identity and worldview were born out of a strong crusading spirit motivated by the eventual defeat of Islam. The transfer of Granada to King Ferdinand and Queen Isabella in 1492 opened a new chapter in world history, although not a radically new one, since it builds on even older hostilities. From that fateful moment, as Spain's subsequent history in the New World shows, anyone who didn't fully embrace Western religious and cultural precepts became unholy, a dangerous alien to be hastily reformed or summarily executed. The cultural options that had marked the history of nations and that allowed for a fragile, but still workable structure of coexistence in al-Andalus—Muslim Spain—gave way to a series of uniform, inflexible, and intolerant philosophies. (Much like the Inquisition, whose ultimate purpose was the saving of souls and the purification of the faith, the modern secular Euro-American worldview rejects the possibility of multiple paths to the "pursuit of happiness.") The fury and zeal of the *Reconquista*, the Christian reconquest of Spain from the Moors, fell on all forms of difference, making American Indians and Muslims interchangeable in the Iberian—and later, Western—imaginary. Indeed, all difference since then has been construed in the image of Muslims, since it was the ideology of the *Reconqusita* that, in many ways, created the ideological foundations of the modern world.

   With the triumph of the nascent West over non-European Christians, Muslims and Native Americans went through several cycles of resistance and defeat, and Islam has been plunging ever since into an abyss of orthodox obscurantism, forever embellishing a past that has been as messy and bloody as any other international civilization that has gone through a similar historical cycle. But in the face of several defeats, Muslim orthodoxy became more virulent and now seems to erupt with frightening violence, not only against Westerners, but also against other Muslims. (The moralizing language of the righteous cuts across all cultures and nations. Didn't Pascal, the seventeenth-century French essayist, warn that those who aspire to being angels ultimately turn into beasts?) Although not directly linked to it, the current wave of religious extremism cannot be dissociated from the failure of globalization, presented as an indispensable part of a packet of democratic reforms, to address fundamental human needs around the globe. As long as the current system remains in place, the West's ideological certainties will continue to be resisted (partly because globalization promises what it cannot deliver), even as many Western remedies are being adopted in a desperate attempt to catch up with the West and to match its powers. Much like the rest of the world's poor, the Muslims' Sisyphean quest for an unattainable prosperity and power aggravates the sense of frustration that fuels violent reactions.

Given the failure of universalist ideologies in the last five hundred years to build structures of peace and dialogue and the bleak prospects awaiting human civilization, a strategic imperative for enlightened communities and the world's political leaders should be the long-term health of the planet and its cultures, not the short-term victory of one nation, religion, or tradition over another. To achieve this goal, we need to have a more accurate sense of the dangers confronting us, measure the limits of our knowledge, and realize that we are all provincial, trapped in social imaginaries that do not allow us to think about what is best for others without projecting or forcing our values onto them. Whether we speak in the name of a god, liberty, or free markets, the time has come to resist the temptation to theorize about or dictate what's good for the whole world, without, of course, relinquishing the common bonds that tie all humans, and, in fact, the whole natural world together. Allowing other nations to live within their means and produce their own food and industries may reduce the profit margins of multinational corporations, but only small-scale, locally based economies, sustained by the ascetic demands of religious cultures and precapitalist traditions, could allow people to live with less without feeling left out or humiliated. By reclaiming their native traditions, people's lives could become richer in more ways than one. Besides, what other options do we have? The planet simply cannot endow the whole world with the levels of affluence enjoyed in the United States, regardless of the political systems in place.

In talking about the effects of Western power on others and how such power produces violent reactions, I do not want the reader to understand that I am accusing Westerners of the evils of history or exculpating others from responsibility. Those who do so accept quite a simplistic view of human motives and assign extraordinary agency to people who are often constricted by their cultural environments and trying to do their best to survive in what they see as an unsafe world. If Western culture has arrogated to itself the global responsibility of converting others to its ways, that does not mean, as I stated earlier, that those who equate their provincial beliefs with a universal human good are necessarily guilty of bad intentions. On the contrary, the globalizing impulse, despite its arrogant connotations, is an implicit admission of the West's connectedness to its Others, an ironic affirmation of the West's deeply held belief that all human history is part of a global plan, although it is one in which the West occupies a privileged place. But there is no denying the fact that Western civilization in the last few centuries has forever changed human destiny. Even those extremists who fight the West in the name of an undiluted Islam rely on a vocabulary that was forged in the West's own (violent) quest for freedom. The only question left, I suppose, is how to rescue the great Western cultural heritage from the forces that undermine it, such as economic systems driven by very short-term and anticommunal interests, and how to convince Muslim extremists that cultural borrowings and cosmopolitanism is the essence of the Qur'anic tradition, one that has been usurped by ethnic and patriarchal chauvinism. After all, no culture or religion is an island unto itself.

I am alluding to issues that will be more fully elaborated in the course of the book. As the quest for freedom continues, Westerners and Muslims are called upon to make a valiant effort to resist the temptation to convert Others, to see Others as needing salvation or death. Those who blame Islam for being conservative need to understand how their own assumptions have fed that conservatism. Muslims must be lured out of their defensive orthodoxy by allowing them, as François Burgat suggested, to participate in a "consensual modernity" with truly universal dimensions, one that is not imposed in the name of a false universality.[5] (Interestingly, just as the world's poor are afraid of being swept up by a Western-imposed modernity, Europeans feel the same about the U.S.-led process of globalization. Even when Clinton was still in office, European polls and publications indicated that Europeans were seriously worried about disregard for their culture by the United States, particularly since they don't identify with many American practices and values.)[6] By surveying various moments in the postcolonial age, by carefully reading key texts, and by showing the double legacy of the West's universalist ideologies, I want to invite readers to consider the argument that only by reducing rampant economic disparities, by deliberately provincializing our outlooks without impoverishing our intellectual pursuits or narrowing the scope of our vision, and by acquiring the courage to search for a formula of coexistence that would allow the world to be one in its multiplicity can we make a difference. The world's free citizens must all unite, as Marc Ferro urged in the conclusion of *Le choc de l'Islam*, to challenge the global inequalities that produce despair.[7] If one adds to these imperatives resisting the temptation to legislate for nations with whose language and cultures we are unfamiliar and accepting our irreducibly provincial dispositions, we will have increased the prospects for dialogue significantly. I know that no self-respecting cosmopolitan wants to be called "provincial," but the truth is, there are no citizens of the world either, because we are all as hopelessly embedded in the traditions or legacies that shaped us. To know the limits of our ways is, in fact, to be closer to our fellow humans in spirit. It is a recognition of what we truly have in common.

Provincial as I am, I have had the good fortune of knowing Jacques Downs, who, once again, by passing on to me a Book of the Month monograph on the history of Islam and the United States during the Revolutionary era, expanded my horizons beyond my expectations. I had been casually interested in the early history of Islam in America, but it was Robert J. Allison's *The Crescent Obscured: The United States and the Muslim World, 1776–1815*, first published in 1995, that enlarged my vistas and led me into the study of Barbary captivity narratives and their historical context. As I stated in my review of the book in the *Journal of American Studies of Turkey* (*JAST*), portions of which are republished here, Professor Allison's book is, in my estimation, a groundbreaking study of U.S.-Muslim relations in the late eighteenth and early nineteenth centuries because it foregrounds much of what is happening today in a richer historical context. I am profoundly grateful to Professor Allison for his scrupulously researched work and for being such a constant source of information and support.

I am also grateful to a number of people who have prompted me to write papers that now form part of this book. Professor Susan Goodman of the University of Delaware encouraged me to write and present on Edith

Wharton's *In Morocco*, for the Edith Wharton Society at the MLA; the University of Minnesota's MacArthur Program and Department of Cultural Studies prompted me to write two papers that I read or discussed when I visited in February and March of 2002; Pamela Nice of the University of St. Thomas and Raj Sethuraju of Gustavus Adolphus College, both in Minnesota, motivated me to write about Islam, culture, and globalization when they kindly invited me to address these issues at their respective institutions. Professor Michael Beard, the co-editor of the journal *Edebiyât*, gave me the opportunity to read and review Abdelrahman Munif's *Cities of Salt* trilogy, now incorporated in this book.

Nabil Matar's passionate engagements with some of my assumptions and his prolific output and truly groundbreaking insights on relations between Arabs and Muslims in the early modern period have enriched my intellectual life, while Paul Baepler's pioneering study of Barbary captivity narratives has been crucial in the elaboration of my more modest project on the subject. My colleagues at the University of New England and its English department made my life rewarding in more ways than they can imagine, while the generosity of my friends and love of my family have sustained me in times of stress and constantly remind that there is no reason for our brief journey on earth not to be all "sweetness and light."

The book's various editors at Stanford University Press have been extremely helpful throughout the process of turning the manuscript into the book you now hold in your hands. Dr. Alan Harvey's initial encouragement and friendly guidance set the tone for a most rewarding intellectual journey. Kim Lewis Brown's meticulous attention to detail ensured the timely production of the catalog copy and delivery of the manuscript to Tim Roberts who oversaw the editorial process with much care and superb professionalism. The manuscript's copyeditor, Bud Bynack, an American Studies scholar and expert on Daniel Webster, used his vast knowledge of the American idiom and culture to straighten out my stylistic lapses and to engage me in a most rewarding (and occasionally funny) conversation. Barbara Roos put together the index in a timely fashion. To them all, and others who worked on the production process, my sincere thanks.

Finally, I still count my blessings for having grown up in a city that quickly disabuses its dwellers of any ambitions they might harbor for perfection. In Tangier, some of us knew that we were too hopelessly human ever to worry about turning into Pascalian beasts. We dreamed of better times, but there were no saints among us.

FREEDOM AND ORTHODOXY

By "colonialism"—another debatable word—we mean all European expansion at least since 1492.

—Fernand Braudel, *A History of Civilizations*

CHAPTER I

Disorienting Theories

Now it does not seem important or even desirable to be "right" and in place (right at home, for instance). Better to wander out of place, not to own a house, and not ever to feel too much at home anywhere, especially in a city like New York, where I shall be until I die.
　　—Edward Said, *Out of Place*

In grateful memory of an Arab American, Christian Muslim scholar who lit our path and passed away in New York City when this book was in the final stages of production.

　　The recent history of imperialism and colonialism, combined with mounting hostilities and suspicions between cultures, particularly between the world of Islam and the "West," have hardened the polarities generated by Edward Said's thesis of Orientalism, although—and one cannot emphasize this enough—such an outcome had never been the intention of the author. Now that the notion of Orientalism has entered the cultural mainstream, its effect has been to conjure a picture of two irreconcilably different worlds—a villainous West, with its white ruling classes, and the world of other, nonwhite folk, wounded by various stratagems of oppression and domination. Orientalism, over time and probably by overuse, has turned into a concept akin to the term "racism," a word that generates a series of conflicting emotions that have the uncanny power of hobbling any lucid critical analysis of a given situation involving whites and blacks in a regime long operating under apartheid rules favoring whites of European descent. The challenge that always arises in such a racially fraught context, such as the one in the United States, is to determine the limits of critique, particularly if critical work on a subject involving blacks is conducted by "whites." At what point does a "white" person's honest critique of a "black" person's work and culture merge into the insidious discourse of racism? Since such boundaries are malleable and totally unpredictable (meaning that they could be manipulated to stifle criticism), well-meaning, nonracist "whites" might find themselves constrained by the larger social conditions of their culture and ironically forced to retreat back into the very racial essences they oppose, instead of opening out into the oneness necessary for a deracialized, truly liberated world. In such an environment, only blacks will be authorized to criticize their culture if "whites" want to avoid the charge of racism.[1] Hence, sensitivity to "black" concerns is itself a form of racial categorization, since such sensitivity recognizes that the races are "different" and implicitly acknowledges the privilege of whites in an apartheid regime.

Something like this, but not quite the same, has been generated by Said's concept of Orientalism, despite the fact that Said's unfailingly nuanced argument nowhere essentializes and is regularly punctuated by disclaimers, caveats, and cautionary emphases on his irreducibly cosmopolitan worldview, his unambiguous rejection of religious fundamentalism, and his unshakable commitment to secularism as the only outlet we have to escape false cultural antagonisms. Said's paradigmatic argument, we must remember, is that a major field of scholarship was strongly shaped by Christian Europe's old antagonisms with Islam and that such animosities began to take the form of objective scholarship (philology, anthropology, and, later, social sciences) that turned into self-perpetuating, guildlike professions in Euro-American universities. Frozen into a distorted essence, the Orient—a dreamlike state that is both fantasy and historically real—appears less as a material place than a legacy of discourse. It is, as is well known, an epistemological category, one whose ultimate purpose is to prove the advanced state of Euro-American cultures.

Just as racism can easily be demonstrated in a thousand details of daily life, there is no doubt that the theory of Orientalism can be amply illustrated in a long list of European and American writings, and it would be numbingly repetitious to try to show the way it works in the present. I still come across good examples of the Orientalist mind, as defined by Said and others, in my home-delivered newspaper or in the myriad magazines and publications that address the topics of Islam, Arabs, or even non-Westerners in general. In fact, the degree of the Arabs and Muslims' self-Orientalizing has become all too shockingly real in many newspapers in the Islamic world. An example that struck me recently, while I was visiting my native Morocco, is the identity discourses in newly established personal ads sections in the printed press. Moroccans are now categorizing themselves racially, with the color black seldom appearing as desirable (at least not in a physical sense). Most frequently, we read that such a seeker of romance or "friendship" is "dark-skinned" or "olive" (*asmar*), and occasionally we come across a lucky person who unhesitatingly describes himself or herself as "white." No place better exemplifies the absorption of the United States' racial categories, forged in the latter's own peculiar history, into the Arab mindset, and yet such descriptions are taken as signs of modernity and openness, even perhaps of Morocco's inexorable march toward democracy, with scarcely anyone noticing or writing about the insidiousness of such a radical change in self-perception or even worrying about the long-term social effects of such mythologized conceptions of the Moroccan/Muslim self. Although one would be hard-pressed to find a good Moroccan who is not against racism, it is through the discursive practices of personal ads that one can measure the extent to which the cultural expressions of one society penetrate and weave their logic around another social reality. Judging from this newly established genre alone, one would have to deduce that Moroccans are becoming more racially conscious—and racist, since race is becoming an openly acknowledged and legitimate factor in establishing human bonds and relationships—in the modern sense of the words.

While rightly celebrated for its paradigmatic influence on a number of scholarly fields, Said's expansive theory has been limited by its lack of attention to three major moments in world history, at least in its post-Andalusian phase. One of the thorniest aspects of Said's theory is, of course, the intractable question of representation. Even Bernard Lewis's famous rebuttal to Said seems most convincing—or least refutable—when he simply decides that the question of representation, at the heart of Said's condemnation of Orientalist scholarship, is a universal "epistemological problem" applicable equally to Orientalists and their accusers.[2] Ross Chambers wrestles with the same issue and resigns to the inescapable fact that unbiased scholarship is (at best) a "necessary illusion," thus proving to be more generous than Amal Rassam, who faults Said for sidestepping the issue and never directly tackling the problem.[3] James Clifford's classic essay on Orientalism sums up most of the objections raised by Said against others. *Orientalism* is beset from the outset by the "predicament" of ambiguity, a condition that is symptomatic of "the new global situation" and not merely reflective of the book's anti-imperialist tenor. The book, in this reading, is rightly qualified as "polemical," partly, one assumes, because it "operates in a number of registers."[4]

I am not interested in discussing the scope of Said's coverage of the Orientalist tradition or in evaluating the growing literature and critical studies on the author,[5] but in the "substantial and disquieting set of questions [raised by Said] about the ways in which distinct groups of humanity (however defined) imagine, describe, and comprehend each other," as Clifford puts it. Said seems to address the issue by choosing not to address it, by embracing the Nietzschean method of suspecting totalities and advocating "cosmopolitan essences." This won't do for Clifford, who wants to uphold a notion of "cultural" difference, especially if cultural differences are "seen as not simply received from tradition, language, or environment but also as made in new political-cultural conditions of global reality."[6] I think Clifford is right to resist such Nietzschean moves, but upholding the notion of culture does not diminish the centrality of the question implicitly raised by Said in his book. Said is not attacking cultures, but the way cultures misrepresent one another and thus aggravate tensions, enmities, and oppression. Can cultures maintain their differences without vilifying their Others?

To pose the question in simpler terms: Isn't identity necessarily an exclusionary act that must have its Others in order to be itself? The discourse (or perhaps structure) of identity is a fundamental existential dilemma that may very well inform some of what Said strenuously critiques in the Orientalist tradition. Othering others, by Said's own admission, is intrinsic to being human. "It is perfectly natural," says Said, "for the human mind to resist the assault on it of untreated strangeness; therefore cultures have always been inclined to impose complete transformations on other cultures not as they are but as, for the benefit of the receiver, they ought to be."[7] But the problem with the Westerner seems to be that he sees the Orient as part of the West and so "the Orientalist makes it his work to be always converting the Orient from something into something else: he does this for himself, for the sake of his culture, in some cases for what he believes is the sake of the Oriental." In other words, Westerners have taken a natural response mechanism of conversion and given it "the self-containing, self-reinforcing character of a closed system." Such universal limitations are compounded by the production and institutionalizing of limited and limiting vocabularies and imagery, imposing and securing distortions and misrepresentations across time. "There is nothing especially controversial or reprehensible about such domestications of the exotic; they take place between all cultures, certainly, and between all men. My point, however, is to emphasize the truth that the Orientalist, as much as anyone in the European West who thought about or experienced the Orient, performed this kind of mental operation."[8] So the problem with the West, let us say, is that it has gone beyond the primitive human impulse to construct Otherness by inscribing such a tendency in a larger ideology of domination. We have now moved from the very personal, the primordial, to the political and ideological. Thus, one of Said's major objections to Orientalism is that it goes above and beyond the universal human proclivity to represent others in such a way as to validate one's own worldview and legitimize one's own being as different/separate from the Other. This is probably Said's most convincing attempt to distinguish between what is "natural" and what is "ideological."

How, then, does one overcome such atavistic propensity ? Said proposes the adoption of what he calls "positive history and positive geography." The problem, though, is that the latter's reliability is hard to ascertain. Said avoids this dilemma by saying that "we need not decide here whether this kind of imaginative knowledge infuses history and geography, or whether in some way it overrides them. Let us just say for the time being that it is there as something *more* than what appears to be merely positive knowledge." Even assuming that Orientalism is a human impulse elevated to the level of ideology, the same existential and ontological questions raised about the issue of identity should nevertheless still apply to nations engaged in the same process of identity making. Why can't powerful nations project their values and define others by them? Why shouldn't James Balfour, for instance, praise Europe's civilizing mission in the Orient or call for integrating Egypt into Europe and thus remove its forbidding strangeness and rescue its people from a long history of tyranny? Couldn't it be true that Egypt, once a great civilization, had "plunged into barbarism"?[9]

The question is this: What if the (bad) Orientalists' diagnosis of Arabs and the Arab condition were truly motivated by a genuine concern for preserving a transnational human patrimony? What if such openly colonialist moves were the paradoxical affirmation of the oneness of humanity, and not its eternal separation into tribal configurations? It's not inconceivable for Arabs to have become too destructive and tyrannical, as Chateaubriand wrote in his *Itinéraire de Paris à Jérusalem, et de Jérusalem à Paris*, to deserve the custody of Pharaonic Egypt, a heritage to which all nations are entitled? "Of liberty," Chateaubriand wrote of the Orientals, "they know nothing; of propriety, they have none; force is their God. When they go for long periods without seeing conquerors who do heavenly justice, they have the air of soldiers without a leader, citizens without legislators, and a family without a father."[10] Or consider H. A. R. Gibb's lecture on "the Arab mind":

The student of Arabic civilization is constantly brought up against the striking contrast between the imaginative power displayed, for example, in certain branches of Arabic literature, and the literalism, the pedantry, displayed in reasoning and exposition even when it is devoted to these same productions. It is true that there have been great philosophers among the Muslim peoples and that some of them were Arabs, but they were rare exceptions. The Arab mind, whether in relation to the outer world or in relation to the processes of thought, cannot throw off its intense feeling for the separateness and the individuality of the concrete events. This is, I believe, one of the main factors lying behind that "lack of a sense of law" which Professor Macdonald regarded as the characteristic difference of the Oriental.[11]

Gibb goes on to provide a cultural explanation for the Muslims' aversion to rationalism, to the utilitarian ethic, and this, of course, becomes a prime example of how Orientalism works through generalizations, oversimplifications, patronizing attitudes, and so on. But, again, what if Gibb were right? After all, one of the seminal books written by an Arab Muslim on the Arab mind comes close to making a similar claim.[12] (To be fair to Said, he states throughout the book that many Arabs have imbibed the Orientalist discourse.) Said then comments: "Already in 1810 we have a European talking like Cromer in 1910, arguing that Orientals require conquest, and finding it no paradox that a Western conquest of the Orient was not a conquest after all, but liberty."[13]

Similar ideological contradictions are found in Karl Marx's writings about the Orient. In destroying despotic Asia, Marx believed that Britain was inaugurating a social revolution. Said wrestles with Marx's views by pointing out that "Marx's style pushes us right up against the difficulty of reconciling our natural repugnance as fellow creatures to the sufferings of Orientals while their society is being violently transformed with the historical necessity of these transformations." Even if we assume that Said doesn't skim over Marx's "rhetorical intentions," as Clifford suggests,[14] this universalist approach to other cultural traditions may very well explain Marx's (in)famous statement on the Orient:

Now, sickening as it must be to human feeling to witness those myriads of industrious patriarchal and inoffensive social organizations disorganized and dissolved into their units, thrown into a sea of woes, and their individual members losing at the same time their ancient form of civilization and their hereditary means of subsistence, we must not forget that these idyllic village communities, inoffensive though they may appear, had always been the solid foundation of Oriental despotism, that they restrained the human mind within the smallest possible compass, making it the unresisting tool of superstition, enslaving it beneath the traditional rules, depriving it of all grandeur and historical energies. . . .

England, it is true, in causing a social revolution in Hindustan was actuated only by the vilest interests, and was stupid in her manner of enforcing them. But that is not the question. The question is, can mankind fulfil its destiny without a fundamental revolution in the social state of Asia? If not, whatever may have been the crimes of England she was the unconscious tool of history in bringing about that revolution.[15]

Clearly such views have the effect of reducing Orientals into one-dimensional beings (only naked force motivates them) and downplay the Orient's long and complex history, the brutal legacies of colonialism that far surpass any sultan's tyranny in his own domain. But couldn't one both agree with Orientalist evaluations or judgments and disagree with their reductionism and belligerence? Marx was certainly not driven by racist feelings or antihuman impulses. He clearly saw colonialism as a necessary prelude to a better life for all humans. His case, more than any other, reveals the paradoxical gesture of Europe's proprietary attitude toward the Orient—that even in its seeming antagonism to the natives, the proprietary gesture also presupposes a common human destiny. Despite power rivalries, both British and French "believed themselves to have [a] traditional entitlement"[16] to the Orient, an attitude (even in its most extreme manifestation of direct colonialism) that appears simultaneously promising and dangerous, for it could potentially reduce old antagonisms or intensify hatreds. Again, Said's objections to such an attitude would make it seem—and I insist that this is not his intention at all—that he wants the world to be one in its cosmopolitanism and yet separated into gated essences.[17]

Understandable as the Euro-American proprietary impulse may be, there is something troubling about a nation claiming other people's histories and land because it just happens to have the military and financial might to do so. Why would an enlightened, civilized Europe take an active interest in the Orient (East and West, for the Americas were also part of the Orient in the conquistadors' imagination) and spend so much energy trying to domesticate it? Why would it want to transform an "alien" space into a "colonial" one if the enterprise were not driven by more than a will to conquer?[18] Said is right to suspect the codification of a rather primitive act of identity formation into a major scholarly enterprise and even a national ideology, even if, as Bernard Lewis would later reply, Muslims also held horribly distorted views of Europeans when the former were comfortably superior to the latter.[19]

Said, then, is justified in calling attention to the ways in which Orientalist scholarship endangers human communication and dialogue, and if his argument is "polemical," it is because the deeper motivations for cultural exclusions are philosophical concerns that are beyond the scope of his inquiry. Still, aside from the intractable question of identity and representation, there are two other significant lacunae in Said's work that have narrowed the scope of his otherwise illuminating theory, ones that are materially historical, but that get little or almost no attention in his "epoch-making book."[20] Not only does Said not spend enough time examining the universalizing tendencies of capitalism, but his almost deafening silence on what Eric Hobsbawm called the "dual revolution" and what Susan Dunn termed "sister revolutions" is rather striking for such an ambitious project dealing primarily with the modern period.[21]

The American and French Revolutions—both of which gradually altered the United States and France's perceptions of themselves as provinces in the world and turned them into full-blown messianic secular forces of enlightenment bent on erasing barbarism from history—were momentous, landmark events that gave rise to uncompromisingly universalist outlooks and invested Americans and Europeans with what Said terms proprietary rights over the whole world, since the whole of humanity, within these new utopian vistas, became tied together into one common destiny. Old boundaries dissolved and gave way to a new *mission civilisatrice*, one that had been successfully executed in the United States, France, and other European nations. These two revolutions turned the French and Americans into the vanguards of a human race still mired in the darker days of pre-revolutionary tyranny. This, at least, seems to be what motivated many Americans and turned them into the agents of their nation's self-proclaimed "manifest destiny." (Note that the expression could have equally been applied to Marx's view of history.) I am not suggesting that the new order arose *ex nihilo*, out of pure revolutionary theory (although this is what Susan Dunn says had been attempted in France and led to the Reign of Terror). The global impulse of the these revolutions (as we shall in the case of the United States) was built on a long and well-established genealogy of Christian messianic literature.

Thus the (deliberately) ambiguous and unsettled concept of Orientalism stretches the debate about Otherness and differences in very productive ways, but doesn't capture the nuances of history or even the differences within the historical West itself. No one theory probably can encompass the various and contradictory streams that run through the veins of a particular culture. However, one can do better with the equally nebulous and elusive notion of the "social imaginary," a theory of cultural behavior that is capacious enough to register differences within the same historical moment. The various historical moments that make up what I am here calling the West's post-Andalusian age (the early period of conquest, wars of independence from European mother countries, and the acceleration of the capitalist mode of production in the twentieth century) produced different, even conflicting, imaginaries without, for instance, altering substantially the structure of Europe's identity, the Orientalist ideology, or the anti-Muslim impulse that has gone into the making of an otherwise imagined Western civilization.

The secular West is still being defined more by what it *claims* not to be than with what it has in common with other civilizations. This doesn't mean, of course, that the secular West is the only civilization that sees itself as a unique, exceptional culture that, however, tries to universalize its values and thus, paradoxically, erase its (geographical) uniqueness—Christianity and Islam have always had universalist aspirations that, in many cases, justified the conquest of peoples—but I will try to argue that with the demise of Andalusian Islam in 1492, a qualitatively new world came into being, and it is this fissurous order that is increasingly endangering human civilization today. Neither Said's Orientalism nor a strictly economistic Marxism can provide a convincing explanation for what is unfolding in the present: The first concept is too restricted to the domain of representation, while the second is too mechanistic to justify persistent patterns of exclusion amid cultural mutations since 1492.

Only the hard-to-define idea of the "social imaginary," something like the Hegelian notion of the "spirit of the times," the *Zeitgeist*, or Georg Simmel's *Stimmung* could serve as a more useful paradigm. It allows us, as Michel Maffesoli puts it, to speak of "unicity" or "whatever brings various elements into coherence, while, at the same time, leaving them in their specific qualities, and maintaining their oppositions. This is the 'contradictorial'—the contradictory elements are not transcended but are maintained as such." This "*all-encompassing imaginary* strongly determines individual attitudes, lifestyles, ways of thinking, and the various interrelations (social, economic, political, ideological, or religious) which constitute life in society. It is the matrix, in the fullest sense of the term, ensuring their gestation and presiding over their birth." All social activity is determined and individuality is constrained by it.[22] As Simmel remarked, "the individual feels himself drawn into the bubbling 'ambiance' of the mass as if by a force that is exterior to himself, indifferent to his individual being and will. At the same time, however, this mass is composed exclusively of such individuals."[23]

The social imaginary appears first as a *sermo mythicus* whose instances are conceived and operate in the plural and thus contradict the narrow concepts of culture imagined by cultural apologists. Gilbert Durand, in his "The Implication of the Imaginary and Societies," states that "the functional polytheism which appears in the conflicts of the individual is even more vigorous in the instances of the collective psyche. This factor pushes us to mistrust the monotheistic simplifications found in culturalisms." The concept allows us to formulate a theory of cultural differences without reducing such cultures to immutable essences, as many culturalists tend to do. Irrational and inscrutable, much like the "totemic principle" operating in clans, the social imaginary infuses everything.[24] This helps explain why Marx and many anticolonialists today cannot ultimately transcend their Eurocentric social imaginary, despite their progressive politics and commitment to human emancipation.

The legendary intellectual Cornelius Castoriadis elaborated the concept in his *L'institution imaginaire de la société* (1975) by unveiling its capacity to contain an infinite number of variables in one particular cultural moment.[25] Although often in sympathy with Marx, Castoriadis nevertheless manages to show the ways in which (as one might expect) Marx was constrained by his own social environment and couldn't easily escape it, despite Marx's strong historical-materialist bent. In fact, the insurmountable paradox in Marx's worldview is that although Marx is (implicitly) aware that he is part of particular historical moment, he still extrapolates from it to project a pattern of iron laws—albeit with room for variations—onto all of (human) history. Yet we know that the logic of the capitalist mode of production, with its system of social relations, is not—and has never been—universal. Not only this, since Marx's historical materialism emanates from a capitalist regime, it is, ironically, part of the capitalist worldview, for its basic assumptions—that, however sublimated their desires may be, humans are motivated primarily by economic necessity—are fundamentally bourgeois. Through the prism of the "social imaginary" one can see how "capitalist elements" are "deeply ingrained" in the "substance" of "present Marxism," partly because Marxism transforms "causal relations" into "laws" and thus excludes the element of "unpredictability" (which includes creativity or conscious activity that disproves theory) in favor of a rigid economic determinism. As a rationalist "closed dialectic" that reduces experience to "rational determinations," Marxist philosophy imposes its system on history and cannot avoid its "anthropormorphism or socio-centrism."[26] Hence, for Castoriadis, a proper dialectic is nonmaterialist, contingent, and includes both what is accessible and what is not:

> A 'non-spiritualist' dialectic must also be a 'non-materialist' dialectic, in the sense that it refuses to posit an absolute Being, whether as spirit, as matter or as the totality, already given in principle, of all possible determinations. It must eliminate closure and completion, pushing aside the completed system of the world. It must set aside the rationalist illusion, seriously accept the idea that there is both the infinite and the indefinite, and admit, without for all that giving up its labour, that all rational determination leaves outside of it an undetermined and non-rational remainder, that the remainder is just as essential as what has been analysed, that necessity and contingency are constantly bound up with one another, that 'nature' outside of us and within us is always something other and something more than what consciousness constructs, and that all of this is valid not only for the 'object' but also for the subject.[27]

This is the only way to come to grips with history, since Marxism itself is the product of its own context:

> The development of Marxism as a theory took place within the intellectual and philosophical environment of the second half of the nineteenth century. This period was dominated, as no other in history, by 'scientism' and positivism, triumphantly borne by the accumulation of scientific discoveries, their experimental verification, and especially, for the first time on this scale, 'the rational application of science to industry'. The apparent all-powerfulness of technique was 'demonstrated' daily, the face of entire countries transforming rapidly by the extension of the industrial revolution. What appears to us today in technical progress not only as ambiguous, but even undetermined with respect to its social significance, had not yet emerged. The economy presented itself as the problem of society. The milieu offered both the materials and the form for a 'scientific' theory of society and of history; it even made this a requirement, by predetermining to a large extent the dominant categories.[28]

Thus the freezing of Marxist theories through a sort of contextual transcendence is not only by definition anti-Marxist and deadening, but it also
transforms what was once a revolutionary fusion of philosophy (abstraction) and politics (action) into dogmatic application—"the utter petrifica-
tion of theory" and "bureaucratic politics."[29]

People do not escape or transcend their social milieus, even if they
try to do so by breaking down the social into its constitutive parts. For one
thing, the social cannot be thus reduced, since "society is not a thing, not
a subject, and not an idea—nor is it a collection or system of subjects,
things and ideas," and the "domains of social activity are not genuinely
separable." Moreover, "there is no articulation of social life that is given
once and for all, neither on the surface nor at a greater depth, neither really
nor abstractly. This articulation, whether with respect to the parts it posits
or to the relations established between these parts and between the parts
and the whole, is in every instance the creation of the society in question."
The "social imaginary is not a substance, not a quality, not an action or a
passion," and "social imaginary significations are not representations, not
figures or forms, not concepts." The social, then, must be imagined as a
"*magma*, and even as a *magma* of *magmas*," by which Castoriadis means
"not chaos but the mode of organization belonging to a non-ensemblist diversity, exemplified by society, the imaginary, or the unconscious." "A
magma is that from which one can extract (or in which one can construct)
an indefinite number of ensemblist organizations but which can never be
reconstituted (ideally) by a (finite or infinite) ensemblist composition of
these organizations." The magmas of each society are thus organized in a
nonreproducible way.[30]

Having posited the notion of a "magma" that contains, but does not
necessarily reflect the institutions of society, Castoriadis can then move beyond Marx's determinism to argue that there is a tenuous relationship between base and superstructure, that machines, for example, become capitalist tools *only* when the social imaginary of capitalism has invaded and
overthrown other social imaginaries (the capitalist penetration of "precapitalist" societies is well known). The overall effect of capitalism is not to sell
commodities, but to produce "capitalist people," "that is to say, of socially
fabricating individuals for whom what does and does not count, what does
and does not have a signification, for whom the signification of a given
thing or a given act are henceforth defined, posited and instituted in another way than in traditional society." This is understandably a controver-

sial proposition, one that seriously dematerializes traditional Marxist assumptions and raises questions about the "production" of a particular "social imaginary." This is why I started this discussion by reminding the reader that the "social imaginary" ultimately runs into the same conceptual hurdles as Orientalism and cannot successfully answer all the questions it raises. But the concept allows us to think of social spaces differently, as irreducible magmas that shape all human and social activity, and yet, like all enduring myths, that do not add up to the sum of their parts. Indeed, capitalism must become the *sermo mythicus* (so to speak) of a society. It must transcend the here and now, merge into the realm of the ethereal and intangible, and suffuse every fiber of the social order if its privileged mode of production is to become real. Capitalism, in other words, must acquire the status of God in traditional, noncapitalist societies, an entity that "has no referent other than the signification God," one that is "central element in the organization of the world for a monotheistic society."

Central significations are not significations 'of' something—nor are they, except in a second-order sense, significations 'attached' or 'related' to something. They constitute that which, for a given society, brings into being the co-belonging of objects, acts and individuals which, in appearance, are most heterogeneous. They have no 'referent'; they institute a mode of being of things and of individuals which relate to them. In themselves, they are not necessarily explicit for the society that institutes them. They are presentified-figured through the totality of the explicit institutions of society and the organization of the world as such and of the social world which these institutions serve to instrument. They condition and orient social doing and representing, in and through which they continue as they are themselves altered.[31]

In Western capitalist societies, in which everything converges into the production of "commodities," the sphere of the "economy" renders capitalism the "central social signification" and thus, as stated, replaces the role of God in (monotheistic) traditional societies.[32]

In departing from Said's theory of Orientalism (or rather by expanding out of it) and by emphasizing the contextuality of Marxist theory, I want to show that the emergence a certain European imaginary is crucial to understanding cultural relations and the West's view of Islam in the post-Andalusian period. The immediate phase following the collapse of the last Islamic bastion in al-Andalus will be discussed in my next chapter, but here I want to highlight the historical forces that shaped the West's attitude toward Islam during the period Said examines in his book. Modern Orientalism emerged precisely when, under the impact of the "dual revolution" (1789–1848), large parts of the world were being "transformed from a European, or rather a Franco-British base."[33] The vocabulary that defines much of our consciousness (terms such as "industry," "freedom," "middle class," and "liberal," including the language of oppositional discourses) was coined within this sixty-year time span and was initially stamped by the implicit worldview of the conquest-bound capitalist bourgeoisie.[34] The upsetting of the feudal world with its peasantries and the rise of this business class relying on improved maritime technology not only brought the feudal order to and end, but it was also accompanied by the rise of sciences and Enlightenment ideologies, including the secular triple mantras of liberty, equality and fraternity:

A secular, rationalist and progressive individualism dominated 'enlightened' thought. To set the individual free from the shackles which fettered him was its chief object: from the ignorant traditionalism of the Middle Ages, which still threw their shadow across the world, from the superstition of the churches (as distinct from 'natural' or 'rational' religion), from the irrationality which divided men into a hierarchy of higher and lower ranks according to birth or some other irrelevant criterion. Liberty, equality and (it followed) the fraternity of all men were its slogans. The reign of individual liberty could not but have the most beneficent consequences. The most extraordinary results could be looked for— could indeed already be observed to follow from—the unfettered exercise of individual talent of reason.[35]

The magical effect of such an unmistakably bourgeois discourse is that it also was, theoretically and morally, beyond reproach, since the virtues it articulated were truly universal and could not be contested without making oneself vulnerable to the charge of supporting tyranny (a situation that continues to bedevil many critics of Eurocentrism today, including the Universal Declaration of Human Rights crafted by Westerners for the world). Indeed, even when the powerful states of China and Islam began to succumb to European colonialism in the nineteenth century, their people were already fighting back by appropriating the same bourgeois vocabulary of freedom coined by their colonial oppressors.[36]

One of the virtues of Eric Hobsbawm's study of the dual revolutions is that he pays equal attention to Britain's Industrial Revolution, which had the same pulverizing effect as the political one in France. Up until the last decades of the eighteenth century, no society had been able to overcome the vagaries of nature in the production process. Since then, however, mechanization and automation have been on a steady march to render human labor and scarcity obsolete, even while increasing human redundancy, general misery, and alienation. In addition to the mechanization of labor, low wages and free-trade policies were instituted as necessary measures to overcome the endemic problem of the falling rate of profit. Home and world markets were expanded in order to sell the ever increasing volume of commodities, while the protective Corn Laws were summarily abolished in 1846. The cotton industry involved the world and the colonies in an insidious fabric of exploitation, greed, and fabulous wealth. Although all raw materials were extracted and imported from abroad, India and Egypt were compelled to deindustrialize, and outright occupation of other people's lands was increasingly becoming unavoidable. The freedom-loving bourgeois was from the very outset ethnocentrically global, his expansionist ideology underwritten by the universalist ethos of the American and French Revolutions, whose remarkable effect was to erase the apparent contradiction of simultaneously celebrating freedom and colonizing others, of imagining a better future while ravaging the earth in the pursuit of short-term profit.

Hobsbawm, who dismisses the American Revolution as a mere local, moderate dispute, describes the French Revolution as the most radical in modern history, one that inspired the non-Western world, including the world of Islam, and that gave it its ideology for modern nation building and a vocabulary to protect its sovereignty. Although French, the "tremendous and earth-shaking idea of liberation" introduced by the revolution was global and encompassed all humanity.

For Frenchmen, as for their numerous sympathizers abroad, the liberation of France was merely the first installment of the universal triumph of liberty; an attitude which led easily to the conviction that it was the duty of the fatherland of the revolution to liberate all peoples groaning under oppression and tyranny. There was a genuinely exalted and generous passion to spread freedom among the revolutionaries, moderate and extreme; a genuine inability to separate the cause of the French nation from that of all enslaved humanity.[37]

Because the world's liberal intellectuals had sympathized with the revolution, at least until its Jacobin phase, the new régime reciprocated by granting honorary citizenships (including citizenships to American luminaries such as Washington, Hamilton, Madison, Joel Barlow, and Tom Paine). By 1810, France was ruling directly or indirectly over large parts of western Europe, forever abolishing feudal institutions and introducing new revolutionary ones, including the radical nation-state. Thus, the French Revolution was not only unique, but, as Hobsbawm insists again and again, "a universal event" from which no country was immune.[38]

The impact of the "dual revolution" was fateful. The commodification of land imposed by the bourgeois elites (except in England and the United States where the only obstacles came from the Indians) was resisted by most social classes (landowners and peasants alike). But the bourgeois triumphed, feudalism lost, and entire populations were displaced and emigrated to cities and countries where they mortgaged their labor to industries.[39] Meanwhile, the ever improving technologies of industry and communication fuelled a population explosion that, in turn, added further stimulus to the economy. The rate of economic and social change accelerated after 1830. And when Egypt tried to industrialize, the first nonwhite country to do so, the Anglo-Turkish Convention of 1838 effectively defeated Mohammed Ali's highly ambitious venture by imposing foreign traders on the country. (Interestingly, we are still being told that there is something intrinsic to Islam that prevents "modernization" or that Arabs' backwardness is due to their lack of democracy.)

The example of Egypt shows that henceforth the world could be divided only between those who control capital flows and others, for one of the most enduring effects of the age of dual revolution was the division of the world between "advanced" and dependent countries, variously called "underdeveloped," "Third World," or even "developing."

Except for Western Europe (minus the Iberian peninsula), Germany, Northern Italy and parts of central Europe, Scandinavia, the USA and perhaps the colonies settled by English-speaking migrants, the rest of the world was, apart from small patches, lagging or turning—under the informal pressure of western exports and imports or the military pressure of western gunboats and military expeditions— into economic dependencies of the west. Until the Russians in the 1930s developed means of leaping this chasm between the 'backward' and the 'advanced', it would remain immovable, untraversed, and indeed growing wider, between the minority and the majority of the world's inhabitants. No fact has determined the history of the twentieth century more firmly than this.[40]

The postrevolutionary period belonged to bourgeois parvenus—the term "middle class" was first used around 1812—who pursued the four principal paths of business, education, the arts, and war to reach up the newly opened social ladder. It was also a period of "emphatic secularization," since the ideologization of religion and "the secularization of the masses" were unprecedented in human history. In both America and France, Christianity became irrelevant, thereby heralding the triumph of the bourgeois elites in imposing their own ideologies on "a much vaster movement of the masses." Thereafter, most working class and socialist revolutions of the nineteenth century would be secular (the word "socialism" was coined in the 1820s). Enlightened British administrators in India consciously fought superstition and stamped out suttee and other violent rituals. Yet, at a time when Christianity was contracting (except in sectarian Protestant movements, whose revivalism may have inspired Marx to make his famous comment on the opiate of the people), Islam was expanding. Still largely unaffected by the secular vocabulary of nationalism, Muslims such as the Wahhabis of Arabia and the Senousi movement in Libya were still relying on religion to wage their own anticolonialist battles. The short-lived Arab nationalism was a later, urban movement reflecting its social origins in the European bourgeoisie.[41]

While Hobsbawm downplays the significance of the American Revolution as mostly a parochial affair, Susan Dunn has shown its far-reaching effects, and how, in fact, it inspired some of the great heroes of the French Revolution. The French were initially intoxicated by America's experiment, so much so that, in 1789, a newspaper considered the new American republic "the hope and the model of the human race."[42] One of France's revolutionary heroes, Marquis de Lafayette, began his heroic itinerary by deserting his wife and country to serve in the cause of American freedom. After leaving France, he wrote his wife from aboard the ship *Victoire*: "The happiness of America is intimately tied to the happiness of all humanity; America will become the respected and secure haven of virtue, honesty, tolerance, equality, and a peaceful freedom."[43]

The American Revolution was considered the most important event since Columbus discovered the continent. "The America Revolution was not only *à la mode* in Paris; it had become virtually a new religion," wrote Dunn. "Washington, Franklin, and Jefferson acted as the apostles, and Jefferson's Declaration of Independence replaced the Bible."[44] Although the French Revolution would eventually come to see itself as vastly more radical and dissociate itself from the American conservative revolution—its sister revolution—both revolutions endowed future liberation fighters with the language of freedom. Frederick Douglass had to remind his audiences of the principles of the American Revolution and the virtue of the republic's founders, while a century later and half a world away, Ho Chi

Minh extolled America's Founding Fathers and their declaration, and used both in the 1940s to justify his country's claims for independence from France. He expected Franklin D. Roosevelt to be sympathetic (which he was), but FDR couldn't oppose his European ally. Much later, and after he had been branded a Communist and defeated the French, Ho wrote again to President Dwight Eisenhower, reminding him of the legacy of Washington and Lincoln. Indeed, as early as 1919, at the peace conference in Versailles, Ho had tried to meet President Woodrow Wilson, architect of the League of Nations, to present his "eight points" defending the civil rights of the natives and calling for equal treatment. At that time, Ho was not calling for the end of colonialism, just for fair treatment. But he was ignored by President Wilson and treated respectfully by French socialists. In this way, Ho was awakened to bourgeois hypocrisy and the duplicity of the French, whose egalitarian culture had attracted him to France in the first place. Disabused of the hopes he had placed on France, Ho left for Moscow (where Robespierre had been highly regarded by the Bolsheviks) and eventually returned to Vietnam. Committed to his nation's "freedom," Ho may very well have become another Jacobin in his mindless pursuit of his noble objectives, spending most of his life fighting the very nations that had inspired him but that, in the process of history, had become "fiercely antirevolutionary."[45] Ho's example shows that extremism is often the act of last resort, the symptom of the failure of dialogue, and almost always invariably in modern history, it is inspired by the very liberal West that condemns it.

Ho Chi Minh's case sounds a familiar echo in our own age. Even as the Mandelas of the world continue to invoke Washington, Jefferson, and Lincoln,[46] the United States, France, and all the great bourgeois nations continue to pursue policies that are antithetical to their own democratic traditions because they have not yet awakened to their own provincialism, nor have they been able to separate the universal, but abstract, notion of freedom from the grip of capitalism that undermines such a lofty ideal. And since they haven't, the project of the Enlightenment has turned into a negative force in history, its moral principles summarily cancelled by the relentless power of a destructive economy. We now have the case of two universalisms clashing—one moral and the other economic—without anyone seriously addressing this deadly impasse.

The social imaginary born out of the "dual" and "sister" revolutions was capacious enough to contain various views of Islam and the Orient, which is what explains the seemingly contradictory attitudes toward the subject in both Europe and America. Even as they disagreed on the meaning of the Orient, Western writers, much like the political systems that ruled them, were still, however, imbued by the social imaginaries that nourished them, and were, in one way or another, responding to the new register launched by the three revolutionary moments. Thus, when the Yemeni scholar Mohammed Sharafuddin takes Said to task for casting the shadow of his skepticism, "both political and spiritual, over the possibility that some conscientious and high-minded writers may be born out of a society that has been defined as imperial," he, like most of Said's critics, and in fact, like Said himself, is most likely pointing out to what is lacking or deemphasized in Said's work, and not (despite his argument) to some error in Said's analysis. For Said—to the extent that his seminal book focuses on certain works—is right, and his theory powerfully accounts for the sort of Orientalism he examines. But because Said's theory restricts itself to a particular, not always representative discourse, one does not always get the impression that Western writers were part of this revolutionary period, one characterized by "innovative as well as [. . .] conservative tendencies." Since taking into account "what was possible in the age" is indispensable to understanding the literature of Orientalist writings, Sharafuddin opts for what he calls "realistic Orientalism," a concept that, in his view, opposes Said's and allows for a complementarity of cultural attitudes to exist within the same historical moment.[47]

It is true that history accounts for many of the shifting attitudes toward Muslims and that the dynamic and changing Orientalist tradition is also best read in light of historical transformations. The declining threat of the Ottoman empire and the rise of industrialization may have transformed the image of Islam in the West and cleansed it from any of its negative associations. This may explain why a new, positive literature began to appear toward the second half of the eighteenth century (roughly the starting point for Said's thesis), one that was inspired by direct observation and was not infrequently at odds with prerevolutionary views of the Orient. In his *Législation orientale* (1778), Abraham-Hyacinthe Antiquetel-Duperron, a long-term resident of India, bluntly stated that the attribution of despotism to the Orient is a distortion that "provided the excuse for Europeans such as the English in India to confiscate native lands and wealth. If no private property existed under despotism, then the conqueror could take everything in the country because it had belonged to the defeated despot."[48] Later, Edmund Burke would reiterate the same view when, after surveying the history of Islam in India, he asserted that "nothing is more false than that despotism is the constitution of any country in Asia. . . . It is certainly not true of any Mohammedan constitution." Indeed, Burke went further:

The greatest part of Asia is under Mohammedan governments. To name a Mohammedan government is to name a government by law. It is a law enforced by stronger sanctions than any law, that can bind a Christian sovereign. Their law is believed to be given by God, and it has the double sanction of law and of religion which the prince is no more authorized to dispense with than any else. And, if any man will produce the Koran to me, and will but show me one text in it, that authorizes in any degree an arbitrary power in the government, I will confess, that I have read that book and been conversant in the affairs of Asia, in vain. There is no such a syllable in it; but, on the contrary, against oppressors by name every letter of that law is fulminated.

Lord Byron, Lady Mary Wortley Montagu, James Bruce, and others all praised the civility and civilization of Arabs and Muslims.[49]

Yet it was out of this same revolutionary cultural matrix and this millennial, universalist vision that Marx wrote his seemingly disparaging views of the precolonial Orient, an event that clearly illustrates why the question of Otherness in the modern period is as much about difference as it is about sameness, for the revolutionary impulse that globalized Anglo-French philosophies ultimately considered humanity and its future as one and the same. Having deemphasized the pulse underwriting much of the colonialist history of the last two centuries, Said recommends de-Orientalizing, if only to subvert the entrenched and highly institutionalized academic discourse that has had well-documented negative effects on better human relations and a better understanding of world cultures. But such a solution cannot work if the much stronger forces of history—the naturally universalist tendencies of both Christian millennialism, Enlightenment ideals, and capitalist ideologies—are not seriously interrogated and dismantled. I am well aware that Said's de-Orientalization cannot happen without, to some extent, foregoing the common destiny and oneness assumed by the three tendencies mentioned above. But as I hope to show in the rest of this book, we have no choice but to embrace a theory that allows for irreducible cultural differences in a common human civilization.

CHAPTER 2

Other Worlds, New Muslims

> The discovery of gold and silver in America, the extirpation, enslavement
> and entombment in mines of the indigenous population of that
> continent . . . are all things which characterize the dawn of the era of capi-
> talist production.
> —Karl Marx, *Capital*

> Wheron I vow'd
> That, if our Princes harken'd to my prayer,
> Whatever wealth I brought from that new world
> Should, in this old, be consecrate to lead
> A new crusade against the Saracen,
> And free the Holy Sepulchre from thrall.
> —Alfred Tennyson, "Columbus"

> European thought in the sixteenth century concerned itself with two types
> of aspirations: the secular pursuit of the ideal and the religious pursuit of
> salvation and the Kingdom of God, and within those two streams there
> were great and devastating disagreements. Both excluded the value of non-
> European thought.
> —John C. Mohawk, *Utopian Legacies*

Six months after the deadly terrorist attacks on New York and Washington D.C., and after thousands of arrests and the defeat of the Taliban in
Afghanistan, three articles appeared in major U.S. periodicals that, taken
together, could have made the reader wonder about why Islam had been
reduced to such low depths and so massively associated with fanaticism
and suicide bombers. In its issue of 8 April 2002, *U.S. News and World Report* featured a beautifully illustrated article on the unspeakable atrocities
committed by self-proclaimed Crusaders in Jerusalem and the Middle East
and contrasted such cruelties with the magnanimity of Saladin, the Mus-

lim general who repelled the Christian reign of terror.[1] Describing this event as the first major clash between Islam and Western Christendom, the magazine told readers that not only doesn't Saladin get much press in the West, but also that the metaphor of the Crusades (undiplomatically evoked by President Bush soon after 9/11) had long endured in Europe's consciousness and was, in fact, deployed by British colonialists when they retook possession of Jerusalem in the early twentieth century. "The colonial powers," wrote the magazine, "glorified the Crusades as their ideological forebears." And yet, despite these devastating encounters, Europeans came back home with new tales and whetted rich Europeans' appetites, as David Stannard put it a decade earlier, for "exotic foreign luxuries—for silks and spices, fine cotton, drugs, perfumes, and jewelry" and thus for gold,[2] stimulating, in the process, a new economy that would propel Europe out of the darkness that had set it on the path to religious fanaticism. Hardened Crusaders had enlisted to fight Islam, but many returned from these religious wars as emissaries for the more advanced civilization they had sought to topple. It was an ironic outcome that would change the very character of Europe.

Almost at the same time this article appeared, María Rosa Menocal, director of the Whitney Humanities Center at Yale, wrote an opinion piece for the *New York Times*, based on a book she had just published, extolling the liberal, refined, and remarkably multicultural culture of the westernmost parts of Islam: Muslim Spain, or al-Andalus. Described by a nun from Saxony as "the ornament of the world," al-Andalus not only tolerated differences, but accepted life with contradictions, both within individuals and communities. "Much that was characteristic of medieval culture was rooted in the cultivation of charms and challenges of contradictions—of the 'yes and no,' as it was put by Peter Abelard, the provocative 12th-century Parisian intellectual and Christian theologian." Jews and Christians were able to develop their own arts and philosophies—and thus strengthen their own distinct identities—from within this flexible cultural mix.[3]

Yet, despite its remarkable achievements, al-Andalus was not the only refined place for a human being to be: Thousands of miles west of Spain, the still-undiscovered lands of America had reached a level of civilization that was also unmatched in all of Europe. Around the time the two articles were published, the *Atlantic* magazine featured an article about the New World before Columbus and listed some of the wondrous accomplishments of indigenous American cultures throughout the continent. Agricultural production and innovation, urban design, health, and the quality of life were so superior that when the author of the article asked seven scholars who had studied this subject whether they would have preferred, given the choice, to be European or Indian at that time, they all chose to be Indian. The Indians were found not to be passive beneficiaries of an abundant nature, but skillful trustees of a fragile environment who were doing much to improve it. They were, as one might say of certain Muslim rulers of al-Andalus, such as 'Abd al-Rahman III and Al-Hakam II, "keystone species" of a well regulated, balanced, and harmonious civilization in which all differences were integrated in a cohesive, but fragile fabric.[4]

The average reader of these three unrelated articles might have been excused for wondering why such a world came to an abrupt end or for asking "What Went Wrong?" to use one of Bernard Lewis's titles after September 11, 2001.[5] The sad fact is that in 1492, with the defeat of the last Islamic kingdom in Spain, both worlds, old and new, embarked on a long and painful process of violent change that, in time, almost totally erased the set of memories associated with either Christian fanaticism or the still-unsurpassed culture of what Spanish historians call *convivencia* (living together despite irreconcilable religious differences) in al-Andalus.[6] That such articles were published at a critical juncture in U.S. and world history, a time when the "clash of civilizations" thesis hovered ominously over human destiny and the divide between West and Islam seemed unbridgeable, should have reminded us of the basic notion that—despite their insistence on their defining uniqueness—religions are not immutable. Whether internally or in their relations with others, cultures and cultural relations were lived differently before 1492, proof enough that there are no inherent features that condemn religions or cultural traditions to a fate of permanent clashes.

The defeat of Islam and the "conquest" of America in 1492 were interrelated events that culminated a long process of increasingly strident Christian missionary wars against Islam in Spain. This is not surprising, given the fact that, as Richard Fletcher put it, the Iberian peninsula was the area of Mediterranean Europe with the "most prolonged and intimate encounter between Christendom and Islam before a Christian power became eventually dominant."[7] The modern world, with its new sensibilities, was forged in this border zone, a place in which two worldviews, two faiths, reached their natural geographical and, perhaps, theological limits.[8] Fletcher reminds us that, contrary to what is often believed, and despite Menocal's description, tolerance in such a region was far from being a *fait accompli*, completed, or even unthreatened by the constant drums of zealotry. To be sure, Andalusian *convivencia* did produce some of the most enduring cultural legacies of the human civilization. Muslim rule, when stable, liberated the creative energies of all three monotheistic religions by removing burdensome taxation, liberating slaves, and doing away with "the overgrown estates of the great nobles and churchmen."[9] It is not without reason that Hispanic Jews cheered the invading Muslim armies and their victory in the eighth century and that many Christians celebrated Arab culture as a better alternative to rigid Christian orthodoxy, but still, Islamic culture was not without its exclusivism. Even the most liberal Muslim jurists refused to allow Muslims to live under Christian rule, recommending *hijra* (migration) instead of submitting to a minority status.[10] Perhaps such a theological stance was justified, given the fact that such Muslims were always threatened (much as Jews must have felt throughout history) by the dominant culture's tendencies toward extremism and scapegoating the socially vulnerable: "The Christian conquerors of al-Andalus in the twelfth and thirteenth centuries treated the indigenous Muslim peoples with a mixture of toleration and persecution. There is sufficient sediment of material here, unfortunately, to muddy the waters of Spanish historical studies with 'rival' cases put for 'tolerance' or 'intolerance,' and burdensome celebrations or laments over the 'Spanish character.'"[11]

So the myth of a golden era of multicultural relations or of Islamic tolerance should not lead us into believing that there were no tensions among religious communities, or that religious communities were always unified against others. There were too many crossovers not to complicate the mythical picture of al-Andalus, and my point here is not necessarily to present the high achievements of a Muslim polity, and thus, by inference, highlight the superiority of Islam over Christianity. In this epic struggle of faiths, no one ultimately appears better than the other, although modern history has placed the burden of restraint on what is commonly known as the West, which since the fall of Granada in 1492 has had a remarkably free hand in deciding much of the world's fate. Indeed, the modern world of European supremacy began with the triumph of Christianity—and the defeat of Islam—in Spain.

The *Reconquista*, which was a long, continuous process consisting of many events[12] and which was shaped by the long tension with bordering Islam, was accelerated by the fall of Constantinople in 1453 and did not stop until the Muslims capitulated in November 1491 and Abu Abdellah Mohammed XI, known as Boabdil, Granada's last king, surrendered the keys of his magnificent city and palace on 2 January 1492.[13] This was an event that was celebrated across Europe, particularly since French, Swiss, English, and other mercenaries had eagerly joined the Spaniards in their war on Muslims and were awarded the exalted status of veterans by the Spanish monarchs. A play was even staged in Naples on 4 March to commemorate the defeat of the Muslims in Spain.[14] Yet, despite the triumphalism with which such an event was greeted, the terms of surrender stipulated in the capitulations were "extremely liberal,"[15] which made the Muslim defeat somewhat more palatable. The new governor and the new archbishop of Granada, Iñego López de Mendoza and Fray Hernando de Talavera, were liberal men of goodwill who made life easy for the Muslims,[16] but Talavera's toleration was soon to be eclipsed by the unyielding conviction of the more influential archbishop of Toledo, Francisco Jiménez de Cisneros, that all Muslims must be baptized in the Christian faith or else be mercilessly hounded and persecuted. Alonso de Santa Cruz who recorded Cisneros's practices in his *Chronicle of the Catholic Monarchs* attributed later uprisings of the Moriscos ("little Moors," the disparaging term used for converted Muslims) to these new harsh, intolerant measures.[17] In fact, only two years after the fall of Granada, Pope Alexander VI (the name and title adopted by the Spanish nobleman Rodrigo de Borja after he had "bribed, threatened, argued, and blackmailed" his way into the office on 10 August 1492),[18] extended the system of taxation known as *cruzada* to finance this undying crusading spirit.[19] Despite Talavera's efforts to honor religious differences, the capitulations of November 1491 were "unilaterally declared to be null and void" only eight years after they went into effect,[20] and Cisneros pressured Queen Isabella to promulgate a decree that would force the Moors to choose either conversion or exile. But the queen didn't need much convincing: So infused was she with the Christian crusading spirit that her dying request in 1504 to her husband Ferdinand was to devote himself "unremittingly to the conquest of Africa and to the war for the Faith against the Moors."[21]

Things were looking increasingly grim for the embattled Muslim community. They were confronted with the prospect of a minority status for the first time in Muslim history, a situation unequivocally rejected by practically all Muslim scholars, who, like most of their Christian counterparts, preferred a state of apartheid to such risky arrangements.[22] Although Christians experienced none of the anxiety felt by defeated Muslims, they were at a loss on how to handle their case, and the best precedent they could find was the one they had used with the Jews.[23] Mosques and books were burned under Cisneros's authority, and this provoked even more revolts among the Mudejars, Muslims living under Christian rule, who now realized that they were fighting for their existence.[24]

By 1500, "the process of forcible conversion and of the destruction of the distinctive culture of al-Andalus was under way."[25] Not only were Muslims forced to wear distinctive attire (an earlier directive in 1215 had already been used by the pope to distinguish Muslims and Jews),[26] but even when they had converted and become Moriscos, eating couscous, speaking Arabic, wearing henna, and singing were considered heretical acts.[27] The list of suspicious activity was expanded to include not eating pork, "dying with one's face turned to the wall, wearing clean clothes on Saturday, [and] cutting open a lamb's leg from top to bottom."[28] Even bathing, which had been introduced by Muslims to Spain, was now suspected of being "a mere cover for Mohammedan ritual and sexual promiscuity,"[29] and so baths were ordered closed by Philip II.

More rebellions erupted in the following century, but the Moriscos were merely biding their time against an increasingly orthodox regime. The Edicts of Faith published by the Inquisition in 1524 and periodically supplemented by a series of royal ordinances had, in effect, established a police state comparable to the most vicious political regimes of the twentieth century, one in which the confession of one's transgressions and the policing of neighbors and the reporting of suspect practices became legal requirements. And yet such measures were still not enough: By the early seventeenth century, according to some estimates, at least a million Muslims had been expelled from Spain.[30]

The post-1492 persecution of Moriscos was part of a growing war on heresy. Catholic Spain had now become the bastion of the old order against the emerging threat of Protestantism, and because religion has no physical markers, it was virtually impossible to distinguish Catholics from others. With Islam defeated and Catholicism becoming the quintessential component of Spanish identity and nationalism, infidelity and heresy were treated as major crimes against the state, akin to treason. The *Repertorium inquisitorum* of 1494 stated that "infidelity is of the order of enmity. Enmity toward God is therefore of the order of infidelity. In consequence, we correctly call 'infidels' the heretics and apostates of our time, because their behavior toward the divine majesty reinforces betrayal and evasion of the truth."[31] The specter of Islam's collusion with Lutheranism, Illuminism, and Erasmianism compounded the already inbred threat of religious difference and led to greater orthodoxy in the Church. The Holy Office of the Inquisition was deployed to root out all heresies and secure the purity of the faith by promoting a culture of fear: "Fear bred fear," wrote J. H. Elliott, "and it was a measure of the propaganda success of the Inquisition that it persuaded the populace to fear heresy even more than the institution which was designed to extirpate it."

With Spain's intensified vigilance and suspicion, the Muslims' different attire, ghettoized dwellings, and even their conversions were considered insufficient measures to guard against the specter of subversion. The Moriscos looked disconcertingly Spanish and thus could not be singled out merely on the basis of looks or race. "Their physical resemblance to other Christians forced the Spanish state, via the Inquisition, to keep raising the bar of national identity, from conversion to Christianity, to the adoption of 'Christian' cultural practices, to genealogical purity."[32] New screening methods, new background checks, ones that would differentiate true Christians from impostors, had to be devised. As Deborah Root put it,

the indeterminability of faith apparent in the Inquisition's inability to determine dissimulation, and its effort to circumvent this by continually increasing its demands for proof of orthodoxy, meant the definition of orthodoxy could migrate to genealogy: Moriscos were not and could not be "truly" Christian because of their ancestry, and they were by definition reduced to impenitent heretics and dangerous outsiders. A polarity had been constructed that became impossible to deal with except by "amputation" and the "casting out" of the deviants.[33]

Because sixteenth-century Spain as a whole, and Granada in particular, experienced an intense anxiety to affirm a purely Christian identity,[34] Christianity, the religion of love, instituted a racial genealogy, allowing only those who could prove their faith generations back to be free of suspicion. The purity of faith was now blended with the purity of blood, or *limpieza de sangre*.

By the middle of the sixteenth century, orthodoxy in Spain thus was coming to mean not only the profession of a strictly orthodox faith, but also the possession of a strictly orthodox ancestry. Admittedly, there were limits to the power of the *linajudo*, the official checkers of pedigrees—

more, perhaps, than those of the inquisitor. The test of *limpieza* was difficult to enforce in the upper reaches of society, and any family that had ob-
tained a *hábito* and taken the vows of the Church's military orders was automatically placed beyond the power of the investigator. But the obsession
with pure ancestry had the general effect of confirming in the popular
mind the view expressed by Philip II that there was a correlation between
heresy and non-Christian background, and it helped to place power still
more firmly in the hands of a narrow and exclusive class of traditionally
minded Old Christians, as they were called, who were determined to bind
the country close within the confines of a conformity that they themselves
had defined. It was these men, highly influential in the Church, the religious orders, and the Inquisition, who had taken charge of the destinies of
Spain by the fateful decade of the 1550s.[35]

Religious extremism and racial purity were thus joined into a new
ideology that is, in many ways, the hallmark of the post-Andalusian age,
one whose effects would be devastating to all non-Christian peoples for
centuries to come. Interestingly enough, at the very moment of Christian
triumph over Islam and the concomitant conquest of the New World,
Spain produced nationalist criteria that would be, in many ways, the foundation of modern racism and anti-Semitism, almost as if the gains of
(re)conquest could best be safeguarded though such measures. (The violence of the Inquisition was the measure of the impurity of the Spanish no-
bility and the upholders of the Spanish faith, including someone of the
stature of Torquemeda.)[36] An entire ideology of discrimination was forged
to extirpate difference and ensure conformity, and although Protestantism
was emerging as another threat, it was Islam, with its recognizable villainous face and its historical challenge to Europe, that served as the template
for Europe's Other.

In *The Conquest of America* (originally published in French as *La
Conquête de l'Amérique* in 1982), Tzvetan Todorov made the most persua-
sive case for the significance of this historical event in establishing a structure of difference. For him, the urgent question of the Other can best be
examined in the momentous encounter of the Old and New Worlds. Admittedly an arbitrary choice, the fateful date of 1492 still nevertheless defines (if it doesn't inaugurate) much of the modern world. "We are all the
direct descendants of Columbus, it is with him that our genealogy begins,
insofar as the word *beginning* has a meaning." Seemingly interested in gold

or meeting the Grand Khan of China, Cristobal Colón's ultimate motive, stated from the very start in his journal, is nothing less than the reconquest of Jerusalem.[37] Having cleansed itself from its own Other (Muslims and Jews), Christianity must now recreate the world in its own image. Christopher Columbus's own logbook, as abridged by Las Casas, makes these connections clear:

On January 2 in the year 1492, when your Highnesses had concluded their war with the Moors who reigned in Europe, I saw your Highnesses' banners victoriously raised on the towers of the Alhambra, the citadel of that city, and the Moorish king come out of the city gates and kiss the hands of your Highnesses, and the prince, my Lord. And later in the same month . . . your Highnesses decided to send me, Christopher Columbus, to see those parts of India and the princes and peoples of these lands, and consider the best means for their conversion. . . . Therefore having expelled all the Jews from your domains in the same month of January, your Highness commanded me to go with an adequate fleet to these parts of India. . . . I departed from the city of Granada on Saturday May 12 and went to the port of Palos, where I prepared three ships.[38]

It took a few months for Columbus to persuade the Spanish monarchs to sponsor his trips, a venture that they had refused to authorize or even take seriously. Why they changed their minds is not quite clear, but there is not doubt that Columbus's voyage was seen as part of Spain's larger war with Muslims and the defeat of the Ottomans. (Interestingly, Columbus took with him Luis de Torres, a Jew who spoke Arabic, since he expected the Grand Khan of Cathay to converse in that imperial language of high culture.)[39] Elliott thinks it safe to speculate that "the close coincidence between the fall of Granada and the authorization of Columbus's expedition would suggest that the latter was at once a thank-offering and an act of renewed dedication by Castile to the still unfinished task of war against the infidel."[40] That Cristobal Colón's own name combines the twin missions of evangelicalism and colonialism is one of the most remarkable coincidences or, even mysteries, of history.[41]

The indigenous people of the Canary Islands, the Guanjes or Guanches, precariously situated between two worlds, would be the first to suffer the fury of Spain's crusading spirit, and from then on, the new continent, reached on October 10 of that same year,[42] would gradually turn into a vast battlefield of heathens whose conversion would not cease until most had perished in "the greatest genocide in human history."[43] (The Jews had been suddenly ordered expelled from Spain on the day before

Columbus sailed out.)[44] The capture of souls and lands, combined with newly developed conception of Christianity, one in which the purity of faith and blood/race were indistinguishable, meant that an even mightier crusading arm would fall on the new Muslims of America. In fact, there is no doubt that the indigenous people of the Americas were almost instantly transformed into Muslims, since Christian Spain's quintessential notion of difference had always been embodied in Islam. Semiotically and ideologically, the world would henceforth be divided into a pure, civilized, Christian, white, enlightened, and capitalist world and a world of Others invoking the ghostly presence of Muslim infidels.

The discovery of America was a world-shattering event. It was, in the words of Francisco López de Gómara, author of *Historia general de las Indias* (1552), "the greatest event since the creation of the world (excluding the incarnation and death of Him who created it)." And Gómara had no doubt about the purpose of the discovery: "The conquest of the Indians began after that of the Moors was completed, so that Spaniards would ever fight the infidels."[45] Even Adam Smith, to this day claimed by enthusiasts of laissez-faire capitalism to be their prophet, agreed with such an assessment, adding that access to the East Indies through the Cape of Good Hope is the only other event that rivals it.[46] David Hume described the discovery of America as "really the commencement of modern History." Such discoveries opened up new worlds to a confined European population trapped in the worst social conditions imaginable and exposed them, "if not for the first time at least in uniquely dramatic ways, to a number of non-European cultures."[47]

In his moving study of Christopher Columbus and his legacy, Kirkpatrick Sale describes fifteenth-century Europe as a dismal continent enmeshed in a macabre culture of violence and death, a place rife with apocalyptic forebodings and millenarian prophecies. "Judicial cruelty," the Inquisition (instrumental for creating the nation-state that Spain was to become), crime, and political violence were part of what Johan Huizinga called "the violent tenor of [European] life."[48] Europe was also ravaged by disease (plagues, leprosy, ergotism, scurvy, chorea, smallpox, measles, diphtheria, typhus, tuberculosis, and influenza) and famine (recurrent episodes throughout the continent). "Most people," adds Stannard, "never bathed, not [even] once in a lifetime." It was this world that Christopher Columbus left in 1492, a world "wracked by disease—disease that killed in massive numbers, but importantly, that also tended to immunize survivors. A world in which all but the wealthy often could not feed themselves and in which the wealthy themselves hungered after gold. Little wonder, then, that the first report back from the Atlantic voyage, purportedly to the Orient, caused such sensations across the length and breadth of Europe."[49]

New ideologies and outlooks were emerging, including a philosophy of humanism that elevated men above all else and endowed them with divine and even imperial powers. In Lauro Martines's formulation, this humanism was meant "to provide upper class citizens with a sense of unity and direction of their lives. And this was a consciousness oriented more frankly toward worldly events." Money and power were presented as uncomplicated ideals to be pursued, while a new form of rationalism led to, in Schiller's expression, the "de-godding of nature" as everything was gradually being desacralized in this new intellectual climate. "The task of rationalism through science was to show—no better, to *prove*—that there was no sanctity about these aspects of nature, that they were not animate or purposeful or sensate, but rather nothing more than measurable combinations of chemical and mechanical properties, subject to scientific analysis, prediction, and manipulation."[50] A culture of science with what Egon Friedell called its "daemonic emotion" was impatiently bursting forth. This was the time when the checks on unbridled materialism were conveniently removed—usury revalued—and capitalism and the nation-state were at the stage of embryonic development. (In 1492, Elio Antonio de Nebrija, the royal historiographer, "published a grammar of the Castilian language, the first such work ever compiled for a European vernacular." Anecdotally, he seems to have known that language was the natural component of imperialism.)[51] The combination of all these trends would give birth to a distinctly European culture that would eventually "prevail throughout virtually all the earth."[52] What Friedell called "one of the most rudimentary, childish, and primitive periods in the history of the human spirit"[53] was being celebrated as a new era of freedom for Europeans and a model for future human civilization.

Kirkpatrick Sale, David Stannard, Robin Wright, and others have given us detailed descriptions of the conquest of indigenous cultures and peoples in America, initially carried out by the same hardened warriors who had fought the Moors in southern Spain. Once the Guanjes of the Canary Islands were defeated (and set on the quick road to extermination), the paradisiacal world (in Columbus's own terms) of America opened up to colonization. "Here, for the first time that we know," wrote Sale, "are the outlines of the policy that not only Spain but other European countries would indeed adopt in the years to come, complete with conquest, religious conversion, city settlements, fortresses, exploitation, international trade, and exclusive domain. And that colonial policy would be very largely responsible for endowing these countries with the pelf, power, patronage, and prestige that allowed them to become the nation-states they did."[54]

The *Atlantic* article with which I began this chapter confirms what had long been known in the world of scholarship, that such a paradise was no *terra nullis*, but a constellation of heavily populated and highly advanced societies, flourishing under a variety of systems. The new world, by some estimates, was home to approximately one hundred and forty-five million people or one-fifth of the human race.[55] The population of Mexico alone surpassed those of Britain and Spain combined (approximately five and eight million respectively). When Hernando Cortés first saw the island metropolis of Tenochtitlán, capital of the Aztec empire and the site of present-day Mexico City, the city had a population of three hundred and fifty thousand and was vastly bigger and more beautiful than any city he had ever seen or known about.[56] Built on water and connected through a network of causeways, it so mesmerized the conquistadors that they thought they were in a dream. Bernal Díaz del Castillo, Cortés's companion and chronicler of the conquest of Mexico, wrote that "it was like the enchantments they tell in the legend of Amadis, on account of the great towers and [temples] and buildings rising from the water, and all built of masonry." They were struck by the city's cleanliness and order, its public services, running water, floating gardens, overflowing markets, architecture and public artwork, colorful costumes, soaps, even deodorants and breath sweeteners. "Most powerful Lord," wrote Cortés to his king,

in order to give an account to your Royal Excellency of the magnificence, the strange and marvelous things of this great city and the dominion and wealth of this Mutezuma, its ruler, and of the rites and customs of the people, and of the order there is in government of the capital as well as in other cities of Mutezuma's dominions, I would need much time and many expert narrators. I cannot describe one hundredth part of all the things which could be mentioned, but, as best I can I will describe some of those I have seen which, although badly described, will I well know, be so remarkable as not to be believed, for we who saw them with our own eyes could not grasp them with our understanding."[57]

Everywhere the Europeans went, they marveled at the accomplishments of indigenous civilizations. Their pyramids rivaled those of Egypt, and their structures, such as the Mayan Temple IV at Tikal, would remain the "tallest structure in the Americas until the Washington Capitol dome was built—eleven centuries later."[58] The rapacious soldiers who toppled the great civilizations of the Incas and the Aztecs were so struck by their sophistication that they ascribed fabulous qualities to them. "To men who had seen Mexico and Peru, nothing seemed unlikely of impossible. Their minds endowed the mysterious land with an entire geography of avarice: El Dorado; the Fountain of Youth; the Seven Cities of Cíbola. Such fantasies doomed them to roam, marauding like Huns until they dropped." In May 1539, when Hernando de Soto, Pizarro's lieutenant, landed on the "flowery lands" (Florida) of North America, rampaging his way to the Mississippi, which he "discovered" and where his dead corpse—probably infected—was sunk, he was the "last" European to witness pre-Columbian North America before its decimation by microbes and conquests. By the time the English arrived, the so-called tribes had become "remnants of once-powerful states." Only deer had multiplied—humans had suffered irreparable damage.[59] Indeed, in the mere span of one century, two hundred thousand Spaniards had settled in America, while between 60 and 80 million natives—if not more—were dead. "In the course of human history," wrote John Mohawk, "there were many periods when people demonstrated what best can be called a depraved indifference to human suffering, but the Spanish treatment of the Indians and the subsequent Spanish, English, and Dutch treatment of African slaves in surely a textbook example of what the phrase can mean." [60] And, as Stannard put it, "the carnage was not over."[61]

The power of narrative was added to that of Spain's conquering sword to rally public opinion back in Europe and further seal the fate of indigenous cultures. Columbus's Santangel Letter, mixing fantasy with fact, had such an impact that, in 1493, the pope, in his Bulls of Donation, granted newly discovered lands to Spain. Columbus instituted the *repartimiento* system, apportioning natives among Spanish settlers for the purpose of gathering gold, in 1498–99, which evolved into the *encomienda* system controlled by the Spanish court when other metals were added in 1503. A ranchero system inaugurated a "red-meat dependent society," while Santo Domingo would become the first city in New World "to be stamped with the orthogonal grid system." The name of the newly discovered continent, what Cristóbal Colón called "Otro Mundo," emerged slowly, initially wrongly associated with Amerigo Vespucci, for the latter never used the term. Although much of his life was controversial, Columbus's legacy, according to early accounts, surpassed that of Hercules, who, according to legend, opened up the Mediterranean. And while the exact location of his remains is still contested even today,[62] in time, the myths of emerging capitalist European cultures were woven around the man. (The term "venture" for capitalist enterprise was first used in 1584.)[63]

Having defeated the Spanish Armada in 1588, insular England, relatively protected and with a capital less tied up in defense and border wars, inherited the Columbian legacy (myths of fabled lands of gold) and became intent on supplanting Spain in the New World.[64] The Genoese Giovanni Cabotto (known in the English-speaking world as John Cabot) had witnessed Cristóbal Colón's triumph in 1493 and had convinced Henry VII to sponsor his trip in 1497 and 1498. Since no Asia was found, however, interest in such expeditions gradually diminished before Christopher Newton, leading a fleet of three ships and somewhere between 140 and 150 men and boys, was dispatched by the Virginia Company of private stockholders. They left a few days before Christmas 1606 and, after a stormy beginning, reached Chesapeake Bay on 26 April 1607. Jamestown (named in honor of James I) was founded on Virginia, a vast stretch of land named by or after Queen Elizabeth (who probably wasn't virgin).

Sale insists that that early accounts leave no doubt as to the real motive of such risky voyages: gold, land, and exploitation. Literary and other discursive metaphors represented America "as the succulent maiden to be seduced, deflowered, and plundered by a virile Europe." One need only read John Donne's poem "Elegie: Going to Bed" to sense this:

> Licence my roaving hands, and let them go,
> Before, behind, between, above, below.
> O my America! My new-found-land,
> My kingdome, safeliest when with one man man'd,
> My Myne of precious stones, My Emperie,
> How blest am I in this discovering thee![65]

The secularization of thought through further scientific exploration removed traditional restraints and made pacts with the devil attractive. The immensely popular play by Christopher Marlowe, *The Tragical History of Doctor Faustus*, based on a true story, expresses this new imperial sprit.

> O what a world of profit and delight,
> Of power, of honor, of omnipotence . . .
> All things that move between quiet poles
> Shall be at my command.[66]

After decades of famine, death, and general misery in their new environment, European settlers established the cash-crop, land-devouring economy of tobacco and were forced, in the course of time, to declare war on the Powhatans and practically wipe them out. Because they had not found the bullion they had sought, land became their principal source of wealth, a process that was expanded to the commodification of all nature. Thus, gradually, the precontact peoples north of Mexico were decimated and/or radically transformed by this new political economy.[67] The Aztecs, like all Indians, had no references to make sense of their murderous antagonists' culture and behavior: "They picked up the gold and fingered it like monkeys," they noted. "The truth is that [the Spaniards] longed and lusted for gold. Their bodies swelled with greed, and their hunger was ravenous; they hungered like pigs for that gold."[68] Montezuma, who had expressed fear and hopelessness upon learning about the nature of the invaders, guided them to his valuable treasures, but the Spaniards took only gold and burned everything else, no matter how precious it may have been in Aztec culture.[69] Thus, Spanish violence, greed, and epidemics combined to defeat the Aztecs, whose once brilliant city now lay in ruins. A poem titled, "The Fall of Tenochtitlan," published in *Cantares mexicanos* laments the Aztec fate thus:

> Weep, my people:
> Know that with these disasters
> We have lost the Mexican nation.
> The water has turned bitter,
> Our food is bitter![70]

No one has chronicled the horrors of what followed the fall of Tenochtitlan more eloquently than Bartolomé de Las Casas in his account, *The Devastation of the Indies*. If Hispaniola is any indication of America's other advanced parts, the continent was densely populated by "the most guileless, the most devoid of wickedness . . . the most humble, patient, and peaceable" people in the world. Las Casas marveled at the Indians' gentle disposition, their cleanliness and lack of interest in material goods. Making up "the great majority of mankind," such selfless people were not "arrogant, embittered, or greedy." And yet, "into this sheepfold, into this land of meek outcasts there came some Spaniards who immediately behaved like ravening beasts, wolves, tigers, or lions that had been starved for many days." The Christians' "unjust wars" against the Indians were "more diabolical than any wars ever waged anywhere in the world." Tens of millions of Indian men, women, and children were tortured, butchered, and abused in unimaginably grotesque ways, all for the sake of profit. And the Spaniards' "intolerably gross behavior" was matched only by their "enormous appetites—one man eating at a single meal more than would suffice for a family of ten Indians in a month." (In Venezuela, the Spaniards were joined by the equally voracious Germans.) Las Casas concludes his report with an even gloomier picture of the future. "I believe," he stated,

no, I am sure that what I have said about such perditions, injuries, and horrible cruelties and all kinds of ugliness, violence, injustice, thefts, and massacres that those men have perpetrated in these parts of the Indies (and are still perpetrating), I am sure that what I have described is only the ten-thousandth part of what has been done, in quality and quantity, by the Spaniards in the Indies, from the beginning until today.[71]

The Indians did their best to resist the wholesale plunder of their continent. With the total destruction of Aztec civilization, the *Mexicas* used syncretism to encode their values in the colonizer's culture. Is it mere coincidence that Juan Diego, a baptized Aztec, had a vision of the Virgin Mary on the old site of Tonantzin, or Coatlicue, the Lady of the Serpent Skirt, in 1531? While the Indian-looking Guadalupe was on her way to becoming the patron saint of all the Americas, Mexicans of Spanish extraction, the Criollos, adopted Aztec food staples and their aesthetic. Indeed, Ronald Wright chooses the date on which Coatlicue was unearthed, 13 August 1790 in Mexico City, to locate the birth of a mestizo Mexican consciousness. And how could the Spaniards not be impressed by native cultures and even adopt them as their own? So struck by pre-Hispanic native art were they that many "European theologians had long been puzzled, even disturbed, that the Bible made no mention of America."[72]

The Maya, whose terrain was less hospitable and less profitable, chose outright resistance over the centuries. Like the Incas, they "employed their scheme of revolving ages" to tough out colonization.[73] In the Books of Chilam Balam, the arrival of the white man spelled disaster:

With the true God, the true *Dios*,
Came the beginning of our misery.
It was the beginning of tribute,
The beginning of church dues . . .
The beginning of strife by trampling on people,
The beginning of robbery with violence,
The beginning of forced debts,

The beginning of debts enforced by false testimony,
The beginning of individual strife.[74]

Everywhere on the continent, the natives struggled to maintain their culture. The Inca leader Tupa Amaru, beheaded in 1572, had advised his people to keep their traditions alive, even while they seemed to surrender to European ways. "I know that someday, by force or deceit, they will make you worship, and when that happens, when you can resist no longer, do it in front of them, but on the other hand do not forget our ceremonies. And if they tell you to break your shrines, and force you to do so, reveal just what you have to, and keep hidden the rest."[75] Ghost dances were used for this purpose.[76] The Incas also resorted to writing down their views. Felipe Wamna Puma's utopia, *The First New Chronicle and Good Government* (with its twelve hundred pages and four hundred drawings) argued for a multicultural world under the symbolic and prestigious, but not political power of King Philip III of Spain and the Holy Roman emperor. "You should consider that all the world belongs to God," he wrote Philip, "and that thus Castile is of the Spaniards, and the Indies of the Indians, and Guinea of the Negroes. Each of these are the lawful owners of their lands." Puma's political geography of the world, which in addition to the Indies (America) and Guinea (Africa), included Rome (Europe) and "Grand Turkey," was too humanely polycentric for messianic European Christians driven by the lethal motives of conversion and conquest even to understand, let alone accept. It was a plea that has yet to be fully heard.

The Cherokee elder Onitositah (Corn Tassel) also tried to convince Europeans that people are different. After pointing out to the white man's greed of land and the use of force in acquiring it, he rejected European universalist claims (often the ideological justification for plunder and enslavement) and the imposition of European cultural norms on Native American cultures. "You say: Why do not the Indians till the ground and live as we do? May we not, with equal propriety, ask: Why do not the white people hunt and live as we do?" Onitositah wanted the Europeans to understand that cultures are different, and such differences ought to be respected as part of a natural plan. "The great God of Nature has placed us in different situations. It is true that he has endowed you with many superior advantages; but he has not created us to be your slaves. *We are a separate people!*"[77] But his peaceful effort didn't prevent the new American presidents, Thomas Jefferson and especially Andrew Jackson (whose life was saved by a Cherokee elder during his war against the Creeks), from delegitimizing the Cherokees' claim to separate nationhood and eventually driving them out of their ancestral lands in a sordid human episode remembered as the Trail of Tears (1838–39), despite two separate Supreme Court decisions in 1830 and 1832 allowing the Cherokees to be "domestic dependent nations." Andrew Jackson was simply intent on a "final solution" to the Cherokee problem.[78]

While the Cherokees were displaced, the Iroquois relied on the neutralizing effects of the syncretic vision of Handsome Lake, an old, alcoholic man who came back to life from the brink of death in 1799. Handsome Lake's vision, the *Gaiwiio* (Good Message), urged the Iroquois to live on and reject the destructive practices (abortions, alcoholism, profit making, etc.) that were destroying their cultures.[79]

Even in its defeat and dislocation, the Cherokee nation managed to impress Europeans. Rebuilding itself after the destruction of the Civil War, it drew the attention of Senator Henry Dawes of Massachusetts, who said: "There is not a pauper in that nation, and the nation does not owe a dollar. It built its own capitol . . . its schools and hospitals. Yet the defect of the system was apparent. They have got as far as they can go, because they hold their land in common. . . . There is no selfishness, which is at bottom of civilization."[80] Such a conception of civilization was confirmed by another Indian leader, Chief Sitting Bull of the Hunkpapa Sioux, who, after touring Europe in the 1880s, stated that "the White man knows how to make everything, but he does not know how to distribute it."[81]

I have said earlier that the power of narrative was deployed by the Spaniards to process and manage the conquered, and it is through these narratives that one glimpses the overlapping of Indians and Moors in the conquistadors' imagination. Todorov's semiotic study of the conquest as a question of otherness is a classic illustration of how the European enterprise was undertaken with signs. It remains, in the words of Anthony Pagden, an "important contribution to our understanding of the clash of cultures in the Americas in the early sixteenth century."[82] Todorov notes that Columbus treated the indigenous people of the New World as either angels or savages. Either the Indians were seen as humans capable of assimilation, or they were dismissed as radically different and inferior. Like most Europeans who came after him, Columbus made no effort to understand the culture of the people he had "discovered": "What is denied is the existence of a human substance truly other, something capable of being not merely an imperfect state of oneself. These two elementary figures of the experience of alterity are grounded in egocentrism, in the identification of our own values in general, of our I with the universe—in the conviction that the world is one." Columbus eventually established subtle differences among the Indians, between "potentially Christian Indians and idolatrous Indians, practicing cannibalism; and between pacific Indians (submitting to his power) and bellicose Indians who thereby deserve to be punished; but the important thing is that those who are not already Christians can only be slaves: there is no middle path." That was as far as Columbus could go: Otherwise, he simply had no interest whatsoever in Indians as Indians. He had discovered a continent, but no Indians.[83]

The conquest of America's great civilizations was due not to European superior weaponry or forces (although those played a significant part), but to the Indians' inability to read European signs, or rather, to a confusion of signs on both parts. After relating the well-known history of Cortés's conquest, Todorov says that the Spaniards' superior weapons, horses, or even unwitting bacteriological warfare do not explain their victory. The Indians—both Maya and Aztec—simply lost control of communication. Because the Aztec world was preordained, predetermined, known through "cyclical divination," prophecies (the projection of the past onto the future), auguries, and omens to explain unexpected occurrences, nothing was supposed to happen out of order. Everything had an explanation, even if it had to be a posteriori. And since individualism didn't exist and everything was overdetermined, sacrifice and defeat were accepted as part of a cosmic plan, a worldview that was particularly helpful to the Spaniards, since they appeared as superhuman deities. The Aztecs looked for explanations in the world of gods; the Spaniards' communication, meanwhile, remained at the human level. Not that the Indians were not great speakers and rhetoricians—they were;[84] but, again, since theirs was a highly structured universe, they couldn't improvise, even to address a threat as enormous as the one they were confronting. Their esteemed orator, the *huehuetlatolli*, could speak only through the unquestioned authority of ancestors.[85] Meanwhile, the easy defeat of the Indians only confirmed the Spaniards' conviction that they were the bearers of the true religion. Duplicitous and seized by gold fever, they saw themselves as God's chosen and so won a dubious battle. As Todorov comments,

this victory from which we all derive, European and Americans both, delivers as well a terrible blow to our capacity to feel in harmony with the world, to belong to a preestablished order; its effect is to repress man's communication with the world, to produce the illusion that all communication is interhuman communication; the silence of the gods weighs upon the camp of the Europeans as much as on that of the Indians. By winning on one side, the Europeans lost on the other; by imposing their superiority upon the entire country, they destroyed their own capacity to integrate themselves into the world. During the centuries to follow, they would dream of the noble savage; but the savage was dead or assimilated, and this dream was doomed to remain a sterile one. The victory was already big with defeat; but this Cortés could not know.[86]

Like Columbus, Cortés was motivated by a strong Christian impulse. His banner, with its "white and blue flames with a cross in the middle" contained a Latin motto mixing the Cross and conquest: "Friends, let us follow the Cross and with faith in this symbol we shall conquer."[87] To Christianity's universalist, egalitarian, and uncompromisingly monotheistic impulses, differences were deviations to be rooted out, punished. Unlike precontact native religions, Christianity accepted only one god and unequivocally rejected the sort of polytheism exemplified in the Aztec temple of Coatescalli (The Temple of Diverse Gods) that had been commissioned by Montezuma on the eve of Spanish conquests. And yet, it was the Spaniards' inflexible ideology, their simplemindedness and orthodox rigidity, that allowed them to triumph over a much larger army, for, as Todorov puts it, "intransigence has always defeated tolerance."[88] Thus, the fervor of faith opened the way to the pursuit of worldly gain, religion providing the impetus for irreligion, so to speak. Indeed, the notion of private property, hitherto tolerated, in the words of R. H. Tawney, as a "concession to human frailty," by the sixteenth century had evolved into one of the hallmarks—if not the only hallmark—of civilization among both Catholics and Protestants. According to Stannard,

The concept of private property as a positive good and even an insignia of civilization took hold among both Catholics and Protestants during the sixteenth century. Thus, for example, in Spain, Juan Ginés de Sepúlveda argued that the absence of private property was the one of the characteristics of people lacking "even vestiges of humanity," and in Germany at the same time Martin Luther was contending "that the possession of private property was an essential difference between men and beasts." In England, meanwhile, Sir Thomas More was proclaiming that land justifiably could be taken from "any people [who] holdeth a piece of ground void and vacant to no good or profitable use," an idea that also was being independently advanced in other countries by Calvin, Melanchthon, and others. Typically, though, none was as churlish as Luther, who pointed out that the Catholic St. Francis had urged his followers to get rid of their property and give it to the poor: "I do not maintain that St. Francis was simply wicked," wrote Luther, "but his works show that he was a weak-minded and freakish man, or to say the truth, a fool.[89]

"In theory," writes Todorov, "and as Columbus wished (and even Cortés, of whom this is one of the most 'archaic' mental features), the goal of the conquest is to spread the Christian religion; in practice, religious discourse is one of the means assuring the conquest's success: end and means have changed places."[90] The key question of course, is whether the two are truly separable, or whether they are the two faces of the same coin. Religion in this case seems to function like any modern ideology (such as human rights and democracy) that justifies intervention and war; yet it is also more than that. To say that religion was cynically used to justify more worldly pursuits would not accurately reflect the ideological blend that animated most Spaniards of that time. Although Marx's suspicion of self-professed aims cannot be disputed,[91] I do think that contradictory tendencies can coexist within the same individual or even nation. Columbus's goal *was* to recapture Jerusalem somehow, and Queen Isabella's passion *was* the spread of Christianity and the defeat of Islam. When Bernal Díaz del Castillo said "We came here to serve God and the king, and also to get rich,"[92] he was in effect describing the social imaginary of his nation.

Convivencia, then, was not part of the Spaniards' vision. No sooner had they defeated the Aztecs than they proceeded to erase the astonishing linguistic diversity of their conquered lands by imposing the Aztec language of Nahuatl as the national native language (something the Aztecs would have never thought of doing) to prepare for the universalization of Spanish. Language was considered crucial in the consolidation of empire and the triumph of Spanish ideology. As suggested earlier, the defeat of Arabs, the expulsion of Jews from Spain, and the discovery of America were complemented by "the publication of the first grammar of a modern European language—the Spanish grammar of Antonio de Nebrija" who matter-of-factly wrote in his introduction that "language has always been the companion of empire."[93] On the face of it, it would seem that Spaniards were motivated by understanding, but the knowledge they sought was part of their lethal arsenal. They were merely interested in an "understanding-that-kills," a knowledge that facilitates plunder and conquests.[94] "There is ... dreadful concatenation here," writes Todorov, "whereby grasp-

ing leads to taking and taking to destruction, a concatenation whose unavoidable character we want to question." Todorov then asks the question
whose answer eludes us still: "Should not understanding go hand in hand
with sympathy? And should not even the desire to take, to profit at another's expense, simply a desire to preserve that other as a potential source
of wealth and profit?"

The conquerors found Mexican civilization most impressive, sur-
passing anything they had seen and known about in the old world, and yet
they set out to annihilate it because, like Columbus, they had failed to see
the humanity of their conquered subjects. "Cortés is interested in Aztec
civilization, and at the same time remains altogether alien to it. Nor is he
the only one; this is the behavior of many enlightened men of his time."
Their knowledge was exploitative, opportunistic, and devoid of the humaneness of dialogue. Because of this inflexible Spanish ideology, seventy
million died in about fifty years, a "hetacomb" that far surpasses even "the
great massacres of the twentieth century."[95] Although the responsibility of
the Spaniards is often debated, particularly by relativists eager to equate all
forms of violence and thus take away from the specificity of European aggression against the Indians, there is no doubt that the weakening of the
native populations through slavery and its effects made them vulnerable to
all sorts of premature deaths. In order to justify their genocidal mission, the
Spaniards annihilated a culture of sacrifices through large-scale massacres,
both bloody practices emanating from radically different worldviews—for
a massacre is what one inflicts on other, distant colonies, whereas a sacrifice is a more intimate social affair closely tied to a shared cosmology.[96]

Confronted by their own brutality, the Spaniards devised a bizarre legal maneuver to justify their actions. In 1512, the royal jurist Dr. Juan
López Palacios Rubios drafted the *Requerimiento* (the "Requirement")—
described by Pagden as "surely the crassest example of legalism in modern
European history"—to be read by the conquistadors to Indians before seal-
ing their fate, one way or the other.[97] In the words of Patricia Seed, it was
an "ultimatum," a hybrid text, inspired by the eighth-century Maliki
school of Islamic jurisprudence (the earliest of the four main schools in
Sunni Islam) then prevailing in much of Northern Africa and Andalusian
Spain. Maliki law stipulated that the option for conversion be given to a
population before war is declared on them, but the *Requerimiento* didn't include the Muslim liberal provisions for a conquered people.[98] The conquistadors would begin by invoking "the King, Don Fernando, and of

Dona Juana, his daughter, Queen of Castile and Leon, subduers of the barbarous nations," claiming that they, the conquistadors, had come to notify
and inform the natives "as best we can, that the Lord our God, living and
eternal, created the heaven and the earth, and one man and one woman, of
whom you and we, and all the men of the world, were descendants, and all
those who come after us." They would go on to say that the world is divided into many nations, but that God made St. Peter "superior" and the
"head of the whole human race, wherever men should live, and under
whatever law, sect, or belief they should be." Although his seat is in Rome,
the pope's jurisdiction in fact covers the whole world and allows him to
"judge and govern all Christians, Moors, Jews, Gentiles, and all other
sects."[99] The *Requerimiento*, "a study of the mentality of the Crusades," in
the expression of John Mohawk,[100] proved that Iberian Catholics were the
rightful possessors of America, since, ultimately, it had been bestowed on
them by Jesus himself. It was read loud to the Indians upon contact, and
the Indians were given the two options of accepting the truth of the document and becoming serfs in the colonial system or rejecting the document
and, as punishment, becoming slaves. That Indians could not understand
Spanish didn't matter.

Respectable and conscientious jurists and philosophers more or less
justified Spanish intervention as a way to end Indian barbarism, since even
the most liberal and well-intentioned scholars believed in inequality and
the unqualified benefits of Spanish rule. The Indians were depicted as
grotesquely savage and sub-human. Here, for instance, is how Tomás Ortiz, a Dominican, described them to the Council of the Indies:

On the mainland they eat human flesh. They are more given to sodomy than any
other nation. There is no justice among them. They go naked. They have no respect
either for love or for virginity. They are stupid and silly. They have no respect for
truth, save when it is to their advantage. They are unstable. They have no knowledge of what foresight means. They are ungrateful and changeable. . . . They are
brutal. They delight in exaggerating their defects. There is no obedience among
them, or deference on the part of the young of the old, nor of the son for the father.
They are incapable of learning. Punishments have no effect upon them. . . . They
eat fleas, spiders and worms raw, whenever they find them. They exercise none of
the human arts or industries. When taught the mysteries of our religion, they say
that these things may suit Castilians, not them, and they do not wish to change
their customs. They are beardless, and if sometimes hairs grow, they pull them
out. . . . The older they get the worse they become. About the age of ten or twelve
years, they seem to have some civilization, but later they become like real brute

beasts. I may therefore affirm that God has never created a race more full of vice and composed without the least mixture of kindness or culture. . . . The Indians are more stupid than asses, and refuse to improve anything.[101]

Gonzalo Fernández de Oviedo, Spain's official historian and foe of Las Casas, echoed much of Ortiz's details is his history of the West Indies, describing the Indians as "naturally lazy and vicious," "a lying shiftless people" given to idolatry and sodomy whose "chief desire is to eat [and] drink." Oviedo's contempt for the Indians is such that he asks: "What could one expect from a people whose skulls are so thick and hard that the Spaniards had to take care in fighting not to strike on the head lest their swords be blunted?"[102]

In 1551, when the humanist Aristotelian philosopher Juan Ginés de Sepúlveda, considered by some as the "father" of modern racism, debated the Dominican bishop of Chiapas, Bartolomé de Las Casas, on the issue of Indian rights in Valladolid, he affirmed a natural hierarchy of cultures that permits the higher forms to dominate the lower ones. "How can we doubt," Sepúlveda asked, "that these people—so uncivilized, so barbaric, contaminated with so many impieties and obscenities—have been justly conquered by such an excellent, pious, and most just king as was Ferdinand the Catholic, and by such humane nation and excellent in every kind of virtue?"[103] Indeed, in *De regno et regis officio*, a treatise on good government addressed to Philip II, Sepúlveda distinguished between three categories of humans, with people capable of self-government on top of the hierarchy and the "barbarous and inhuman" (a category that includes Turks and Indians as "inculti") at the bottom.[104] In his dehumanizing rhetoric, Sepúlveda didn't forget the natives' unforgivable vice of not even having private property.[105] Las Casas, meanwhile, who opposed the *Requerimiento* (partly because he knew it replicated Muslim law and principles) resorted to the Christian principle of equality under Christ—a prevalent view in the royal court—that all humans are to be treated equally, assuming they receive the message and adopt it.[106]

Despite Las Casas's profuse praise of the Indians, Todorov thinks that his portrait of the Indian (at least the one that emerges out of this debate) is poorer than Sepúlveda's, for at the heart of Las Casas's defense is the assumption that Indians are amenable to Christianity through less drastic measures. The Indians are good because they are not quite Muslim. Unlike the "Turks and Moors, the veritable barbarian outcasts of the nations," they are predisposed to Christianity. Although Las Casas professed to love the Indians, Todorov wonders whether we really can love someone if we know little or nothing of his identity; if we see, in place of that identity, a projection of ourselves or of our ideals? We know that such a thing is quite possible, even frequent, in personal relations; but what happens in cultural confrontations? Doesn't one culture risk trying to transform the other in its own name, and therefore risk subjugating it as well? How much is such love worth?

We know how Las Casas felt toward Indians, but "we know virtually nothing of the feelings of the Indians of the period toward Las Casas, which, in itself, is already significant."[107]

Still, despite this lacuna, one must assume that as much as he was shaped by his period's social imaginary, Las Casas was able to operate at a different register of consciousness and thus to contribute to the prophetic literature of people resisting domination. Las Casas went through several transformations: there is the Las Casas who released the Indians in 1514, there is the Las Casas who became a Dominican monk in 1522–23 (i.e., after he had released his Indians), and then there is the Las Casas of the post-Valladolid debate. True, prior to this, Las Casas had imagined equality for the Indians within a Christian doctrine, but later, in his *Apologética historia,* he resorted to "religious anthropology" and "perspectivism,"[108] not only to show that sacrifice has a history in Christianity, but that, in fact, it can be the sign of ultimate devotion and religiosity. It is only the incomprehension of rites and languages that make others look inferior:

A man will be called barbarian in comparison with another man because he is strange in his ways of speaking and because he pronounces the other's language badly. . . . According to Strabo, Book XIV, this was the main reason the Greeks called other people barbarians, that is, because they pronounced the Greek language improperly. But from this point of view, there is no man or race which is not barbarian in relation to another man or another race. As Saint Paul says of himself and others in 1 Corinthians14:10–11: "'There are, it may be, so many kinds of voices in the world, and none of them is without signification. Therefore if I know not the meaning of the voice, I shall be unto him that speaketh a barbarian, and he that speaketh shall be a barbarian unto me." Thus, just as we consider the peoples of the Indies barbarians, they judge us to be the same, because they do not understand us.[109]

In his old age, Las Casas reached a level of cultural maturity that would be echoed in Italy by another Dominican monk, Giordano Bruno, author of *De l'infinito universo e mondi* (1584), arguing that the world has no privileged center or margins. "There is in the universe neither centre nor circumference, but, if you will, the whole is central, and every point also may be regarded as part of a circumference to some other central point." For such an antitotalitarian perspective, the Inquisition had Bruno arrested, condemned, and burned in 1600.[110] There were other Spaniards who viewed the Indians benevolently and imagined them within a scheme of their own making (utopian, Christian, etc.), but the case of Las Casas remains quite intriguing: Despite his strong antipathy for Islam, he admitted that Islam's rejection of coercion in matters of faith made it more tolerant. In his *The Only Way*, a treatise that was not published until the twentieth century, he confessed that the Prophet Mohammed "forced no one to join his belief," for "so long as they remained subject . . . he forced them no further."[111] Perhaps equally daringly, he suggested that the king of Spain renounce his possessions in the Americas.

As America was being "discovered," other voices, both Spanish and Indian, emerged to reject European absolutism and call for a dialogue of cultures, either through hybridization or simply by allowing the natives to practice their own traditions. The Dominican Diego Durán, who lived in Mexico from the age of five or six and thus grew up practically Mexican, wrote *Historia de las Indias de Nueva España y Islas de la Tierra Firme* between 1576 and 1581 to study Aztec religion and culture, but the book wasn't published until the nineteenth century. As a rigorist Dominican (unlike the more realist Franciscans), he was most angered by the "religious syncretism" of the Aztecs, since such syncretism allowed the conquered Indians to keep their culture and faith and insert them into Christian practices. Yet the more Durán studied preconquest Aztec traditions, the more resemblances he found with his own, to the point that he claimed Quetzalcoatl to be the "common father of the Toltecs and the Spaniards."[112] He went as far as to claim that the Aztecs must have been one of the lost tribes of Israel. Thus, Durán became a cultural hybrid in the process of evangelization, unable to maintain his proclaimed purist ideology.

The Franciscan Bernardino de Sahagún, who arrived to Mexico at the age of thirty, spent the rest of his life doing the work of a typical scholar: learning Nahuatl and teaching and researching the history of the Aztecs. He spent forty years working on his *Historia general de las cosas de Nueva España*, an exceptional and structurally complex work of scholarship written in Nahuatl and Spanish and illustrated with drawings. After weighing the pros and the cons of the conquests, he came out against them:

Since all these [idolatrous] practices ceased upon the Spaniards' arrival, who made it their task to trample on all customs and on all ways of governing themselves the native possessed, with the claim to reduce them to living in Spain, as much in the divine practices as in human affairs, by the mere fact of considering them as idolaters and barbarians, we destroyed all their ancient government. . . . But now we see that this new organization renders men vicious, produces in them very bad inclinations and worse undertakings which render them hateful to God and for man as well, not counting diseases and the shortening of human life.[113]

To Bernardino de Sahagún, Aztec strength derived from living under structures that reflected their culture: "If it is true that they attested to still greater aptitudes in times gone by, either in the administration of public affairs or in the service of their gods, it is because they lived under a system closer relationship with their aspirations and their needs." For espousing a liberalism and tolerance that mirrored Talavera's with the Moors in Spain,[114] the Spanish authorities reacted immediately by condemning and censoring the book, "this unique monument to human thought," as Todorov puts it, and cutting the scholar's funds. So concerned were the Spanish authorities about Sahagún's multicultural perspective that a royal edict was issued in 1577 to decree ignoring the book.[115] Sahagún may have been against hybridization, but he set the tone for a dialogue that is most relevant to us today.

Both Talavera and Sahagún accepted theological differences as part of a larger natural scheme and saw no reason to force "others" into a belief system or way of life that simply was not suitable to them. Because they had such an expansive view of the world, one they somewhat shared with the Indian leaders such as Tupa Amaru and Onitositah, they were defeated. The question for them then—as it is for us now—was: Could Catholic Spain, and by extension, the Christian West, live side by side with different cultures and traditions without forcing non-European others into traumatic and ultimately unproductive conversions, whether to a faith or to an economic doctrine?

The *Reconquista*, with its "sacred patriotic struggle to wrest power from alien hands and restore Christian dominion," was ultimately "irresistible" and served Spain throughout much of its history, extending all the way to Franco and even beyond. "The sickle [may] have replaced the crescent," wrote Fletcher in his history of al-Andalus, "but the enemy's symbol retained the same menacing shape." The administration of (re)conquered Muslim lands (such as the *repartimiento* and *encomienda* systems)[116] became the basis of Spain's policy in the Americas, as we have seen. And so when an overseas empire was acquired in the sixteenth century, models and precedents existed for the guidance of those whose task was to rule it. In this as in so much else there was little that was new about the so-called "early modern" period of the sixteenth and seventeenth centuries. Colonial Mexico, Peru, and Brazil were medieval Andalusia writ large. Much that is central to the subsequent experience of Latin America follows from this.[117]

Indeed, Viceroy Francisco de Toledo, who ruled in Peru and sought to refute Las Casas's claims against Spain's illegitimate mission in the New World, inspired a treatise in 1571 arguing, as Hanke puts it, that "the Indies were given to Spain as a reward for her eight centuries of warfare against the Moslems."[118]

In her study of post-1492 Spanish narratives, *Mimesis and Empire*, Barbara Fuchs notes that the structure of villainy comes out of the same cultural matrix that had defined Christian/Muslim relations prior to the discovery of America. Fuchs opens her book by quoting Stephen Clissold's account of the entrance of Viceroy Francisco de Toledo into Cuzco, Peru, in 1570 to show that a "time-honored Mediterranean script is produced in an American setting, casting the natives of the New World as the Islamic bogeymen of the Old," although, by that time, most Indians had already been baptized Christian. Why, then, would Indians play roles whose purpose was to legitimize or encourage Spanish violence? "Perhaps," Fuchs speculates, "the 'infidel' Indians are simply standing for their unbaptized brethren, or perhaps their very participation in the Spanish performance marks the success of the Conquista."[119] In any case, these images "make their appearance in actual New World performances as well as in the *relaciones*," the accounts of the conquest.

Noting that sixteenth-century Spain still saw itself fighting Muslims at a variety of fronts (Ottomans, Barbary corsairs, and even the dangerously Spanish-looking Moriscos at home), she suggests that literary forms of resistance to the *Conquista* produced in America echo or parallel those depicting the Morisco struggle in Spain. For instance, she examines Alonso de Ercilla's thirty-seven-canto poem, *La Araucana* (1569–97), which deals with Chilean natives' uprising against Spaniards, and Ginés Pérez de Hita's two-volume *Guerras civiles de Granada* (1595, 1604), which examines the Moriscos' uprising in Spain, to show how both authors struggle with their sympathies for the heroic, "indomitable," and chivalrous Other, although both Others (metaphorically the same) would eventually be defeated, either through forced conversion or by expulsion. (The Moors were ordered to be expelled from Spain in 1609). Since, in the words of Pagden, "the struggle against Islam offered a descriptive language which allowed the generally shabby ventures in America to be vested with a seemingly eschatological significance," Indians were imagined as extension of either the defeated Moors or the still-troublesome Moriscos.

The substantial Spanish literature of conquest served to enhance this sense of continuity, by redescribing the actions of the most celebrated of the conquistadors in the language of the Spanish border ballads. In their own eyes, and in those of their readers, men like Hernán Cortés and Francisco Pizarro were simultaneously the heirs of Caesar and El Cid, the great eleventh-century hero of the Reconquista, for whose soul it was customary to dedicate a mass on first reaching the coast of America. And contiguity with the Reconquista implied, if not divine sanction, at least divine favour. Few of the conquistadors could claim to be executing God's will; but most assumed that God openly favoured their cause. How else could the extraordinary conquests first of Mexico and then of Peru be explained? Little wonder, too, that a disingenuous old soldier like Bernal Díaz could claim to have seen St. James of Compostela, the "Moor-slayer" and patron saint of Castile, fighting alongside him.[120]

So interchangeable were Muslims and Indians in the conquistadors' minds that they called Indians "Muslims" and Indian temples "mosques." At one time, according to Bernal Díaz's account, the Spaniards even considered naming the first city they saw Great Cairo.[121] The cleanliness of the Aztecs was also associated with the Moors, and when battling the Indians, "the Spaniards often invoked the aid of holy figures such as the Virgin Mary or St. James, known in Spanish as Santiago Matamoros, patron saint of Spain against the Moors" (rechristened Mata-indios to better suit his new or renewed role).[122] Indeed, Europe's own identity and the emergence of the nation-state were effects of this clash with Islam. As Fuchs states it,

The confrontation with Islam, in its many incarnations was crucial for Europe's cultural construction of itself as a geographic and imperial center. Spain, especially, underwent the double experience of acquiring an empire while holding Islam at bay and investing enormous energies into excising Moors and Moorish culture from the newly constituted nation. The consolidation of the state—both as unified metropole and as overseas empire—was predicated largely on the attainment of religious and ethnic homogeneity. But it was not always easy to distinguish Islamic other from Christian self.[123]

In his fast-paced, galloping history of Mexico, Ramón Eduardo Ruiz describes the Spanish conquest of America as the "last crusade." If by this is meant that the conquest was Spain's last great imperial triumph, one could agree, but the new crusade that was launched by Columbus and Cortés has never truly ended, each episode provoking more resistance among the new "Muslims" while confining the latter's outlook into ever more crippling orthodoxies.

The triumph of Spain over infidels of course, did not mean the total obliteration of the defeated people's cultures. As stated earlier, many aspects of pre-Columbian culture were adopted as part of the new Criollo national identity, and the abundance of silver led to art forms inspired a baroque architecture that drew on Arab and Muslim motifs, such as the cupola, tile designs, and the patio.[124] But the *Reconquista* and Columbus's conquests were a fateful moment in history: "a rootless man" seemingly born on the sea, who never experienced what the Spaniards themselves termed *querencia,* organic attachment to a particular environment,[125] Columbus was a fitting person to spearhead the penetration of a restless Europe into the civilizations of the New World, an assault in which the exploitation of humans and nature would become the foundations and measures of success and "progress."

Most humans had shown destructive tendencies and used violence, but the nature and quality of this new enterprise were markedly different. "No civilization prior to the European had occasion to believe in the systematic material progress of the whole human race," wrote William Woodruff in *The Impact of Western Man,* "no civilization placed such stress upon the quantity rather than the quality of life; no civilization drove itself so relentlessly to an ever-receding goal; no civilization was so passion-charged to replace what is with what could be; no civilization had striven as the West has done to direct the world according to its will; no civilization has known so few moments of peace and tranquility."[126] As Columbus was lionized and mythologized and various groups of immigrants vied to claim him, the continent he discovered was exploited by Europeans. The conquerors celebrated their victories in parades and holidays, "but as is inevitable with any war against the world of nature, those who win will have lost—once again lost, and this time perhaps forever."[127] The era of direct colonialist occupation has ended, but much like Columbus, Cortés, and indeed most of Christian historians and defenders of the Indians, the West, which has grown out of this historical moment, still seeks knowledge for power, although such knowledge only perpetuates violence and imperils human relations. A language of dialogue, one that truly transcends cultural barriers, has yet to be implemented, although, ironically, at this juncture in history, the multilingual poor, out of necessity, are ahead of the privileged rich. They talk to survive and work, not to dominate.

I will say more about this at the end of the book, but it might be helpful to remember that Las Casas had prophesied a disastrous future not just for the conquistadors who committed the inhumane acts he so passionately recorded, but for the entire country of Spain, since it benefited from the murder of the Indians and the devastation of their lands.[128] Little did Las Casas know that most of Western European nations, one by one, would scramble for extraterritorial colonies and subject the native populations to varying degrees of inhumanity and degradation, or that the passions of the *Reconquista* would still be shaping the world more than five hundred years after the Moors surrendered the keys of Granada and the poetic palace of Alhambra to the Spanish monarchs. It was this period, more than any other, that established the patterns of relations between the West and its others, between the West and Islam. When trying to explain the larger goals of his history of Spain between 1250 and 1500, L. P. Harvey says:

Relations between the various regions of the Islamic world and the West (with all its divisions) have occupied a disproportionately large amount of space on the agendas of our twentieth-century international bodies. Those relations have usually been characterized by mutual incomprehension, often by exasperation and recrimination. It has always surprised me that so little attention has been paid to the period at the end of the Middle Ages when Islam was in the process of being eliminated from Europe. Many of the attitudes that help generate modern misunderstandings were formed at this time. The crusading endeavors of Europeans in the Middle East are certainly formative influences on those attitudes, but contact, largely hostile, between Christendom and Islam went on much longer in the Iberian Peninsula. The experience of Islam in Spain needs to be understood.[129]

Of course, Spain's claims and treatment of new cultures were animated by a certain medieval universalism, a "presumed right over the entire world"[130] that was rooted in Roman and Christian legal doctrines, although some were inspired by Muslim law. Spaniards, and Europeans in general, could understand the New World only through familiar lenses. Like anyone confronting an unfamiliar scene, they "had to classify before they could properly see; and in order to do that they had no alternative but to appeal to system which was already in use. It was indeed the system, not the innate structure of the world, which determined what areas they selected for description."[131] In the late eighteenth century, such a view would give way to more nationalist aspirations, although imperial nations would still rationalize their undertakings through recourse to universalist principles, assumed to be good for all people at all times and places. "As commerce had replaced conquest," writes Anthony Pagden, "so enlightenment would replace evangelization and the crasser forms of cultural domination."[132] Although historical circumstances and social priorities would change over time, Europeans and their descendants continued to see themselves burdened with the mission to civilize and, if need be, to conquer those who refused total assimilation. The doctrine of blood purity, combined with any variety of post-Andalusian universalism, jeopardized the lives and cultures of all those who didn't fit into this exclusivist matrix. Getting rid of the Moriscos in Spain in the early seventeenth century was the mere prelude to a process of "españolidad" founded on persecuting difference as heresy. No sooner had the Moriscos been expelled that one Salazar de Mendeza stated: "In order for Spain to stay clean, it remains to do the same with the Gypsies." The necessity to exterminate Muslims (articulated by the pope in 1265 on congratulating James following his conquest of Murcia) had now been extended to other different people.[133]

CHAPTER 3

Empire of Liberty

The old idea of American Christians as a chosen people who had been
called to a special task was turned into the notion of a chosen nation especially favored. In Lyman Beecher, as in Cotton Mather before him . . . this
tendency came to expression. As the nineteenth century went on the note of
divine favoritism was increasingly sounded. Christianity, democracy, Americanism, the English language and culture, the growth of industry and science, American institutions—these are all confounded and confused. The
contemplation of their righteousness filled Americans with such lofty and
enthusiastic sentiments that they readily identified it with the righteousness
of God. . . . It is in particular the Kingdom of the Anglo-Saxon race, which
is destined to bring light to the gentiles by means of lamps manufactured in
America. Thus institutionalism and imperialism, ecclesiastical and political,
go hand in hand.
—H. Richard Niebuhr, *The Kingdom of God in America*

Almost a century after the discovery and conquest of the Americas by
the Iberians, the English joined in the adventure, bringing with them a set
of prejudices that were both similar to and different from those that had
motivated Latin Catholics. With minor exceptions, the English were motivated by new wealth and a disdain for the "savages" who roamed the otherwise free land of North America, but they also had a different religious
perspective, and although they considered Muslims to be rivals, they did
not inherit the intense hatred that Spaniards had for the Moors.

Nabil Matar's groundbreaking book on this subject clearly shows that
there was no correlation between England's real encounters and dealings
with Muslims (the "Moors" of North Africa, the "Turks" of Ottoman
Turkey, and people of the Levant) as recorded in government documents,

prisoners' depositions, and commercial exchanges and the anti-Muslim nationalist consciousness propagated in plays and pageants of the Age of Discovery ("the period that corresponds in England to the time between the
Elizabethan period and the beginning of the Great Migration in the Caroline period"),[1] which reduced the otherwise formidable and threatening
Muslims to the same barbaric status conferred on the militarily much
weaker North American Indians. Remarkably, the designation "barbarian"
for Ottomans and North African Muslims was used for the first time in
English during this period, a time when, paradoxically, much about the
greatness and strength of Islam was widely known and acknowledged.[2]
Unlike the Spaniards, who projected the Moorish status onto the unsus-
pecting indigenous peoples of the Americas, the English, who had dealt
with Muslims as equals, reversed the transfer process and started applying
to Muslims the set of pejorative designations devised for the Indians. This
transfer or superimposition of native alterity on Muslims expressed England's own anxiety about Muslims and its failure to defeat or conquer
them. It was in such a political juncture that the terms "Indian" and
"Moor" became strategically interchangeable.

While the English were failing at converting the "heathen" natives of
the New World to Christianity, European Christians were abdicating their
faith and converting to Islam. During the Age of Discovery, the English
knew more about Muslims than they did about either the Jews or the Indians. Whether through strategic military alliances (against Catholic
Spain), exchange and ransom of prisoners of war, friendship treaties, or
spectacular ambassadorial visits to the city of London, the Moors and
Turks were visible "not just in the literary imagination of English drama-
tists and poets, but in the streets, the sea towns, the royal residences, the
courts, and the jails of Elizabethan, Jacobean, and Caroline England and
Wales." Hundreds, perhaps thousands of Muslims visited England and
Wales throughout this period in one guise or another. And while miscegenation with Jews and American Indians was unmentioned, the marriage
of English women to Muslim men was acceptable, if not desirable.[3]

Meanwhile, thousands of Englishmen and Britons traveled and lived
among Muslims. Soldiers and pirates seeking valor, honor, and professional
opportunity joined Muslim armies and contributed their superior technological knowledge to their often renegade-manned navies. They worked for
Muslim rulers and not infrequently converted to Islam. To these two
groups of fortune seekers, to the traders who spied on the Persian and

Turkish clothing and dying industries to improve English standards, and finally to the scientists and physicians who were popular in Muslim courts, Morocco, Spain's Muslim archrival, was "the most attractive and accessible location in the Muslim world."

Not all Britons who had encounters with Muslims chose to convert or to live among them, however. Those who had been captured and freed by ransom or exchange of prisoners submitted depositions—debriefings, as they might be called today—that reaffirmed their "religious and national identity" and that served as "intelligence reports" on Muslim navies and societies.[4] Although captivity narratives didn't excite the English literary imagination as much as they did the French and Spanish, these "texts of confrontation" are "the first realistic documents in English that are situated within the conflict between Christendom and Islam." The captives' knowledge of Islam and Muslims was "unparalleled," and their accounts portrayed a fuller and more complex picture of Muslim societies. "The captives provided the English reading public with precise, sometimes sympathetic, sometimes not so sympathetic, but most importantly, empirically derived information about the Muslims." Out of these various accounts and encounters emerged the picture of a challenging and threatening Islam, even while England was busy crossing oceans and expanding its reach and realm of "discoveries."[5]

Ignored by most scholars, the England-Moorish North Africa–North America triangle sheds significant light on the uneven processes of constructing Otherness. Well into the middle of the seventeenth century, Britons remained wary of settling what they often considered to be a wild, uncivilized, and inhospitable New World, which is why many undesirables were forced into emigrating there; yet during the same period, so many Britons chose to live and work among Muslims that royal proclamations were issued to lure them back to England. For these lower-class British sailors, traders, renegades, and captives, the Mediterranean was safer, its societies were metropolitan, and captivity was more rewarding than indenture. (In fact, the *Mayflower* had traded in the Muslim Mediterranean before taking "pilgrims" to New World.) Opportunities in Islamic lands were so clearly better that, during the Caroline period, Britons living among Muslims constituted the largest expatriate community. No wonder the study of Arabic became important.[6]

It was Muslim strength that excited the fear of the New World British settlers and led them to reverse the process of imposing Moorish otherness onto Indians and reimagine the Muslim as a savage barbarian. But first, they had to justify their settlement of the Indians' lands. Branding them as infidels, Britons declared their land a *vacuum domicilium* in need of (re)naming and (re)settling, or (re)populating. Such a policy was easier to implement in the New World, since Muslim lands had long been named. "In the Muslim dominions, the Old was real and the New superficial; in America, the New was real and the Old was savage, unnecessary, and eradicable, just as Patuxet had been eradicated to give way to Plymouth." The major exception was the Levant or Palestine (the Holy Land), in which the English saw only "the cities of biblical history."

In any case, whether in the Levant or North Africa, Arabs were seen as intruders, while rightful ownership was attributed to the industrious and trading pre-Muslim civilizations such as that of the Romans in Carthage. To this new discursive process of renaming was added a whole arsenal of negative images, including the emphasis on the deviant sexuality of Muslims (initially associated with Indians) and the call for holy war.[7] Nation building and ideologically charged pageants used holy-war themes (Francis Bacon was a major propagandist in this genre while in prison),[8] for "in the Mediterranean as in New England, the English were fighting a holy war in defense of God's English Zion." Writers continued to use this motif well into the middle of the seventeenth century, when European national interests and rivalries made such a concept rather obsolete. Yet as the notion was dying in England, it was being revived in New England, where the Turk and the Moor were seen to have crossed the Atlantic. For the New England colonists, the "Holy War was still in progress in both 'Canaan' and 'New Canaan.'" As Matar puts it, "Zion was the Kingdom of God on all the earth, an earth cleansed of Indians, Papists, and Mahometans in a way that is godly and holy."[9]

By the end of the seventeenth century, the process of superimposition was complete, and the discourse of infidel alterity was translated into colonialist ventures and arguments. All nonwhite Others had to be evacuated from the illegal occupation of holy biblical and once-flourishing pre-Islamic lands. Daniel Defoe's view of Muslims not as infidels in need of conversion, but as barbarians who impeded British trade and therefore whose lands called for European colonization, reflected the new eighteenth-century attitude. In his *A Plan of the English Commerce Being a Compleat Prospect of the Trade of this Nation, As Well the Home Trade as the Foreign*, first published in 1728, Defoe described North Africans as inheritors not of the great Carthaginian or Roman civilizations, but of the lowly Vandal culture.[10] "These Mahometans, as I have said of the Turks," wrote Defoe, "have very little Inclination to Trade, they have no Gust to it, no Taste of it, or of the Advantages of it; but dwelling on the Sea-coast, and being a rapacious, cruel, violent, and tyrannical People, void of all Industry or Application, neglecting all Culture and Improvement, it made them Thieves and Robbers, as naturally as Idleness makes Beggars: They disdain'd all Industry and Labour."[11] While Indians were being dispossessed of their lands, Arabs were increasingly seen as the illegitimate settlers of Roman and Carthaginian lands. By the late eighteenth century, the "contrast between a sordid present and a glorious past, whether of Rome or Zion, resulted in the illegitimization of the present, whether of Indians or of Muslims, and aspiration toward a glorious future by the chosen and the American."[12] A few decades later, about a century after the publication of Defoe's views on Muslims and commerce, the French occupied Algiers.

Matar's insightful study clearly shows that the Europeans invariably carried their cargo of prejudices against the Moors wherever they landed. They saw the world through this old prism, one that separated the world into godly Christians and infidel Moors. Whether in Mexico, Peru, or New England, the New World was conceived and built against the backdrop of Europe's long rivalry with Islam. But unlike the Spaniards, who had to confront the Moors in endless battles and whose culture had been irreversibly shaped by the centuries-long close-range conflict with Islam, England's battles with Islam were confined mostly to the issues of piracy, the captivity of English sailors, and the embarrassing defection of so many renegades. The New World English colonists' view of Islam was decidedly of a different nature, and thus had a different future in North America, both during the colonial era and in the early days of independence.

Despite Spanish and English attempts to establish a new world free from Muslim trouble, Islam was introduced to the Americas by the very people who fought and condemned it. They brought them as slaves. Ladinos,[13] forcibly converted Senegambian Muslims, were imported as early as 1501, and later other Muslim slaves from West Africa were brought to the New World. Islam thus became, in effect, the second monotheistic religion to be introduced to the New World after Catholicism. "It preceded Lutheranism, Methodism, Baptism, Calvinism, Santeria, Cantomble, and Voodoo to name a few." From the start, Spain was uneasy about the unruly Muslim slaves, and within fifty years passed no fewer than five decrees prohibiting further importation of Muslims. (Sometimes Jews and mulattos were excluded, too.) Still the Muslims came, the logic of demand and supply being what it was. The latest conservative estimates of the number of Muslim slaves who were ultimately brought into America is somewhere between two and a quarter and three million, a considerable number even by today's standards.[14]

From the information available so far, it appears that Muslims formed a sort of cosmopolitan elite within the slave population.[15] Although they came from all social strata, many were highly literate, urban, and well-traveled men. Accustomed to dignified treatment in their home societies, they developed a reputation for intractability, aloofness, and rebelliousness, along with a disdain for Christianity. They found their white captors ignorant of Africa and Islam and even of their own Christian religion. Many assumed leadership roles in several major uprisings and revolutions. There is now serious speculation that Muslims played a major role in the success of the Haitian Revolution, and the Bahia revolt of 1835 in Brazil was entirely led by Muslims. Often better educated than their white masters (a fact noticed even by Theodore Dwight, secretary of the American Ethnological Society), they were "indomitable opponents" whose goal was always to return to their native lands of Islam. Against overwhelming odds, they saved money, procured paper, and continued to write in Arabic. One Benjamin Larden (or Larten), a slave in Jamaica, wrote an entire Qur'an from memory. Job Ben Solomon, a runaway slave from Maryland, did the same while crossing the Atlantic to England and added three other copies while in that country. In fact, this proud Muslim slave, who so impressed people that he gained his freedom and eventually returned to Senegal, wrote a memoir that is considered the "oldest text in African American literature."[16] In England, he consorted with major intellectuals and may have met Sir Isaac Newton and Alexander Pope. He also translated documents for several major scholars, including the cofounder of the British Museum and probably George Sale, the author of the first major English translation of the Qur'an. Other Muslims slaves in the Americas also wrote autobiographies and religious documents.

These proud "servants of Allah," as Diouf titled her masterly treatise on the subject, puzzled many white observers, who scrambled for a nongenetic scientific explanation. The Muslim was not considered truly African and was deemed to have benefited from his contact with the almost white Arabs and Moors. In 1864, Theodore Dwight wrote an essay on

Africa and quoted scholars saying that millions of Africans had "been raised to a considerable degree of civilization by Mohammedism, and long existed in powerful independent states."[17] Indeed, so struck by the power of Muslim slaves was the French count Joseph Arthur de Gobineau, author of the infamous *On the Inequality of the Human Races* (1855), whose views inspired the notion of Aryan superiority, that he considered Muslim slaves the Aryans of Africa.[18]

While black Muslims were enslaved in North America and across the continent, the early English settlers of America were already warning against the fraudulent religion of Mohammed and complaining about Muslim attacks on American ships. John Smith, John Winthrop, and William Bradford deplored Turkish and Moorish aggression on American or British vessels, Bradford suggesting that Moroccan pirates were "almost within sight of Plimouth." Such fears were not totally unfounded: James Fenimore Cooper estimated that "the very first regular naval action in which an American vessel is known to have engaged did involve a Barbary rover." Joshua Gee's fragmented narrative of his captivity in Algiers in the 1680s, well known to his contemporaries, published for the first time only in 1943, set the tone for a literary genre that would come into full favor in the first decades of the Revolution.[19] Cotton Mather, the Congregationalist clergyman from Massachusetts, wrote in 1698 that "wee had many of our poor Friends, fallen in to the Hands of the Turks and Moors, and languishing under Slavery in Zallea [Salee]." In his famous sermon *The Goodness of God Celebrated*, delivered in 1700, he said that "between Two and Three Hundred" New Englanders had been imprisoned by the "Emperour of Morocco."[20]

Indeed, no one exemplified the colonists' dealing with Indians and Muslims better than Cotton Mather, as Matar's study shows. While he preached to "Christian Indians," about the goodness of the English for introducing them to Christianity ("It was great compassion in the English, not only to offer you many comforts of the life, but also to show you the way that leads to ever lasting life"), he wrote to the "English captives in Africa," imploring them not to relinquish their Christian religion and turn renegade. "We had rather a *Turk* or a *Moor* should continually Trample on you, than the *Devil* should make a prey of you," he exhorted. His anxiety over the threat of Islam as a rival faith was such that he went to great lengths to prove the truth of the Christian religion in his pastoral letter. He lists there in painstaking detail the miracles of Jesus and even states that the Qur'an itself acknowledges the superiority of Christianity.[21] In his *The Christian Philosopher*, Mather described Mohammed as the "thick-skull'd Prophet" and prayed "May our Devotion exceed the Mahometan as much as our Philosophy."[22]

This view persisted throughout much of the eighteenth century. John Trenchard and Thomas Gordon's *Cato's Letters* (1723), probably the most influential English political tract on the Revolutionary generation, also presented Mohammed's religion as violent and threatened by reason. Constantin-François Volney's treatise on the negative effect of Islam on civilization, *The Ruins, or a Survey of the Revolutions of Empires*, which was first published in French in 1791, was translated into English in 1792 and appeared in two more English translations and two American editions. Even President Jefferson, with Joel Barlow, translated and published it in Paris in 1802. It was, in a sense, Jefferson's warning to his nation. In fact, there was what one might call a "bipartisan" consensus on the evils of Islam: All parties during the American Revolution (Tories and Patriots, Republicans and Federalists) used it as a foil against which to define their agenda and to chart out their visions of freedom. "The Muslim world," in Robert Allison's expression, "was a remarkably useful rhetorical device that could be used by libertarians like Mathew Lyon and Thomas Paine and by conservatives like John Adams and Alexander Hamilton."[23]

Allison shows that the worlds of literature and culture did their part to uphold such a view. In an essay on Arabic literature, the French historian and economist Jean Charles Leonard de Sismondi surveyed the once rich cities of Baghdad, Fez, and Marrakesh and noted how they had become deserts.[24] In 1806, the Philadelphia *Aurora* noted the decadence that had befallen Morocco in the previous three hundred years due to its lethargy. An anonymous Englishman's biography of the Prophet Mohammed, *The Life of Mahomet*, initially published at the end of the eighteenth century, was reprinted in the United States in 1802 to warn against tyranny and monarchy. Voltaire's *Le fanatisme ou Mahomet le Prophete* (1742) was translated by James Miller under the title of *Mahomet* and premiered in New York as a play entitled *Mahomet, the Impostor* in 1780.

"European and American writers came to the same conclusion about why the Muslim world remained backward," observed Allison. "A wicked religion had fostered bad government, and bad government thwarted social progress. Instead of encouraging industry and enterprise, these governments fostered ignorance, which bred indolence." Muslims were starving, indolent, and apathetic slaves to tyrannical rulers. The absolutist Ottoman sultan was seen as despotic and incompetent, hostage to his janissaries. Thus, as "the American people debated the Constitution in 1787 and 1788, anti-Federalist critics, not surprisingly, used the image of Turkish despotism to attack the proposed government." In such a climate, Americans didn't fail to read in captivity narratives, plays, and other writings that Muslim women were equally oppressed by the same tyrannical laws that denied "property rights and sexual autonomy."[25]

Despite this overwhelmingly negative picture of Islam, it is not entirely clear that American attitudes constituted a classical case of Orientalism, since American Orientalism, as Fuad Sha'ban has shown, is both derivative and native. As a chosen people, Americans embraced the daunting task of regenerating the fallen Promised Land even before they landed on the new continent. And it was not only the Holy Land (i.e., a land predominantly inhabited by Arabs and Muslims) that they sought to rescue, but in time, and with the secularization of the Protestant temper, such an ambition expanded to other parts of the world under the all-embracing mission of Manifest Destiny.[26] Page Smith was right when he wrote that "the Protestant Passion" is the "driving force of American history," one that creates an "insatiable desire to redeem mankind from sin and error."[27] As a people who had entered into a solemn "covenental relationship" with God, Americans enforced their commitments in "compacts" and "constitutions," obligating members of this community of grace "to spread the light" through evangelization.

This Christian imaginary shaped much of American politics and role in the world. As Sacvan Becovitch argued, the colonial Puritan hermeneutics of New England turned out to be a remarkably resilient myth that eventually became a way of interpreting all of United States culture and history. Its rhetoric "provided a ready framework for inverting later secular values—human perfectibility, technological progress, democracy, Christian socialism, or simply (and comprehensively) the American Way—into the mold of sacred teleology." Only the Southern myth of the New World as an unspoiled paradise "stood fundamentally opposed to the hermeneutics of Puritan American identity."[28] The American Revolution and Independence were seen, for instance, as the unfolding of a providential plan. Daniel Webster's statement that Christianity "must ever be regarded among us as the foundation of civil society" expressed "the prevailing sentiment among his contemporaries and was echoed later by such statements as that made by President Eisenhower that 'without God there could be no American form of government, nor an American way of life.'"[29] Business was integral to this godly worldview. Jonathan Edwards's statement that "the changing of the course of trade, and the supplying of the world with its treasures from America is a type and forerunner of what is approaching in spiritual things, when the world shall be supplied with spiritual treasures from America" established American commerce as the indispensable engine for this prophetic tradition.[30]

Although Christianity had left its imprint on the secular American Revolution and the nation to which it gave birth, many of America's founding generation were more directly influenced by the legacies and philosophies of the Enlightenment and the vision of a common humanity living in peace and solidarity. As with Christian utopianism, although it was mostly a state of mind, a psychological attitude, the "cosmopolitan ideal" of the Enlightenment allowed its adherents to believe in "human solidarity and uniformity throughout the world" and encouraged them to "the numerous humanitarian reform movements of the eighteenth century."[31] As self-proclaimed citizens of the world, Enlightenment enthusiasts disdained petty nationalisms and were avowed universalists who read voraciously and wrote prolifically, revered the classics, and considered dilettantism a strength. Regular patrons of literary salons and coffeehouses, they emphasized the importance of literature, particularly world literature, and used cultural comparisons and the comparative method to criticize their own societies.[32]

Although such speculation was not unique to the Enlightenment, it was the first time that the practice of making cultural comparisons with non-Western peoples assumed an important role in the discussion; moreover, it was the first time that a cultural view had to be truly global in both an ideological and geographical sense.

The Enlightenment men of letters who popularized cross-cultural comparisons in their literary works recognized the effectiveness of this approach. In fact, the philosophes made a deliberate cult of their transnational awareness, and this cosmopolitanism, in turn, strengthened and motivated their intellectual movement. Their ideal supposedly applied anywhere in the world.[33]

David Hume expressed this approach best when he stated: "We are apt to call *barbarous* whatever departs widely from our own taste and apprehension: But soon we find the epithet of reproach retorted on us."[34]

Globalists, but not necessarily multiculturalists, Enlightenment intellectuals also liked to codify, using Latin to ascribe uniform names to plants and species across cultures. They shared scientific information freely, even across conflict boundaries, and developed an interest in race matters, assuming, of course, the white Caucasian to be the norm. Because they didn't know enough about other cultures, they were guided by a "highly intellectualized concept" based on Eurocentric assumptions. Still, Enlightenment historians did widen the parameters of civilization by resisting their own ethnocentric tendencies and revering the East for its ancient arts, and, as did Voltaire, hailed it for giving birth to Western civilization.[35]

As might be predicted, the question of religion was widely discussed and, consistent with their views, almost all Enlightenment thinkers espoused a form of "rational theism." Jesus was duly placed "in the cosmopolite's hospitable pantheon [of ethical models] that also included Socrates and Confucius," Voltaire's favorite hero. Since their views were more philosophical than religious, they found the laic tenets of Freemasonry—despite this secrets cult's penchant for exotic rituals and pageantry and for conducting meetings in a linguistically eclectic and "unpronounceable phraseology"—most congenial. Theophilanthropy and *bienfaisance* were their creeds. Like others, Benjamin Franklin hated slavery and actively participated in its demise by helping found abolitionist societies both in England and America. Abolitionism and penal reform were part of their larger ethos of tolerance and cultural understanding.[36]

The world society they envisioned could be realized only through a system of international, self-regulating and wealth-generating free trade, not the provincial self-serving protectionist policies of mercantilism. "Americans such as Franklin, Benjamin Rush, Philip Freneau, and Joel Barlow saw world trade as eradicating national prejudices, and their colleague Thomas Paine felt that 'if commerce were permitted to act to the universal extent to which it is capable it would extirpate the system of war and produce a revolution in the uncivilized state of governments.'" The merchant thus became the ideal cosmopolitan type, whose agency would help establish this happy state of affairs.[37]

Correspondingly, and consistent with their theory of openness, the *philosophes* championed free and unrestricted immigration, tolerated the nation-state as a necessary evil, despised vulgar patriotism, and considered themselves to be fighting for the entire world's liberty, as Franklin saw himself during the Revolution. "The guarantee of mankind's 'fundamental liberties' in all countries became a vital concern of the political cosmopolitan ideal." The optimistic cosmopolites could not foresee the perversion of their ideals, even though skeptical Enlightenment thinkers such as Edmund Burke, Johann Herder, and especially Jean Jacques Rousseau were already scoffing at the unattainable wishes of alienated elite philosophers. Nevertheless, the *philosophes* still dreamed of a world of justice in which nations would be subjected to the same moral rigors expected of citizens and, as Kant dreamed, would be united under a federation of republics, a cosmopolis that would promote human rights.[38]

Thus, the Enlightenment era—roughly between 1688 and 1789—produced a generation of utopian thinkers, using French as their lingua franca to participate in a republic of letters whose goal is to promote secular truths and world peace. It was a short-lived vision: By the 1790s, the dream of a cosmopolis was eclipsed by the terrors of the French Revolution and the Napoleonic Wars. The emerging nationalism championed national literatures at the expense of a wider vision, a trend that was exacerbated by the German Romantics, as well as by the rise of democracy and mass literacy. The Enlightenment spirit did survive in many socialist movements, but it was isolated and contained by these new economic and political forces.[39]

It was out of the two powerful universalist matrices of Protestant messianism and Enlightenment thought that the American Revolution was forged. Armed with such convictions, and endowed with seemingly inexhaustible resources, the United States became a magnet to the oppressed and a beacon of hope and salvation to the rest of the world. American nationalism, infused with religious visions and secular ideologies, was to be spread, exported, duplicated, and imposed on others, even though in time Americanism grew more complex. In retrospect, it seemed that America had always had a "manifest destiny," a covenant with history to help nations dissolve the chains of tyranny and darkness by spreading "the light of the Gospel and American Revolutionary ideas."[40]

Despite America's ideological exceptionalism, Sha'ban still reads the popular prejudice against Islam in nineteenth-century writings as mostly inherited from Europe and thus as an extension of the (premodern) European Orientalist tradition. Robert Allison and Malini Schueller also have implied, in one way or another, that the traditions of Orientalism were transported into the new continent and continued to fuel the old European animus against Islam, whether in literature or in politics. This may have been the case later in the nineteenth century, as the United States sought to justify its expansionist ideology in terms of culture or civilization, but this, I would argue, cannot be said of the earlier days of America, particularly of the first two or three decades after the American Revolution. Orientalism implies a set of attitudes and a particular mindset that do not truly explain America's relations with Islam at that time. In fact, the American Revolution succeeded in de-Orientalizing the American imagination, particularly as Americans came into increasing contact with Muslims in North Africa and elsewhere. The American Revolution also hastened the demise of slavery and servility in all its forms. I will address this issue after detailing the studies that make a strong case—whether explicitly or not—for the Orientalist thesis.

No one has studied the relations between Islam and the nascent United States in as a comprehensive manner as Robert Allison in *The Crescent Obscured*. Having inadvertently witnessed the outbreak of the Iranian Revolution in 1978 (assumed to be antithetical to progress and liberty), Allison was inspired to study his nation's own revolution. But as he proceeded to do so, he found that "images of the Muslim world appeared everywhere"[41] and that Americans, who had indeed inherited Europe's attitude toward Islam and Muslims, were anxious to avoid the pitfalls of Islamic societies. As was the case after the 9/11 terrorist attacks, the reading public was inundated with literature on things Islamic, all of which ultimately designed to show that "the Muslim world was a lesson for Americans in what not to do, in how not to construct a state, encourage commerce, or form families."[42] The only issue that complicated America's sense of its own high morality (and on which it appeared worse than the Muslims) was the issue of slavery—which stained the otherwise ideal republic.

In the years following the Revolution, Americans were anxious to have access to the Mediterranean for trade, but the Barbary states, urged on by both Britain and France, attacked American vessels and demanded tribute. The conflict had reached such dangerous proportions that the appearance of three Moroccan-looking men at the shores of Virginia prompted that state to enact legislation that would become the prototype of the Enemy Aliens Act of 1798, allowing the U.S. president to deport aliens whose countries were at war with the United States. (Ironically, the federal act was considered abusive by the state of Virginia.) The appearance of these men occurred after Algiers had declared war on the United States in 1785 for failing to negotiate a tributary policy. While the U.S. government was still debating whether to pay tribute or not (Jefferson was against it, while Adams was for it), the sultan of Morocco, Mohammed ben Abdellah, negotiated a treaty with Thomas Barclay in the summer of 1786 requiring no tribute from the United States and thus made the Atlantic and the Straits of Gibraltar safe for American ships.[43]

Of course, Morocco's isolated case didn't solve the problem of the other three Barbary states—Algiers, Tunis, and Tripoli. Although Americans continued to fight over issues related to the nature of the new republic—most importantly whether to build a navy and risk endangering civil liberties by creating a standing military force—a fleet was built, even while the government continued negotiating with the Barbary states. In 1800, Jefferson, who once equated the Algerines with Indians (since both were used by the British against the United States) and for whom opening up the Mediterranean was part of the Revolution, became president.[44] Within five years, and after a series with skirmishes with Tripoli, the United States was able to subdue that nation and even bring back to New York seventeen Tripolitan prisoners—"real *bona fide* imported Turks"—for display in theaters.[45] For this single military exploit, the Americans were praised by Pope Pius VII for doing "more in a few years [to defeat Muslims] than the rest of Christendom had done over centuries."[46] Even the British Lord Nelson is reported to have commended U.S. action.

America's wars with Tripoli between 1801 and 1805 and the exploits of figures such as Andrew Sterret, Daniel Frazier (known as Reuben James), William Eaton, and Stephen Decatur became the stuff of legend. Andrew Sterret's August 1801 victory at sea against Tripoli was the basis of a play, *The Tripolitan Prize; or, American Tars on an English Shore*, performed in New York in November 1802. William Ray's poem "Ode to Liberty" (written while Ray was captive in Tripoli) was published in 1805. Joseph Hanson's poem "The Musselmen Humbled, or a Heroic Poem in Celebration of the Bravery Displayed by the American Tars, in the Contest with Tripoli" appeared the following year. "Testimonials to the heroes of Tripoli," writes Allison, "ranked them beside the Revolutionary fathers and placed the post-Revolutionary generation in a new heroic light. The Revolutionaries had beaten the British; this generation had bested the scourge of Christendom." Colorful figures such as William Eaton, a former consul to Tunis who assembled a group of Arab, Albanian, and Greek mercenaries, in addition to a few marines, and marched across northern Libya to capture Derne in 1805 and depose Yusuf Qaramanli, partly inspired James Ellison's play *The American Captive, or Siege of Tripoli* (1811).[47] Even America's national hymn traces its lineage to this conflict with Muslims. Francis Scott Key composed a poem in honor of Decatur in 1805 that later became the prototype for the U.S. national anthem:

> And pale beam'd the Crescent, its splendor obscur'd
> By the light of the star-spangled flag of our nation
> Where each flaming star gleam'd a meteor of war
> And the turban'd head bowed to the terrible glare
> Then mixt with the olive and the laurel shall wave
> And form a bright wreath for the brow of the brave.[48]

Malini Johar Schueller's suggestions that the "cultural mappings" of American Orientalist discourse began in the post-Revolutionary period and that they are central to America's burgeoning identity are, naturally, hard to contest.[49] To be sure, American writers described different Orients, all juxtaposed to a masculine, morally upright, but crisis-prone and "anxiety-ridden" proto-imperial nation. Such oppositions, however, were destabilized by "questions of national incoherence" and the inevitable—and problematic—presence of African Americans, Native Americans, and immigrants, as Jefferson himself noted. Literary Orientalism was thus not merely "a displaced site of racial issues," but, of all genres, the one that "most significantly challenges, even as it evokes, imperialist constructions of national identity and of the Orient, as well as the racial hierarchies at home." The same may be said of gender hierarchies. Like several writers who tackled the issue of Americans' captivity in Barbary, women such as Susanna Rowson used the Orient in *Slaves in Algiers* to critique gender construction in republican America. Rowson's narrative works to accomplish the imperial goals of hierarchalizing races and nations, but she also uses the "Oriental setting to break free of conventions at home" and to show that the harem is, in fact, a space of female bonding.[50]

Although post-Revolutionary America sought to break ties with Britain, it kept the colonizer's imperial outlook, relying on the discourse of liberty (as opposed the British civilizing mission) to accomplish its postcolonial goals. "An understanding of how literary Orientalism works in the early period of the nation's history is therefore crucial in comprehending both the global dimensions of definitions of nation and the dual nature of early U. S. culture as both postcolonial and colonizing." In other words, one cannot overlook the role of the American Revolution in globalizing

America's founding missionary zeal. As soon as the American Board of Commissioners for Foreign Missions was formed in 1811, missionaries conflated "Christian conversion and cultural conversion" as identical goals. "For instance," writes Schueller, "religious conversion, the ostensible rhetorical concern, is linked with market-driven concerns, such as the advantages of industry over idleness. Even Christian societies in Eastern nations were thus considered objects of conversion, because their morals were considered to be lax" and, as Schueller later shows, made impure by their unconcern for racial and cultural purity, anxiety producing-issues in America.[51]

There is no doubt that America's attitude toward Islam was shaped initially by its founding Christian/Protestant vision (inherited from a long history of Christian/Muslim polemics) and given a much quicker momentum by the success of the American Revolution and the establishment of a new independent nation. Because the American Revolution was uncompromisingly and doubly universalist in outlook, it addressed not merely colonists rebelling against an intractable British government, but also indirectly the entire world fighting injustice and tyranny. At least, that is how Americans read their revolution, and that is what motivated them to break out of their national confines to redress wrongs around the world.

Although rooted in the foundational Protestant imaginary, the American Revolution was a radical and world-shattering event in American— and world—history. Gordon Wood's and Joyce Appleby's studies on the Revolution's effect on national life and character make it clear that the United States' relations with the world, including with Muslims, were greatly influenced by the new American creed of liberty.[52] To give us a sense of how radical the American Revolution was, Wood reminds us that just before it was launched, the two million Americans in the British colonies lived in a hierarchical world of dependencies and social obligations that were sanctioned by religion and by monarchical and aristocratic worldviews. In such a typical premodern culture, patriarchal supremacy was naturally accepted, including the infantilization of household dependents (children, women, servants, and slaves). With the exception of a few Quakers, Americans accepted black slavery "as the most base and degraded status in a society of several degrees of unfreedom." Notions of "liberty" were confined to the aristocratic prerogative of freedom from work and from the degrading practice of trade or commerce. Such freedom entailed the obligation to buy from farmers and workers and to extend patronage to (talented) lower classes. In such an aristocratic world of honor codes (slander lawsuits and duels were outcomes of such a culture), one understands Benjamin Franklin's insistence on right appearances.[53]

By the time of the Revolution, however, a new generation of politicians was "no longer willing to abide the insincere dissembling of that older monarchical courtier world." Republican ideas and practices, which first appeared as reform movements under the monarchy, would change this worldview radically. Best suited for the prevailing Protestant spirit in America, republicanism was also the ideology of the Enlightenment, stressing public virtue, disinterestedness, and the value of liberal learning. As the monarchical worldview came under increasing stress from demographic explosions, human mobility, loosening of communal ties, and the emergence of a commercial culture (farmers producing surpluses for distant markets, the transformation of traditional meaning of contracts, credit, and debt [the decline of patronage], the use of paper money, etc.), republicanism was the only revolutionary concept able to accommodate these momentous transformations. The American Revolution was thus prompted by ascending aspirations for a better life, not by a revolt against intolerable wretchedness, especially since Americans were better off than their European counterparts, and "most American farmers owned their own land."

A new, enlightened, and benevolent paternalism called into question most of the patriarchal practices fostered by monarchical culture, (from relationships within the household to those between governor and governed. Labor was redefined as the source of prosperity and well-being, not as one's inevitable lot in life. This led to new anxieties about losing one's acquired wealth, which in turn precipitated a yearning for equality. Dependency was therefore equated with slavery, laws of primogeniture were abolished, and inheritance and divorce rights were given to women. The master of old became the "boss" (from the Dutch), servants became the "help" or waiters. "Indeed, once the revolutionaries collapsed all the different distinctions and dependencies of a monarchical society into either freemen or slaves, white males found it increasingly impossible to accept any dependent status whatsoever."

As "the most cosmopolitan" generation in their country's history, Americans saw themselves tied with bonds of love and ineradicable humanity with the rest of the world. But how about slavery at home? Didn't that make Americans seem inconsistent and hypocritical? Perhaps. As Wood explains, it is important to realize that the Revolution suddenly and effectively ended the cultural climate that had allowed black slavery, as well as other forms of bondage and unfreedom, to exist throughout the colonial period without serious challenge. With the revolutionary movement, black slavery became excruciatingly conspicuous in a way that had not been in the older monarchical society with its many calibrations and degrees of unfreedom; and Americans in 1775–76 began attacking it with a vehemence that was inconceivable earlier. . . . .

The republican attack on dependency compelled Americans to see the deviant character of slavery and the confront the institution as they never had to before. It was no accident that Americans in Philadelphia in 1775 formed the first anti-slavery society in the world. As long as most people had to work merely out of poverty and the need to provide for a living, slavery and other forms of enforced labor did not seem all that different from free labor. But the growing recognition that labor was not simply a common necessity of the poor but was in fact a source of increased wealth and prosperity for ordinary workers made slavery seem more and more anomalous. Americans now recognized that slavery in a republic of workers was an aberration, "a peculiar institution," and that if any Americans were to retain it, as Southern Americans eventually did, they would have to explain and justify it in racial and anthropological ways that their former monarchical society had never needed. The Revolution in effect set in motion ideological and social forces that doomed the institution of slavery in the North and led inexorably to the Civil War. . . . [54]

The Revolution unleashed popular forces with aspirations for equality and commercial opportunity unanticipated by the patrician republicans among the Founding Fathers. Undermining the old titles of the American aristocracy with their anti-intellectual disposition, Americans now believed that all "men" to be born equal, that social positions and fortunes are accidental. Aware of the power of self-interest in human endeavors, petty bourgeois merchants and illiterate workers began to demand participation in the government and scorned the old patrician belief of government ruled by enlightened gentry. Democracy, for these new Americans, meant "the prevalence of private interests in government." This new view was part of the larger assault on aristocracy and inherited privilege. In this new culture, leisure (the classical attribute of the gentry) was scorned and turned into a parasitic idleness, while labor (scorned in the pre-Revolutionary era) was embraced as "a universal badge of honor."[55] Against the futile attempts of the Founding Fathers to impose restraints, Americans democratized politics and chose to remunerate the holding of public office. Modern political parties were formed to promote interests, and loyalty to them was the best way to win public office or benefit from government patronage.

Westward mobility and strong individualism added more stress to an increasingly atomized and violent society. The businessman (a term first used in the 1820s) emerged as the prototype of the new system. This new social type benefited from the rapid proliferation of banks and other state-chartered corporations (the prerogative of monarchy in the past) and joined the newly established evangelical churches (such as the Baptists and Methodists) and other social associations. Christianity was "republican-ized" as the old churches became insignificant in the competitive scramble for members among the new denominations. And as churchgoing became more of a recreational pastime than a daily obligation, character and morality were emphasized over religious observance.

But economic interest was the ultimate social adhesive in this frag-mented society. Samuel Blodget, the architect who designed the First Bank of the United States in Philadelphia, described commerce and business as the *"golden chains"* that created *"the best social system that ever was formed."*[56] The cult of the self-made man replaced the gentleman as the icon of worthy emulation (Benjamin Franklin's *Autobiography* was reinter-preted in light of the age and deployed to promote this cult). In Webster's *American Dictionary of the English Language* (1828), the meaning of "gen-tleman" was changed to more or less what it is now. Thus, except for slaves in the South, America had become a middle-class nation by appropriating "the principal virtues of the two extremes": It "drained the vitality from both the aristocracy and the work of the working class."

Practical education and morality (such as temperance) were valued over the sort of liberal-arts education and aristocratic virtues championed by early republicans. Women were placed on a new pedestal. "Virtue now lost what remained of its classical association with marital and masculine severity and became more and more identified with enlightened feminine sociability and affection; indeed, virtue at times seemed to mean little more than female chastity."[57] But out of this chaotic, hustling society of unsung masses, there emerged a social harmony, together with a new ob-session with statistics and the collection of facts. By undermining the tra-ditional authority of knowledge and truth and by relying on their own ex-periences and limited fields of observation, Americans became parochial and anti-intellectual. In such a world, only "public opinion" functioned as the truth generated from the aggregate wisdom of the middling sorts. In this brave world that lived out the promise of the Revolution, the early rev-olutionaries, from Washington to Jefferson, were pushed out. They had fallen victim to their own vision.

Appleby's *Inheriting the Revolution* paints a similar picture of Americans born after independence. This new "race of Americans"—as Gouverneur Morris put it—"became agents of change in an era marked by the convergence of political revolutions, commercial expansion, and intellectual ferment that penetrated . . . the most mundane aspects of life." Restless and aggressive, free white men began forging the myth of the self-making man and autonomous individual, "a patriotic icon that differentiated the United States from the savagery at its borders and the tyranny across the Atlantic." Although circumscribed by race and gender categories, the Revolution and the emancipation legislations enacted in Northern states complicated the slave-holders' position, increasingly alienated the South from a threatening union, and emboldened blacks to fight for more freedom. "The widening of economic horizons sparked ambitions that ranged from global proselytizing for Christianity to the liberation of the world's enslaved." Women joined their missionary husbands in preaching the equality of the sexes to infidel Hindus and Muslims, while others preached Christianity to both Indians and frontier Americans. It was a generation infused by America's unparalleled greatness and triumphant spirit of democracy, zealously committed to expressing this inherited freedom in strong universalistic overtones propagated by an explosion in print communication.[58]

As Wood indicates, older notions of authority came tumbling down. The vote became available to people in numbers unprecedented in history. Although Andrew Jackson consolidated the Jeffersonians' gains against an older elite, the tacit understandings of the Founding Fathers were replaced by vituperation and "vitriolic disputes" in public discussions. This disputatious temperament was duly noted by visiting foreigners. One German traveler warned that "this mutual abuse, repeated until disgusting, shall if it goes unpunished become habitual, make the people indifferent to calumny and insult, and destroy all sense of honor; and then freedom of the press may have proved to be a Pandora's box." Ironically, it was in such a giddy democratic environment that the European aristocratic practice of dueling became a popular way to settle political disputes.[59]

Emancipation societies that were formed in the 1780s took the principle of equality seriously and tried to enshrine such principles wherever they could. "More often supported by Federalists than Jeffersonians, these first emancipation successes led to a peaceful abolition that gradually cleansed the North of slavery as it simultaneously divided North and South into separate societies. The old surveyors' boundary between Maryland and Pennsylvania—the Mason-Dixon line—became the symbolic divide between the domain of natural rights and the territory of slavery." Two nations were being formed.

Still, the presence of high moral principles at the country's founding turned perfectly normal patterns of domination into vexed issues. Whether inspired by democratic principles, Christian zeal for perfection, or an enlightened sense of progress, American reformers would not leave the public conscience at peace. . . . The hopes for liberty with equality, justice, and the unimpeded pursuit of happiness were extravagant, yet believable enough to excite the imagination.[60]

Enterprise and economic gain were seen as a legacy of the Revolution and critical components of American democracy. "If the Constitution provided the foundation of America's liberal society," commented Appleby, "the free enterprise economy raised its scaffolding." Entrepreneurship flourished. New industrial cities were built, and the quest for money dominated every other motive in this nascent capitalist economy. "Americans, especially in the North, viewed commercial expansion as the moral and material handmaiden to their liberal society" and "vigorously rejected the aristocratic notion of natural inequality." Of course, such commercial ambitions meant a "widespread willingness to be uprooted, to embark on an uncharted course of action, to take risks with one's resources—above all the resource of one's youth,"[61] and this created a new social fabric that brought atomized individuals together into new affinities and ideologies.

Growing cities and population, demographic mobility, together with the establishment of a first-rate postal system, encouraged a boom in publishing along with literacy and reading. Although the publishing centers were mainly in the big Eastern cities, transportation made all publications available to rural and frontier folk. Female literacy also grew, with more magazines and books addressed to female audiences. Newspaper reading became almost a mania. In 1810, "Americans bought 24 million copies of newspapers annually, the largest aggregate circulation of any country of the world, regardless of size." Careers in writing, journalism, teaching, law, and medicine attracted many, as did military service, preaching, and even art. And Americans entered the professions with confidence and an ingrained awareness that failure is as inevitable as success.[62]

The egalitarian spirit radiated through the entire social fabric ("Landowning and wealth distribution were much more equitable in the

United States than in any other country"), democratizing sartorial traditions (the rich dressed down in an act of "social camouflage") and refine-
ments (for those white men who could afford them), scrambling hierarchies, and, in the process, upsetting the Old World instincts of Federalists
and Southern planters. The president was greeted with a handshake instead of the traditional "solemn bow." In this exciting time of human freedom, many wondered whether slavery "undercut the republic's claim to the
high ground staked out in the Declaration of Independence." Black
slaves—"a full fifth of the nation's population"—were obviously excluded
from this universal human right of liberty. Defensive Southerners rational-
ized slavery by shrouding their culture in nearly obsolete and anti-Revolu-
tionary aristocratic, Christian, and racial ideals, yet for Northerners, the
declaration "signaled the beginning of an international crusade against
slavery." Women, too, demanded rights. Mary Hunt Tyler, Royall Tyler's
"strong-willed wife" and author of *The Maternal Physician: A Treatise on
the Nurture and Management of Infants* (1811), advocated some freedom for
women, even while she subscribed to a strict separation of the sexes. And
so, despite the persistence of inequality, slavery, and racism, "the affirmations of the first generation guaranteed that the move towards greater inequality would exist in tension with the natural rights tradition that they
had expressed in their politics, taught in their schools, and propagated
through their manners."[63]

Even family and intimate relationships were transformed by this
democratic and commercial spirit. Marriages and spousal affections were
celebrated as edifying and inspiring affairs, but relationships between fathers and sons became tense, partly because the old patriarchal system
clashed with the political implications of independence and the youths'
impatience with farm life and growing interest in learning and mobility.
"Leaving home in late adolescence disconnected sons, as well as some
daughters, from the round of filial obligations and cut the ties in that dense
network of associations that had slowly accumulated in mature settlements. Many passed over the threshold to love and marriage in communities that they themselves had chosen. This unanticipated foreshortening of
parental control left a lot of emotion to be redistributed."

Inspired by their own conversions and the revivalist style, people
poured out details of their intimate feelings with abandon. "Americans had
been telling stories about their struggles with self-indulgence, carnal long-
ings, and material distractions since the seventeenth century, for the Puri-

tans, Baptists, and Quakers had planted a strong tradition of experiential religion in the colonies." Such conversions not only severed family ties by sometimes pitting the converted against their own relatives, but they also "provided these awakened Christians with a moral compass, an instrument of rare utility in a society with so much uncharted terrain. The participatory politics and free association claimed by radicals in the 1790s set the stage for reformers of the 1800s who would direct American attention towards the moral ends of nationalism."[64]

Political and religious doctrines led to disagreements whose cumulative effect was to produce a vibrant public sphere, the whole covered in a tone of informality that scorned elite snobbery. Associations and Christian denominations proliferated like brushfire. The paradoxical blend of Jeffersonian (but anticlerical) democracy and the anti-institutional tendencies of the Second Great Awakening (revivalism) eventually led to a "new consensus [that] endorsed liberty [but] rejected free thinking." Indeed, Christianity was being democratized, even while, ironically, a cultural Protestant orthodoxy was being established. Black slaves were also Americanized in this revivalist phase, their roots decisively severed from their African roots. Temperance societies (founded in the 1820s) and sabbatarian movements sought to reform a straying republic. In the early decades of the century, alcohol consumption had reached levels unsurpassed in America before either before or after. And then, alcohol consumption "was cut in half," and the sale of liquor was outlawed in Maine. Christians organized not only to lobby against working on Sunday (an issue that pitted the movement against the postal system), but also to establish Bible societies (the first in 1808) and even a peace society (a first in the world).[65]

Only antislavery efforts encountered a seemingly insurmountable obstacle, although the crusade against slavery remained alive. The booming cotton economy in the South, slave revolts in Haiti, Virginia, and South Carolina in the South, and the contemplation of a biracial society and a diluted white European society in the North complicated the issue. In 1816, the American Colonization Society was formed (partly as a solution to this dilemma), but the number of resettled blacks in Liberia was minuscule compared with the millions of slaves added over forty years. And as early as 1826, free blacks denounced the scheme while demanding equality.[66]

While the question of slavery haunted the new Republic's conscience (John Adams prophetically had warned that "we must settle the question of slavery's extension now, otherwise it will stamp our National Character and lay a Foundation for Calamities, if not disunion"), the nation grew along two polarized cultural and ideological poles. But the commercial, cultural, and economic habits of the North—based on a sense of redefined values, a new code of masculinity, and a sense of optimism derived from the general philosophies of the Enlightenment—eventually spread its distinctive colors over the whole canvas of American life.

The vision of America as having a special destiny for the human race provided the raw material for creating a national myth, an elaboration of enlightenment themes, or what might be called the poor person's enlightenment, directed as it was to liberating ordinary men from the flagrant injuries of inherited privilege. The merger of this goal with the loftier Enlightenment preoccupations with free inquiry, scientific knowledge, and political liberty enabled ordinary and elite reformers to move in tandem. Sharing an ideological commitment to change, the real distances in wealth, education, and opportunity could be rendered a matter of rhetorical, and perhaps even emotional, indifference. Thinking no further than the evils they could perceive, these male reformers had little sense of how women would soon use their philosophical arguments to expand the scope of universal rights.[67]

Having inherited and accepted the consensus on the free market, the darker side of this enterprising North became the noted culture of avarice and a single-minded pursuit of money making. (Washington Irving was first to use the phrase "the almighty dollar.") Unparalleled in the rest of the world, the market in the United States exerted significant social influences, including valorizing a set of masculine traits.[68] In the minds of this generation, both market and freedom were part of an indissociable whole. In his *Annals of Philadelphia* (1830), John Watson stated that "so exalted are our privileges, as a self-governing people, that the fact of our example and happiness is bidding fair to regenerate other nations, or to moderate the rigor of despotic governments throughout the world."[69] This view of moral leadership, not intervention, prevailed even when Congress debated whether to intervene on behalf of Greeks fighting for freedom from Turks:

As this congressional debate reveals, inheriting a revolutionary tradition had thrust upon an entire generation of Americans the responsibility for explicit articulation of what the Unites States stood for. Impossible to ignore, the bequest of the founders catapulted radical philosophical propositions into the center of American public debate, giving every group excluded by prejudice and custom from citizenship potent arguments for their inclusion. Reason and justice were expected to explain social arrangements, an expectation baffled by formal institutions of slavery and common-law traditions that bolstered the authority of white householders over family and employees. Natural law affirmations of liberty and equality gave the union the moral glue it badly needed while promoting a rift between those states that found a way to abolish slavery and those that did not. These contradictions and the conflicts they engendered paradoxically enhanced openness in government, popular political participation, a vibrant print culture, and inclusiveness in public life. Americans seemed to shed old conventions like a snake its skin, coming through with colors brighter than ever.[70]

Of course, contradictions and divisions cut across the land, but the rhetoric of self-regeneration and success, half true, was enough to cast its myth over this emerging and dynamic nation.[71] It was a useful myth that allowed Americans to define themselves against others. In this phase of nation and identity building, Indians, blacks, Frenchmen, Spaniards, and Turks, even British West Indians, served as "negative reference groups." All were, in the words of Roy Harvey Pearce, what Americans "were not and must not be."[72] Expansion, economic growth, and prosperity required new adjustments triggered by the disjunction between a "mythic [Puritan] past and contemporary reality" induced a sense of guilt, which probably fueled the Great Awakening. The "idealized image of English society and culture" and British cultural standards were promoted as the fear of "creolean degeneracy," in the words of Cotton Mather, haunted colonial elites. But as with the early Puritans, cultural borrowing and imitation were unable to assuage the sense of failure at Anglicization and intensified the desire for even more cultural borrowings. Only the Revolution allowed Americans to claim higher moral and political grounds, putting into practice the very ideals the British government had failed to uphold. It was a cathartic event that liberated Americans from their prosperity-induced guilt and their failure to live up to Puritan myths and British cultural standards.[73]

But no subject provoked as much soul-searching as the persistence of slavery in the new "empire of liberty," as Jefferson described the new nation.[74] After all, liberty was "the most cherished right possessed by English-speaking people in the eighteenth century. It was both an ideal for the guidance of governors and a standard with which to measure the constitutionality of government; both a cause of the American Revolution and a purpose for drafting the United States Constitution; both an inheritance from Great Britain and a reason republican common lawyers continued to study the law of England."[75] Slavery was thus a glaring "paradox" in the new social fabric, in the words of Edmund Morgan, but one that could, nevertheless, be explained.

The American concept of freedom was premised on the notion of slavery as both the fate of idle, landless people in a republic and, as in the case of Virginia, a buffer against the threat of multitudes of freedmen without a stake in the system. American revolutionaries wanted free access to maritime trade, yet America's major commodities, such as tobacco, were "produced in very large measure by slave labor." Virginia, which, in 1840 contained 40 percent of slaves in the United States, also, paradoxically, "produced the most eloquent spokesmen for freedom and equality in the entire United States: George Washington, James Madison, and above all, Thomas Jefferson." The latter's continued upholding of slavery may be explained by his strong republican aversion to debt, wage labor, and even poverty, all of which induce dependence (although Jefferson was a debtor all his life). In Revolutionary America, slaves constituted the majority of the population, and so Jefferson simply didn't think that they could stay in the country if they were allowed to become free. (Freedom, it was believed, entails a civic mind emanating from proprietorship.) African slaves helped limit the number of English freedmen in the colony of Virginia and develop an economy that would be the cornerstone of the nascent U.S. trade. In this way, the beauty of American freedom was founded on the horrors of African slavery.[76]

John Reid has argued that the notion of slavery was not necessarily equated with chattel slavery. If anything, chattel slavery was seen as part of a free nation's social landscape and, in fact, as supporting liberty. With more chattel slaves than free people, South Carolina worried about slavery only when it referred to the tyranny of British legislation. Such thoughts were not seen as hypocritical at all. Slavery, in this view, was primarily a British legal concept entailing the absence of the rule of law (liberty), which explains why both licentiousness and tyranny were feared. When America fought for liberty, it was fighting the slavery that was the lot of most Europeans and Turks, for under slavery, the New England clergyman Judah Champion stated in 1776, humans "sink below the primitive standard of humanity. . . . They become stupid and debased in spirit, indolent and groveling, indifferent to all valuable improvement, and hardly capable of any." Both British and Americans used the same damning imagery. As Reid put it, "Slavery was the cause of every evil—ignorance, error, poverty, wretchedness, immorality, irreligion, vice, and, of course, political tyranny." In short, slavery was the fate of most people.[77]

In 1775, Joseph Towers wrote a letter to Samuel Johnson comparing colonial Americans to Moroccans: "If the British parliament, in which the Americans have no representatives, can enact any laws of capital punishment respecting them, can take away life, seize upon property, and tax them at pleasure, are the Americans, in a political view, more free than the inhabitants of the empire of Morocco?"[78] In 1762, the Massachusetts House of Representatives reminded Jasper Mauduit, its agent in London, that "Liberty is not only the Right of Britons, and British Subjects, but the Right of all Men in Society, and is so inherent, that they Can't give it up without becoming Slaves, by which they forfeit even life itself. Civil Society great or small, is but the Union of many, for the Mutual Preservation of Life, Liberty and Estate."[79] Indeed, as Edmund S. Morgan notes in *The Challenge of the American Revolution*, property and liberty were indistinguishable from each other in eighteenth-century Americans' minds, since both presumed the existence of laws.[80] In 1766, the Sons of Liberty were promoting local manufacture as "our best barrier against [British] slavery."[81] Indeed, in the years preceding the Declaration of Independence, the term "slave" was "probably the most frequently used word by both American Whigs and their British supporters, and to no issue was it more often applied than that of parliamentary taxation."[82]

The American Revolution was thus "a great theater for the rhetoric of liberty. People on both sides of the controversy employed the words of liberty as a form of shorthand or code of cherished beliefs with which to argue, persuade, and motivate." The rhetoric of liberty "permitted Americans to defend local institutions by arguing for traditional British values, using the phraseology of English constitutionalism."[83] However complex the term might have been, it is not surprising that abolitionists would use the concept of liberty to fight for their cause. Vague and abstract, assumed to be understood by all free people, liberty was sometimes poetically evoked and praised, as when, in February 1775, the Freeholders of Augusta County addressed Virginia's Continental Congress Delegates thus:

May the bright example be fairly transcribed on the hearts and reduced into practice by every *Virginian*, by every *American*. May our hearts be open to receive, and our arms strong to defend, that liberty and freedom, the gift of Heaven, now banishing from its last retreat from *Europe*. Here let it be hospitably entertained in every breast; here let it take deep root, flourish in everlasting bloom; that, under its benign influence, the virtuously free may enjoy secure repose, and stand forth the scourge and terrour of tyranny and tyrants of every order and denomination, till time shall be no more.[84]

Whereas in Britain liberty meant civil rights without equal access to political representation, by the time of the American Revolution, the notion was expanded to imply the consent of the governed (representation). Anything less than that meant enslavement worse even than chattel slavery. "There is much to be learned about the eighteenth-century British constitution by contemplating the astonishing fact that chattel slavery was said not to be the worst type of slavery," writes Reid, who then asks: "The question that deserves deep cognition is why people familiar with chattel slavery who saw it in daily operation and were witnesses to its dehumanizing harshness could believe that it was a lesser evil than life under arbitrary government."[85]

Regardless of how one answers such a question, the American model of liberty was later celebrated by radical Englishmen, despairing of the growing arbitrary power of their parliamentary system, as the only beacon of freedom left. In 1793, Henry Yorke credited America for saving freedom:

It is not impossible that the nations of the earth would have been at this day sunk in apathy and ignorance, had not the ever memorable revolution of America promoted a spirit of inquiry and discussion, that soon made men long after Freedom. At this period, Reason, with her offspring Liberty, were recalled from their long exile, into the cabinets of Philosophers, and the strangers were welcomed into the homely mansions of Poverty.[86]

Although slavery and liberty may have had different meanings for Americans of that time, the coexistence of both in a new republican structure caused considerable unease among American patriots. By the 1780s, it was fairly reasonable to expect prominent Americans such as Benjamin Rush to espouse antislavery principles for that reason. In 1788, Luther Martin, Maryland's attorney general, stated that slavery was "inconsistent with the *genius* of *republicanism* and has a tendency to *destroy* those *principles* on which it is *supported,* as it *lessens* the *sense* of the *equal rights* of *mankind,* and habituates us to *tyranny* and *oppression.*"[87]

In Gary Nash's explanation, it wasn't the complex definition of liberty that explained the persistence of slavery after the Revolution, but the new state's unwillingness to challenge the slave culture, partly because consensus turned out to be more important than the insistence on principle. The new debt-ridden government was reluctant to pay what would have amounted to $90 million to compensate slaveowners, and the national government was more concerned with national integration efforts. Men like Ferdinando Fairfax, a prominent Virginian protégé of George Washington, wanted to end slavery, but they also wanted to remove blacks from American society. Others, like the prominent Virginia lawyer and statesman St. George Tucker, used the example of black revolts in St. Domingue to warn against a similar rebellion at home. Tucker recommended gradual emancipation—over the span of a century—and the settling of Western and Spanish lands. Because of growing racism and attacks on freed slaves after 1800, the one motive for the founding of the American Colonization Society was to solve the problem of slavery by getting rid of blacks.[88]

Yet foot-dragging and violent solutions did little to snuff out the spark of liberty ignited by the Revolution. According to Nash, until fairly recently, few historians truly appreciated that "the American Revolution represents the largest slave uprising in our history." Not only were many blacks inspired by the revolutionary ideals, but they also saw themselves as God's true chosen people, the real enslaved and oppressed Israelites. Again and again, slaves and freed blacks appealed for redress and justice in America's republican language of inalienable rights. Between the 1780s and 1820s, blacks strove to gain freedom and rights while maintaining their own African identity. To be sure, their attempts to establish independent black (African) churches and other institutions were met with renewed racism, but by redeploying the myth of chosenness, they were able to withstand such denigrations and present themselves as the true upholders of republican principles. In an ironic way, they became "the conscience of the nation" and kept America's contradictions on the forefront of the debate by constantly invoking "the elevated phrases of revolutionary ideology" and "confronting white Americans with the misalignment between their sacred texts and their continued toleration of slavery." Indeed, by doing so, blacks helped post-Revolutionary Americans reach for a better democracy.[89]

White and black abolitionists relied on America's universalist principles to undermine slavery and the slave trade. Both showed how America, the beacon of liberty, was jeopardized by maintaining such a cruel and degrading system. Here is how James Forten, a rare successful black Philadelphia businessman, opened a series of letters to the senate of Pennsylvania in 1813 arguing against putting restrictions on black migrants to the state:

We hold this truth to be self-evident, that GOD created all men equal, and is one of the most prominent features in the Declaration of Independence, and in that glorious fabrick of collected wisdom, our noble Constitution. The idea embraces the Indian and the European, the Savage and the Saint, the Peruvian and the Laplander, the white man and the African, and whatever measures are adopted subversive of this inestimable privilege, are in direct violation of the letter and spirit of our Constitution, and become subject to the animadversion of all, particularly those who are deeply interested in the measure.[90]

Although Muslims were omitted from this note, they were mentioned in the "earliest extant petition to Congress from black Americans," a petition probably drafted by Absalom Jones on behalf of four freed North Carolina blacks threatened with reenslavement. Jones compared the plight of black slaves to captured white Americans in Algiers—for both had witnessed the intoxicating powers of liberty and their captivity only made their suffering more intolerable.[91] Jones's petition shows that the captivity of Americans by Muslims in the Barbary coast of North Africa was often deployed to challenge the American slave system and, not infrequently, compare the two cultures' treatment of slavery.

As early as 1700, Samuel Sewall had used the still insignificant Barbary issue to write and print the first antislavery tract in New England:

Methinks, when we are bemoaning the barbarous Usage of our Friends and Kinsfolk in *Africa*: it might not be unreasonable to enquire whether we are not culpable in forcing the *Africans* to become Slaves amongst ourselves. And it may be a question whether all the Benefit received by *Negro* Slaves will balance the Accompt of Cash laid upon them; and for the Redemption of our own enslaved Friends out of *Africa*.[92]

In 1776, when few Americans were held captive in Barbary, the Congregational minister Samuel Hopkins used what Ben Rejeb calls the "comparative method" in his pulpit in Newport, Rhode Island, to argue that if Americans don't condemn slavery at home, then "the Africans have a good right to make slaves of us and our children. . . . And the Turks have a good right to all the Christian slaves they have among them; and to make as many more slaves of us and our children, as shall be in their power. . . . According to this, every man has a warrant to make a bond slave of his neighbor, whenever it lies in his power."[93] John Jay, foreign affairs secretary, asked directly in 1786: "Is there any difference between the two cases than this, that the American slaves at Algiers were white people, whereas the African slaves at New York were black people?" At the Philadelphia Convention of 1787, the Abolition Society of Pennsylvania appealed to the gathering by saying that "Providence seems to have ordained the sufferings of our American brethren, groaning in captivity in Algiers, to awaken to a sentiment of the injustice and cruelty of which we are guilty towards the wretched Africans."[94]

In addition to being deployed against black slavery in the newly formed United States, the Barbary issue opened up the possibility for many writers to de-Orientalize the American imagination. Several historians and literary critics (Robert Allison, Ben Rejeb, and Paul Baepler, among others) have noted that the main purpose of the Barbary antislave narrative (exaggerated though the term "slave" may be here) was not to rehabilitate Muslims as such, but to use them polemically to wage domestic struggles against slaveholders in the United States. In this reading, the Muslim simply occupies the classical, politically expedient position of the "noble savage," reminiscent of earlier or even contemporaneous Indian captivity narratives, but the ultimate purpose of such narratives is not to defend Islam and rescue Muslims from old prejudices. As Ben Rejeb puts it, once the captive is released, he "returns to rediscover his national identity and celebrate his own culture and political institutions."[95]

While such readings may be familiar to students of all captivity narratives, I want to stretch the fact already noted by prominent historians such as Wood, Appleby, Nash, and others that the American Revolution radicalized the imagination against slavery and eventually led to its demise. I want to add that such an imaginary had an equally radical effect in rescuing the American consciousness from inherited Orientalist prejudices, even while apologies for the slave system continued to be made and the new American nation embarked on fulfilling its millennial mission of redeeming others from ignorance and bondage. Such a progressive legacy is incontrovertibly visible in white slave or Barbary narratives in whose texts the antislave and anti-Orientalist agendas were often joined.

The Barbary captivity narratives depicting the wretchedness befalling American sailors at the hands of (North) African Muslims was a not insignificant genre in the early decades of the American republic. Inexplicably, these have remained unexamined by leading scholars on the African American heritage in the United States, although African blacks were commonly called "Moors" and assumed to be the bearers of Muslim culture.[96] According to Baepler, whose anthology of excerpts of many Barbary narratives was published in 1999, "American publishers issued over a hundred American Barbary captivity editions" between 1798 (the year that John Foss's narrative of suffering in Algiers was published) and 1817, when James

Riley's account of his captivity in what is now Mauritania appeared at the urging of leading American politicians and congressmen. These dates dovetail with Royall Tyler's novel *The Algerine Captive*, published in 1797, a picaresque narrative that is clearly inspired by earlier of earlier Barbary captivity narratives.

That *The Algerine Captive* has been considered one the first consciously authentic American novels shows the extent to which the Barbary coast (African, Muslim lands) shaped American consciousness and culture.[97] A discussion of all the major works inspired by the Barbary issue is impossible to sketch in this chapter, but a reading of a few captivity narratives and the fictionalized accounts based on this genre will reveal that the main ideological aim of this literary movement was not necessarily the demonization of Islam and Muslims, but the consolidation of American nationalism and the defense of republican principles. Barbary captivity narratives, whether real or fictional, partook from the common assumptions of their home culture, presented a complex picture of the African and Arab landscapes, and were used to strengthen the abolitionist cause.

In the preface to his second, 1798 edition of his journal of captivity, written in an Algerian bagnio, John Foss alludes to the evils of slavery and simultaneously warns his readers that the cruelty of Muslims (sons of Ishmael) toward Christians is real and is taught by religion—although he quickly notes that Algerines are harsher toward Christian captives than other Barbary Muslims.[98] Foss endures the "hardest days work" of his life (21) when he is assigned his task and composes a poem on how slavery unjustly and cruelly separates lovers and punishes merchants in which he wonders how long would Americans endure such humiliation:

> How long, Columbians dear! Will ye complain
> Of these curst insults on the open main?
> In timid sloth, shall injur'd brav'ry sleep?
> Awake! Awake! Avengers of the deep!
> Revenge! revenge! The voice of nature cries:
> Awake to glory, and to vengence rise!
> To arms! To arms! Ye bold indignant bands!
> 'Tis heaven inspires; 'tis GOD himself commands.
> Save human nature from such deadly harms,
> By force of reason, or by force of Arms.
> Then let us firm, though solitary, stand,
> The sword, and olive branch in either hand (21).

Forced to blow up rocks and haul them to the harbor, slaves are pun-ished with *bastinadoes* (22–25) and forced to subsist on a daily food al-lowance consisting of bread and vinegar—sometimes oil or olives, if they are lucky to work in a corsair vessel. Foss has seen more than twelve hun-dred Christian captives laboring "with the woeful appellation of slave prey-ing upon their mind" by the time he leaves Algiers (30). He witnesses "scenes of diabolical barbarity—inconceivable among humans—carried out in the name of justice" (38). In the hierarchy of punishments, rene-gades receive the same punishment as Turks, but Jews get the worst treat-ment, forced to wear black and "shoes without any quarters"(39–40, 62).

Unlike the Africans of the age of Carthage and Rome, when agricul-ture flourished and cities rose to "the highest state of luxury," he finds his Algerine captors grossly ignorant (47). Among the few good deeds of Mus-lims is their respect for graves. Contrary to what happens in Christian cemeteries (presumably in his native United States), where graves are opened and "the remains of the dead are tossed about with very little cere-mony," Muslims leave their graves undisturbed, and thus their cemeteries grow very expansive (55–57). The men "spend a great part of their time in bathing, smoking, and drinking coffee" (58) and conduct public business in Arabic, although they speak a variety of languages and idioms (Arabic, Moresco, ancient Phoenician, and the universal Lingua Franca of the Mediterranean, 63).

As an American accustomed to living in a racially divided society, he notices the social hierarchies in Algiers and notes the subtle differences among Turks ("well built, robust people, their complexion not unlike Americans, tho' somewhat larger in statue, but their dress, and long beards, make them appear more like monsters than human beings," 74), "Cologlies" (offspring of Turkish fathers and Moorish mothers, "less in stature than the Turks, and of a more tawney complexion," 73), Moors ("a tall thin, spare set of people, not much inclining to fat, and of a very dark complexion, much like the Indians of North America," 73), Arabs ("of a much darker complexion than the Moors, being darker than the Mulat-toes," 73), renegades, Levantines, and, finally Jews and Christian slaves (63). Foss describes Arabs as "thieves & murderers by profession" (64) and the Algerines, although they claim to be Muslim, as lazy, treacherous, un-trustworthy, "nearly to equal the Spaniards in cowardice," a people who "cultivate the most inveterate hatred against Christians." The men's only virtue is their dexterous management of horses (64–65). Without explaining such contradictory observations, Foss notes that although Islam is the official religion of the state, Algerines tolerate other religions and respect idiots, and, as if to exonerate Islam further, he adds that the Algerines "have adopted the very worst parts of the Mahometan Religion, and seem to have retained as much of it as countenances all their vices" (66).

One of the things that amaze him and other captives is how such people are "so submissive and patient under so excessive and cruel a tyranny" (66). Algiers is a "military republic" where the "Dey is elected by the soldiery" (67) and any assassin who kills the humane and monogamous dey can take his place, and Foss declares that this chaotic situation "ought to teach both rulers and ruled in this happy country justly to appreciate the blessings of liberty and good government" (68). To think that the land that was "once the seat of liberty and scientific improvements" under Carthage and Rome has now been reduced to its present wretchedness is quite disheartening to Foss (69). Turks, he concludes, "profess the greatest contempt for Learning," their education being limited to the Qur'an, writing letters, and some astronomy (75).

Foss relates the history of the corsair state of Algiers from the time of Barbarossa to the present and notes, rather sadly, that it is the good dey himself, "the humane benevolent man; the respectable citizen, and affectionate parent—he who vindicated the sacred cause of liberty, and adorned society by inflexible honor" (120), who rebuffs the U.S. attempt at establishing a treaty with Algiers. Meanwhile, more Americans are captured while Foss is still in Algiers; but when the government finally ransoms them, Foss's pride explodes uncontrollably: "No nation of Christendom had ever done the like for their subjects in our situation," he proudly declares (123). "The Republican government of the United States," he continues, has "set an example of humanity to all the governments of the world" and has forced the admiration of his barbarian captors (123). After many delays and slow diplomacy, Foss finally leaves Algiers on 13 July 1796. Rome's Catholic slaves, abandoned by their governments, marvel at the (American) Protestant spirit—although the ship carrying Foss to freedom also contains 48 ransomed Neapolitans (144–45). After endless peregrinations in the Mediterranean, stops, and quarantines, the ship finally secures a passage to the United States and arrives in Philadelphia on 28 April 1797. A few months later, Foss reaches Newburyport in Massachusetts, the place at which he had initially embarked. Fittingly, then, the narrative concludes with a poem titled, "The Algerine Slaves," written in 1798 by "a citizen of Newburyport."

The poem opens with a call for liberty: "For were e'en Paradise itself my prison / Still I should long to leap the chrystal walls." The poet implores the assistance of the muse in relating the horrors of submitting in wretched servitude to the Turks, "sons of hate," and in bearing "the scoffs, the cruel taunts of those / True sons of Ishmael" (177). Then it recapitulates the story in his preceding narrative—rather concisely—while capitalizing and italicizing the word "slavery" in any tense or form to highlight the ultimate state of humiliation he suffered in Algiers. He adds a captive's prayer calling on the just and free Columbia to "send quick destruction on this unused land" (183) and rejoices at his freedom in the incomparably glorious country to which he returns. While other countries may boast of their wealth and beauty, the independent United States possesses the most precious gift of all: liberty.

> Be thine the boast—Columbia, thine the soil,
> Where freedom reigns, & all the virtues smile.
>
> Tis now he tastes what thousands rarely know,
> The balmy sweets, which from fair Freedom
>   flow;
> 'Tis thine Columbia! Daughter of the skies,
> Thine, thine the land, where freedom's gentle
>   Reign
> Demands the poets and the Captive's strain. (189)

It is interesting to recall that, except in the preface, Foss seems to restrict his demonizing descriptions to the Algerines, who don't live up to the true faith of Islam and that his diatribes against Islam are quite limited. Even then, Foss views Spaniards in the same negative light and has an equally low opinion of Roman Catholics. Only American freedom and Protestantism are unequivocally valued.

Although Foss attributes all grandeur in Algiers to the ancient Romans or Carthagenians, he nevertheless praises the Moorish civilization in Spain. In a footnote, he describes the Moors as descendants of Saracens, who, in Spain, "were superior to all their contemporaries in arts and arms," and he unhesitatingly observes that "learning flourished in Spain [under the Moors' 300-year reign], while the rest of Europe was buried in Ignorance and barbarity." He even accurately notes that the expulsion of the Moors and Jews from Spain after 1492 added significantly to the strength of Algiers and its navy (106). Foss's narrative, then, is not necessarily an anti-Muslim or anti-Arab diatribe, but a tribute to his nascent "empire of liberty" where tyranny had been blissfully extirpated by the Revolution. Except for conspicuous absence in Foss's narrative of the paradoxical issue of African slaves back in his land of freedom, the narrative treats Muslims as any American would his captors. One doesn't sense an inbred hatred of Islam, even if Islam had been associated with tyranny in the political and cultural literature.

In the same year that Foss's narrative was published, a play and one of America's first novels presented the case of America's relations with Muslims, particularly around the issue of slavery, in a rather different light. In May 1797, the *Columbian Orator*, a Boston magazine edited by Caleb Bingham to "inspire the pupil with the ardor of eloquence, and the love of virtue," published a drama in two acts titled *Slaves in Barbary*. The first scene of act 1 opens with the Venetian Amandar's lament at not being able to enjoy the beauties of nature in his bondage. He has been captive for fifteen long months and is owned by the shrewd, Machiavellian, and cruel Oran. Ozro, Amandar's brother and slave in captivity, throws money at Oran and informs him that the Bashaw Hamet has purchased Amandar. Forced, Oran accepts, but not without decrying the Bashaw's softness.

In scene 2, Ozro tells Amandar that upon hearing about his condition and that their brother is on his way to ransom them and restore them to their "disconsolate family," the Bashaw was so moved that he sent the money to purchase Amandar. But Ozro wonders whether they should go back to the Bashaw and trust a Turk, who may have been tempted by the ransom. Reasonable Amandar, though, has hope. He notes that "Tunis, of all the states of Barbary, is famed for its refinement" and that "every Turk is not an Oran" (105). People are not the same. He reminds his brother that not all their countrymen are like Francisco, who released a Turk twice. After all, the play shows that the Bashaw's own guards wonder about their boss's magnanimity and his liking of Christians. One guards even thinks the Bashaw does this to drink wine with the Christians.

In scene 2 of act 2, Bashaw Hamet's humanitarian impulses become clear when he shows kindness and mercy to the captives in a slave auction. An American named Kidnap objects to the Bashaw's fair treatment, while Kidnap's own slave, Sharp, rejoices, leading his white master to exclaim: "Severe reverse! Now, Africans, I learn to pity you" (111). An officer assumes Kidnap to have been "a wholesale dealer of slaves himself; and is just beginning the hard lesson of repentance" (111) and says that the previous night, in his sleep, Kidnap "gave Liberty and Independence for a toast, sung an ode to Freedom; and after fancying he had kicked over the tables, broken all the glasses, and lay helpless on the floor, gave orders, attended by a volley of oaths, to have fifty of his slaves whipped thirty stripes each, for singing a liberty-song in echo of his own" (113). Hearing this, the Bashaw interviews Kidnap about the irony of his dream and asks Sharp about his master. The latter describes his master as cruel and says he would rather be Hamet's or any other man's slave before he goes back to America or to Kidnap. So Hamet orders Kidnap sold to the highest bidder (Sharp would be sold later).

Hamet also intercedes on behalf of an Irish sailor and helps proud Francisco, who comes to ransom his two brothers. Hamet recognizes his former benefactor—for Hamet turns out to be the Turk that Francisco once released—and rejoices at his good fortune that allows him to show his gratitude. The play ends with Hamet saying "Let it be remembered, there is no luxury so exquisite as the exercise of humanity, and no post so honorable as his, who defends THE RIGHTS OF MAN" (118).

Royall Tyler's *The Algerine Captive*,[99] at first published anonymously in 1797, the same year the U.S.S. *Constitution* was launched, one of six frigates commissioned to fight the Barbary states, set out self-consciously to establish a new literary genre that reflects the values of the rising nation, not those of defeated England. It was dedicated to David Humphreys, Esq., a brilliant young officer during the Revolutionary War and author of patriotic poems,[100] not, as was the custom in Europe, to a financial patron (iii–iv). In the preface, which is part of Tyler's fiction, the main character, Doctor Updike Underhill, returns after seven years to a country that has abandoned its somber religious views but has rushed headlong into the equally dangerous fascination with foreign—mostly English—sentimental romances that are "not of our own manufacture." Thus, Underhill's biography is an opportunity to write a critical reflection on American manners and beliefs (v–xiii).

The story begins with the arrival of protagonist's grandfather, Captain John Underhill, an experienced military man, in Massachusetts in 1630. His liberalism puts him immediately at odds with the Puritans, who finally accuse him of committing adultery of the heart, banish him out of Boston (under John Winthrop's governorship), and then force him out of Dover, New Hampshire. He settles in Dutch-controlled Albany (called Amboyna then), Dutchifies his name to Captain Hans Van Vanderhill, and assumes military leadership against the Indians. In this setting, he begets two sons, the eldest of whom goes back to New Hampshire, where the novel's protagonist is born on 16 July 1762.

From the outset, Tyler thus comments on the habit of refashioning identities in the New World and is clearly critical of Puritan or Christian zeal, although he is respectful of ancestors and acknowledges the Puritans' contribution to the Revolution:

Whoever reflects upon the piety of our forefathers, the noble unrestrained ardour with which they resisted oppression in England, relinquished the delights of their native country, crossed a boisterous ocean, penetrated a savage wilderness, encountered famine, pestilence, and war, and transmitted to us their sentiments of independence,—that love of liberty which under God has enabled us to obtain our own glorious freedom,—will readily pass over those few dark spots of zeal which clouded their rising son. (20)

Consistent with republican notions of education, Underhill learns and masters Greek and Latin with a minister, but never makes it to Harvard. Unable to farm—his mind, in quixotic fashion, is overtaken by Greek myths and stories—he teaches, but this, too, turns out to be a disastrous occupation. Unable to use or impress anyone with his Greek, he then studies with a doctor who restores sight to a blind young man. For reading Greek to a young lady, he is challenged to a duel and inadvertently declared a man of honor. In 1785, he completes his medical education and after visiting Boston to procure instruments is surprised to find "the curiosities of all countries" but those of New England in the [Cambridge] college's museum. "I felt then for reputation of the first seminary of our land," he remarks (102–3). He returns home to become a country physician. But after eighteen months of practice, often competing with quacks, Underhill decides to go south where, he is told, "the inhabitants were immensely opulent, paid high fees with profusion, and were extremely partial to the characteristic industry of their New England brethren" (128). On his way, he visits with none other than the illustrious Dr. Benjamin Franklin, the quintessential American for whom the cynical Underhill has the utmost and unequivocal admiration:

To see one, who, from small beginnings, by the sole exertion of native genius and indefatigable industry, had raised himself to the pinnacle of politics and letters; a man who, from an humble printer's boy, had elevated himself to be the desirable companion of the great ones of the earth; who, from trundling a wheelbarrow in bye lanes, had been advanced to pass in splendor through the courts of kings; and, from hawking vile ballads, to the contracting and signing treaties, which gave

peace and independence to three million of his fellow citizens, was a sight interesting in the extreme. (130)

Not able to fit in or find employment in the South (Virginia) with
his Northern temperament, the doctor accepts the invitation to be surgeon
aboard a ship bound to London (with tobacco), and later, on another one
bound to West Africa. Considering all of the United States, north and
south, to be his home (145), he is unimpressed by England. The English, to
him, are a "motley race, in whose mongrel veins runs the blood of all nations, speaking with pointed contempt of the burgo-master of Amsterdam,
the cheerful peasant, the hardy tiller of the Swiss cantons, and the independent farmer of America; rotting in dungeons, languishing wretched
lives in foetid jails, and boasting of *the glorious freedom of Englishmen*
(148–49). He meets Thomas Paine in London and wonders whether Paine,
who, during their interview, speaks highly of the Jewish prophets, might
have written his antireligious *Age of Reason* in a fit of drunkenness (158–61).
From England, he sails to West Africa to pick up slaves on the way to
South Carolina. Once on the coast of Congo, Underhill grows horrified by
the slave trade and the traders' indifference to human suffering. As a Yankee, he is profoundly affected by the inhumanity of the enterprise
(165–67), but as surgeon, he is forced to examine the 150 slaves picked up
at that station:

I cannot even now reflect on this transaction without shuddering. I have deplored
my conduct with tears of anguish; and I pray a merciful God, the common parent
of the great family of the universe, who hath made of one flesh and one blood all
nations of the earth, that the miseries, the insults, and cruel woundings, I after-
wards received when a slave myself, may expiate for the inhumanity I was necessitated to exercise towards these MY BRETHREN OF THE HUMAN RACE. (160–70)

Clearly of Muslim faith (see 174), the male slaves go on a hunger strike
and refuse to eat, but give in when the slavers torture their women and
children (174–75). At Benin, 150 more slaves are added onto an already
horribly filthy environment, especially for the enslaved, who are "used to
the vegetable diet and pure air of a country life" and at home are "remarkable for their cleanliness of person, the very rites of their religion
consisting, almost entirely, in frequent ablutions" (176–77). The ship's
captain thinks the doctor is "moved by some *yankee nonesense about humanity*" (177), while Underhill's clerk tells him that blacks thrown over-
board "love to die" anyway (178).

More than two-thirds of the slaves get sick and start dying (to escape the "wild white beasts"), says the narrator (179). The ship is then ordered anchored near Cape St. Paul, on the Gold Coast. The slaves recover amazingly quickly and pray for Underhill's prosperity, wondering meanwhile why God "put my good black soul into a white body" (180). He encourages a few slaves to escape and is himself later caught (with another black slave) by "several men of sallow and fierce demeanour, in strange habits, who spake a language I could not comprehend" (184). When asked by his captors about his nationality, he states unequivocally that he is American. He is then thrown into a dirty hole and becomes mortified to find out that the black slave walks unhindered on the deck with other sailors (186–87). But this slave turns out to be a kind human being who risks his life by sharing his small portion of food and water with the grateful Underhill: "Is this, exclaimed I, one of those men, whom we are taught to vilify as beneath the human species, who brings me sustenance, perhaps at the risk of his life, who shares his morsel with one of those barbarous men who had recently torn him from all he held dear, and whose base companions are now transporting his darling son to a grievous slavery?" (188–89)

At this point, the narrator grows determined to fight slavery when he returns home and to use the moral and political argument of freedom, "declared to be the unalienable birth-right of man" (189), to persuade his countrymen. The first part of the novel ends with Underhill's astonishment at the "regularity and frequency" of his captors' devotion, whom he has been taught to consider as "the most blasphemous infidels" (190).

Once in Algiers, like the mostly European captives with him, Underhill is bathed, shaved, clothed, and fed, then paraded in front of the dey (Vizier Hassen Bashaw) in a typical Orientalist scene. Then, as someone with no ransom prospects, he is stripped of his clothes and displayed in the marketplace the following day. After telling how he has been examined and purchased like cattle, Underhill cautions American citizens not to condemn his "tameness of spirit" and his failure to assert "the dignity of my nation," since the conditions he is subjected to are seemingly irresistible (12–13). Acting as a historian, he debunks the fantasies of captivity romances and attests to the mundane, hard reality of captivity—although his slave companions are unfailingly compassionate (14–18).

As in the case of Foss, Underhill is surprised that his master—Adel Melic, a former officer in the dey's army—has only one wife.

I found it to be a vulgar error that the Algerines had generally more. It is true they are allowed four by their law; but they generally find, as in our country, one lady sufficient for all the comforts of connubial life, and never take another, except family alliance or barrenness renders it eligible or necessary. The more I became acquainted with their customs, the more I was struck with their great resemblance to the patriarchal manners described in Holy Writ. Concubinage is allowed; but few respectable people practise it, except for the sake of heirs. (20–21)

Unlike other (non-American) slaves, he resists the tyranny of overseers and is condemned to even harder labor. Tired and defeated, he nevertheless lectures his American readers on the "value of our free government" (27). Soon he is approached by an English convert, and although he abhors apostates, is convinced by this former English dissenter to converse with a Muslim scholar, called "mollah" in the novel (28–33). Upon accepting, he is thus relieved from his travails and sent to a heavenly garden where he is bathed, fed, pampered, and his hands and feet decorated with henna. On the eleventh day, he is visited by the "mollah," a 30-year-old native of Antioch converted from the Greek Church. Using Latin (see 56), the "mollah" assures Underhill that the "holy faith he offered to my embraces disdained the use of other powers than rational argument; that he left to the church of Rome and its merciless inquisitors all the honor and profit of conversion by faggots, dungeons, and racks" (39). So kind and gentle is the mollah that the American, for the first time in his life, trembles for his faith and "burst[s] into tears"(40). The conversation takes place for five consecutive days, but to sum it up and make it accessible to the reader, Underhill presents it in the form of it dialogue.

Patiently, the mollah describes the sociology of religion (mostly contextual and inherited), and in response to Underhill's charges explains the divine origins of the Qur'an, the spread of Islam and the unity of Muslims, the miracle of Mohammed, and the violent history of Christianity, which, unlike Islam, is still confirmed by the treatment of slaves:

It is true, they then, and we now, when a slave pronounces the ineffable creed, immediately knock off his fetters and receive him as a brother; because we read in the book of Zuni that the souls of true believers are bound up in one fragrant bundle of eternal love. We leave it to the Christians of the West Indies, and Christians of your southern plantations to baptize the unfortunate African into your faith, and then use your brother Christians as brutes of the desert. (50)

Underhill becomes "so abashed for my country, I could not answer him" (50). But despite further exhortations from the mollah, he chooses to go back to his slave's attire rather than succumb to the mollah's self-assurance and sophisticated arguments (53). He returns to the stone quarry, but, surprisingly, is not mistreated for his obduracy. He learns the lingua franca and some Arabic and starts plotting his escape, but the spectacle of a tortured slave dissuades him. So it finally dawns on him that he is "indeed a slave" and now appreciates the "blessings of freedom" that people "have bled to obtain" in his country (66–67). Soon afterward, he falls sick (probably from malaria) and a taken to a hospital staffed by "good nurses and ignorant physicians" (69). There, he is visited by the gentle mollah, who helps him procure "the quinquina, or jesuit's bark" (72). A few weeks later, he recovers and is purchased by the director of hospital. This would be a good vantage point from which to "observe the customs, habits, and manners, of *a people of whom so much is said and so little known at home,* and especially to notice the medical practice of a nation whose ancestors have been spoken of with respect in the annals of the healing art" (74, my emphasis).

He finds Algerian doctors to be woefully backward in basic surgical skills and has to contend with ignorance, obstinacy, and passive religious prejudice (unlike the Roman Catholic faith [77]). Still, a series of successful operations make him famous, and although Underhill refuses to convert, his master allows him to keep the presents—but not the money—of the grateful relatives of patients.

The narrator sketches out a perfunctory, but unadorned history of the Algerine people—their power struggles, long history of piracy and tributary practices enabled by European short-sighted rivalries, their harassment of American ships—and explains why the United States signed a treaty with that state on 5 September 1795 (85–104). He describes Algiers (105–8) and attributes the frequent political turmoil in that regency to the dey's dependence on tribute as a principal source of revenue. That's why princes who sign peace treaties either have to break them or are deposed—for the terms of a treaty are annulled once the signatory dey is dethroned (109–117). He remarks on the dey's troops, people's clothing and eating habits, marriages, and funerals. While commenting on arranged marriages and the status of women, Underhill tells the reader that he has heard that women enjoy both marital love and freedom behind their disguises (127).

In three short chapters, Underhill, announcing his impartiality and that he will be "neither influenced by the bigoted aversion of Sales and Prideaux, or the specious praise of the philosophic Boulavnilliers," sketches out a mostly accurate account of the early history of Islam—deviating from traditional accounts only when he asserts that Mohammed must have been literate to be a factor traveling to Syria, Palestine, and Egypt (130–31). He concludes his account with this general assessment:

Upon the whole, there do not appear to be any articles in their faith which incite them to immorality, or can countenance the cruelties they commit. Neither their Alcoran nor their priests excite them to plunder, enslave, or torment. The former expressly recommends charity, justice, and mercy, towards their fellow men. I would not bring the sacred volume of our faith in any comparative view with the Alcoran of Mahomet; but I cannot help noticing it as extraordinary, that the Mahometan should abominate the Christian on account of his faith, and the Christian detest the Mussulman for his creed; when the Koran of the former acknowledges the divinity of the Christian faith, and the Christian Messias, and the Bible of the latter commands us to love our enemies. If either would follow the obvious dictates of his own scripture, he would cease to hate, abominate, and destroy the other. (145)

His remarkable tolerance and his inclination toward dialogue don't prevent him from regretting the lack of unity among European or Christian nations to reject the humiliation of tribute and slavery from Algiers. Rather prophetically, Underhill estimates that only colonization of the entire country could subdue this renegade regency. After a series of adventures and mishaps, he manages to escape and land in the United States on 3 May 1795. "I had been degraded to a slave, and was now advanced to a citizen of the freest country in the universe," he rejoices (226–27). As was typical, the former captive is encouraged to write his story.

Thus the story ends on a happy note. The doctor resolves to marry a good woman, continue his practice as physician, and

contribute cheerfully to the support of our excellent government, which I have learnt to adore in schools of despotism; and thus secure myself the enviable character of a useful physician, a good father, and a worthy FEDERAL citizen.

My ardent wish is, that my fellow citizens may profit by my misfortunes. If they peruse these pages with attention, they will perceive the necessity of uniting our federal strength to enforce a due respect among nations. Let us one and all endeavor to sustain the general government. Let no foreign emissaries inflame us against one nation, by raking up the ashes of long extinguished enmity; or delude us into the extravagant schemes of another, by recruiting to fancied gratitude. Our first object is union among ourselves. For to no nation besides the United States can that ancient saying be more emphatically applied—BY UNITING WE STAND, BY DIVIDING WE FALL.

Such exhortations from a dedicated patriot are not surprising, given the fact that the author (born William Clark Tyler) was a highly educated lawyer and judge who played a leading role in repressing the Shays's Rebellion and helped draft the charter for the University of Vermont in 1781.

He was also the author of *The Contrast*, a "comedy of manners" produced in New York on 25 May 25 1787, shortly before the Constitutional Convention. Not only is *The Contrast* the "first American comedy to be produced by a company of professional actors," but it is also "a patriotic play that urges Americans to divorce themselves from the affectations of foreign behavior." Like his pioneering novel, the play stresses American themes and "promotes American virtues and encourages a national literature," "praises American heroes and soldiers," "preaches federal unity and fiscal responsibility," and "attacks luxury, adherence to fashions, and frivolous behavior."[101]

Although *The Algerine Captive,* "the first American novel about life in New England" and "the second American novel about American life," was generally favorably reviewed, one reviewer objected to the chapter that allows the mollah "the best of the argument" and states: "We enter our solemn protest against this cowardly mode of attacking revelation."[102] But Tyler, who seems to have favored religious and political writings in his other work, replied, a least a decade later, by suggesting that his purpose was not only to "to do away with the vulgar prejudices against [Islam],"[103] but also to reveal the imposture of Mohammed and the superiority of Christianity.[104]

In his book on Tyler, G. Thomas Tanselle emphasized that in the 1790s, Barbary piracy was a hot news item that also "helped to unify the American states in a single cause, for meeting the challenge was a matter of national pride."[105] Years after the publication of *The Algerine Captive*, Tyler confirmed in a preface for a proposed new edition that when the novel appeared, American slavery in the Barbary coast "was the common topic of conversation, and excited the most lively interest throughout the United States."[106]

The novel was hailed as an American original by no less a figure than James Fenimore Cooper and was one of the two American novels to be reprinted in England, in both book and serial form.[107] The first installment in *Lady's Magazine* was prefaced with this note: "The narrative is almost entirely founded on facts; and it is the first genuine American production of the kind that has been published in this country."[108] Although it drew no praise for its literary qualities, its Americanness seems to have impressed many readers. For one thing, the book is valuable as "a historical and literary document," and its preface "is one of the important early manifestoes of American literary independence." Indeed, Tanselle argues that the "principal motif of the entire work is the glorious freedom of America." Although provincial, Underhill's "Yankee common sense" allows him to be better convinced by natural, instead of supernatural, explanations of Islam and to impress upon his readers "the advantages of their new government and the greater importance of inner faith than of ritual."[109]

Although Tyler later retracted his favorable treatment of Islam, the literature of Barbary captivity usually presented a positive view of the religion, because much of the hardships and cruelties suffered by the captives was blamed on the zeal and greed of captors, not on the tenets of the Islamic faith. In *Humanity in Algiers: Or, the Story of Azem*, written by "an American, Late Slave in Algiers" in 1801, the author begins by accusing his country of hypocrisy and double standards when dealing with the issue of slavery. He also accuses America of cultural or religious prejudice: "Taught and accustomed from infancy to think our own religious creed the only mark of civilization, we can scarcely think it possible that a Mahometan should possess a feeling heart, or perform a virtuous deed." He thus sets the stage for showing how, contrary to popular preconceptions, his story will demonstrate to every reader that there is "Humanity" in Algiers (4).

When the author, who has been transacting some business in the East India islands, is captured by Algerian pirates on 21 June 1786 and sold to a rich planter, he considers his fate similar to the "thousands in my own country," including those kept by his own father, and so serves his Muslim master faithfully for nine years. When he provides assistance to a city man who falls from his horse, his freedom is purchased by Azem's endowment, a charitable fund set up to release one honest slave every year. Curious, the freed American slave decides to find out about his benefactor before he leaves.

The story of Azem opens on the plains of Natola, near the river Tenun, home of Selictor, a "wealthy husbandman" and his beautiful and educated wife, Sequida. Through the treachery of a confidant, the industrious, kind, and amiable couple suffer a traumatic change of fortune and bankruptcy, and Selictor is jailed before he is bailed out by a benefactor. Upon his release, the couple, with their two sons and two daughters, move to Natola to start a new life. One day, Selim, Sequida's brother, visits and gives them his slave Azem, an enslaved captive, as a gift.

Selictor and Sequida raise Azem as their own child and teach him the Qur'an. Azem develops a spirit of freedom and refuses to obey Selictor's son. To avoid trouble after his death, Selictor decides to sell Azem to

Testador, his neighbor, and divide his price among his four children and his wife. Azem is distressed and contemplates suicide, but, hopeful, he calls on God "that searcheth the heart, and respecteth not the person or colour of man" to look after him. Selictor is saddened, but money dissipates his gloom.

Desperate and imbued with the spirit of freedom, Azem escapes, but a voice commands him to return to his master. He seeks the help of Omri, the kind physician and the executor of Selictor's will, a man of liberal views. Although pained by Azem's condition, Omri is unable to help, but he persuades Pestoli, Sequida's eldest son, that it is better for each member of the family to use Azem's services for one year than to divide the money among the five of them. While the four children have no objection to this proposal, Sequida refuses, fearing that Azem might commit a crime. After her unwavering refusal, she dreams of the Prophet Mohammed offering her a drink in a gold cup and her husband regretting his decision. Omri interprets the dream as God's rewards for assenting to the plan for Azem's freedom, and so Azem is repurchased from Testador and starts his five-year service. After two years, while serving Sequida, who has moved to Arabia with her husband, Azem rescues Narina, their eldest daughter, from being raped by a violently enamored Arab, and so Azem is relieved from the remainder of his bondage.

Now free, Azem remembers his love for Alzina, a teenage servant to one of Testador's neighbors, and how one day he happened upon her, on the rocky and barren edge of their fertile region, lamenting her own enslavement, wishing she had followed her father into the sea rather than accept a life of bondage. When Azem appears to her and comforts her, she tells him that her family is originally from the "northern bank of Senegal," a luxuriant region where they lived in peace until attacked by a neighboring, barbarian tribe. Her brother was taken prisoner and never heard from, while her father escaped to Zara. But six years later, they were attacked again, and she and her father were taken captive. Her father jumped into the ocean, but she was restrained and sold in Tunis to Valachus, her present master, who wants to use her sexually. Now freed and in possession of money given to him by Narina's husband, he hastens to Valachus and asks for Alzina's freedom. But Valachus refuses, and so Azem, once again, seeks the help and counsel of Omri.

Restless, Azem composes a letter to Valachus appealing to his conscience, knowing full well that the state provides no help to the enslaved, who have no rights. The letter is delivered by Omri, and despite the latter's intercession, Valachus refuses. Despondent and heartbroken, Azem sails to Algiers, still hoping to find his parents (he is their only son) (80). In Algiers, he joins a ventures in a ship that is sailing to the "Southern Continent" to trade in ivory and gold dust. Anchoring at the bay of Senegal, Azem ventures inland, takes pity on an enslaved old woman, and ransoms her. She turns out to be his mother, so they return to Algiers. Once there, he leaves again to Omri's house and is surprised to find Alzina waiting for him. He finds out that Valachus had plotted to seduce her by force, but was mortally bitten by a scorpion. But before he died, Valachus had called Omri, apologized, and freed the virtuous Alzina with a purse of 1000 drachms. Azem then rushes back to Algiers to bring his mother to the wedding.

But the marriage never takes place: Azem's mother recognizes Alzina as her long-lost daughter. This miraculous occasion leads Omri to extol the humanitarian precepts of Islam, even wishing for "the light of Islamism to shine forth, in its full splendor, to the utmost ends of the universe! For thus saith the God of all men: 'Of one blood have I created all nations of men that dwell upon the face of the earth'" (98–99).

Azem shares the profits from his last voyage with Omri and spends the next three years getting an education from his kind benefactor. Azem's mother dies in an epidemic. After receiving Alzina's money to invest in his venture as a factor for the company he had joined in his first voyage, he sets out to Algiers, then to Gambia, where he spends some time making money for his company and for himself. He condemns the sale of African captives by their fellow Africans to European factors. On his way back, his ship and its cargo is attacked and sunk by a Spanish ship—now at war with Algiers—and he is taken captive again. Azem manages to maneuver a takeover of the ship and steers it safely to Algiers, but he refuses his part of the booty of slaves.

Having accumulated a considerable fortune, he invites his sister to join him and devotes much of his money to helping the poor and the oppressed, so much so that the lower classes start calling him the "Friend and Father of the Unfortunate." He later marries Shelimah, a childless, wealthy widow, with whom, after a long time, he engenders a son. After Omri's death, Omri's son, Arramel, also joins him, and together they go on a trade expedition to Barca. Meanwhile, the plague devastates Algiers and kills his wife, sister, and child. Azem is devastated, and his health slowly deteriorates.

But before he dies, he appoints Arramel as the executor of his estate, divided between relieving the poor and ransoming one honest slave every year.

It is the same Arramel that the author assists after falling from his horse. Thus, in a remarkable twist of fate, a benevolent black African helps a white American regain his freedom.

A similar theme, combined with the patriotic ardor of Tyler's novel, is conveyed in James Riley's best-selling *Authentic Narrative*,[110] published more than seventeen years after Foss's account. The significance of this most famous and most successful of all Barbary captivity stories has been well documented in Allison's *The Crescent Obscured*. In many ways, the narrative of the shipwreck and capture of American sailors is part of a formulaic pattern that, in Baepler's view, (re)legitimizes the captive's (religious) community and demonizes the un-American/non-Protestant Other. As is typical of the genre, Riley's narrative is preceded by two "Certificates" of authentication (one from a shipmate and the other someone with reliable geographical information on the region), and, as Ben Rejeb has shown for the genre as a whole, the second half of Riley's narrative predictably dabbles "in anthropology, ethnology and sociology."[111]

Although Ben Rejeb argues that such surveys had the cumulative effect of eventually facilitating and justifying colonialism, one nevertheless discerns a comparatist approach that has the opposite effect. The Other's culture appears in certain crucial areas to be healthier and better. Black slaves in Arab culture (whether in the desert or in the city), we are told, can become free and enjoy equal privileges and may even become leaders of their tribes (361, 423). Riley and his companion, Clark, are even mocked by a black slave, Boireck, who deems the white Americans inferior to him. Infuriating the racist Clark, Boireck amuses his Arab masters by poking the white Americans' "sore flesh with a sharp stick, to make sport, and," in Riley's words, "show the Arabs what miserable beings we were, who could not even bear the rays of the sun (the image of God, as they term it) to shine upon us" (92).

The less than black Arab (dark olive, in Riley's scheme of skin-color gradations), often derided for his barbarity elsewhere in the earlier part of the narrative, is presented as a noble savage who is surprisingly literate, one who feels superior to all other men, is rarely sick, and, thanks to a healthy and ascetic diet, lives to an advanced biblical age (376). Indeed, although Riley elsewhere assumes that the ancient greatness of Morocco must have been achieved by nonnatives (267), he attributes the appearance of writing to the wandering Arabs, long before the time of the Greeks (377). Several other positive and historically probable descriptions in the large ethnographic section (nine chapters) turn this narrative into a valuable historical source.

Once the ship is wrecked and the crew members reach the desert shore, they are continually menaced and attacked by natives (variously called "Arabs" and "savages") whose ferocious features fall somewhere between those of an Indian and a black. In these fierce moments of survival, the Americans (whose numbers include one black man and no woman) are saved miraculously and later drift along the barren rocky coast, drinking their own urine and huddling together at night until they eventually surrender to another group of Arabs, hoping to "excite pity" in their barbarous breasts. Predictably, the Americans are instantly enslaved by the wandering Arabs and subjected to a grueling and infernal physical punishment, condemned to cross the hard, rocky desert naked and shoeless under a blazing sun. Although "blistered and burnt," Riley bravely manages to hope for redemption, even extending his hand to his comrades. He tells his masters that he knows the sultan of Morocco, Moulay Slimane (Soulayman), personally, insisting that the sultan "was a friend to me and my nation" (79). The Arabs don't believe Riley, but they save his life until two Moroccan brothers, on their way to buy ostrich feathers, happen upon the group. The elder of the two brothers, Sidi Hamet, listens to Riley's story and bursts out crying, so moved is he by his plight.

Resisted by his brother Seid, Sidi Hamet nevertheless prevails and gambles his capital on the four Americans, who promise to compensate him upon their delivery to Swearah in Morocco. En route, Riley and his four companions discover couscous and kebabs (the most delicious food and best meat they have ever had—better than beefsteak) and notice the cleanliness of Arabs. Riley reflects on the geography of the desert, and all five slaves (for that's what they consider themselves) begin to believe in their redemption when they reach walled towns and rich agricultural regions whose lands are tilled by industrious peoples. The topography of freedom culminates in the sight of the Atlas Mountains, the falling of rain, and the sight of rivers. This land of abundance brings to Riley's mind "the ancient Jewish history," the "land of Canaan," as he later says in the ethnographic section (243, 387). The sense of optimism and hope that seize him at this moment only prepares him for the ultimate sight of freedom, the American flag floating over the still-distant city of Swearah: "at this blessed and transporting sight, the little blood remaining in my veins, gushed through my glowing heart with wild impetuosity, and seemed to pour a flood of new life through every part of my exhausted frame" (295–96). This emotion is matched only by the feeling of seeing "the hospitable and civilized shores of Europe" from the city of Tangier (513–14). On 20 March 1816 he arrives in New York to the warm reception of family and government, which generously pays $1852.45 for his ransom (530).

As I read this fascinating and complex narrative (which even includes a Moroccan/Arabic–English dictionary), I came across observations that we often construe as sure signs of Orientalist prejudice. For example, Riley bemoans how Morocco's once prosperous wheat-exporting cities such as Mogadore and Afidallah have declined as a result of "superstition, fanaticism, and tyranny" (311). Swearah, built by Moualy Slimane's father, Sidi Mohammed, flourished under the founder's liberal policies, but his son's antitrade practices (such as closing major ports, forbidding the export of certain items to Christians, and imposing heavy tariffs) have alienated the Christian community and depressed trade (427–511).

However, this narrative, which was read by more than a million Americans, which influenced an American to name his son Sidi Hamet, and which so inspired Abraham Lincoln that he considered it one of the most influential books in his early life,[112] was, like most other narratives, conceived to promote the universal ideal of liberty that the American Revolution was supposed to enshrine. One almost gets the sense that Moualy Slimane's unenlightened policies are not worthy of men such as Sidi Hamet and others such as Rais bel Cossim, who exhibit a remarkable degree of tolerance and compassion for the enslaved Christians. When Bel Cossim reassures Riley that God won't forsake him and that Muslims, Christians, and even pagans are children of the same heavenly father, Riley looks upon him as a "superior being" (250–51). His savior's tears and his vow to look out for the rest of the crew are all highly emotional moments in the narrative, eventually leading the grateful Riley to make the same vow to fight for the freedom of black slaves in the United States. "Adversity has taught me some noble lessons: I have now learned to look with compassion on my enslaved and oppressed fellow creatures, and my future life shall be devoted to their cause:—I will exert all my remaining faculties to redeem the enslaved, and to shiver in pieces the rod of oppression; and I trust I shall be aided in that holy work by every good and every pious, free, and high-minded citizen in the community, and by the friends of mankind throughout the civilized world" (533–34).

The book itself is dated by the new calendar of American freedom (year 41) and conforms very well to thesis that the Revolution set in motion a process of freedom that has not stopped to this day. Freedom was conceived as a gradual process, just as America, as stated by Gerald Ford in his defense of affirmative action, is still considered to be "a work in progress."[113] The fiction, plays, and accounts based on or inspired by stories of captivity and early encounters with Muslims make it clear that what motivates even the most surprising acts of cultural tolerance and condemnation of slavery is the notion of liberty that has come to define Americanness. If Islam was vilified, it was because it had no democratic institutions, promoted tyranny, and hindered free trade. Such deficiencies were not seen as exclusive to darker-skinned peoples and Muslims. They were easily found among other nations and religions. Otherwise, Islam was often given the high ground on the issue of slavery. The two-act play *Slaves in Barbary* was influential for years. It probably inspired a young slave from Baltimore, Frederick Bailey, who bought a copy and, few years later, escaped, changed his name to Frederick Douglass, and later wrote his own narrative.[114]

American liberty was universal from the start, based on the paradoxical premise that Americans were the vanguard of one human race. To reduce the attitude of such writers and captives to an Orientalist mindset is to misread the manifestations of an epochal moment in human history. After all, even though Islam was viewed in early America as a religion fostering tyranny, the United States dissociated Islam from piracy. The 1797 treaty between the United States and Tripoli (subsequently violated by the latter) stated that:

the government of the United States of America is not in any sense founded on the Christian Religion—as it has in itself no character of enmity against the laws, religion or tranquility of Musselmen,—and as the said States never have entered into any war or act of hostility against any Mehomitan nation, it is declared by the parties that no pretext arising from religious opinions shall ever produce an interruption of the harmony existing between the two countries.[115]

The Manichean theoretical constructs inspired by Orientalist theory (pitting a villainous West against a virtuous Other) have a tendency to both confine thought to prepackaged formulas and define genres and attitudes on too narrow ideological grounds. There is no reason at all to assume that Islam was the exceptional and universal evil in the story of America's making. Revolutionary Americans were more interested in their conception of freedom than in religious polemics. No sphere of activity, not even literature and literary criticism, escaped the impact of the Revolution. In his annual oration to the American Philosophical Society, titled *Discourse Concerning the Influence of America on the Mind* (1823), Charles Jared Ingersoll, lawyer, congressman, district attorney in Pennsylvania, versatile writer, and author of *Inchiquin, the Jesuit's Letters* (1809), proudly but temperately attributed the rising rates of education and professional learning in the United States to the country's ingenious system of political self-representation. Having escaped the barbarism still engulfing Europe, the United States, although still trapped in many colonial habits, was nevertheless in the process of decolonizing itself from "European pupilage." Noting that "the veil of the European beau ideal" had been pierced in the previous ten years, Ingersoll concluded his oration thus: "Let our intellectual motto be, that naught is done while aught remains to be done, and our study to prove to the world, that the best patronage of religion, science, literature, and the arts, of whatever the mind can achieve, is SELF-GOVERNMENT."[116]

Though radical, the American Revolution gave a new and powerful impetus to the universalist impulse—borne out of a long process of differentiation with Islam—that drove the conquistadors and Pilgrims to the new continent. What was good for Spain or America must have been good for those with different religions and cultures, political systems, economic habits, or even languages. Not only that, but a crusading spirit ensured that different people would always be confronted with the traumatizing choices of conversion to the West's current universalist principles or exclusion, and even defeat. The post-Andalusian Euro-American imaginary remained broadly consistent, but it manifested itself historically in different forms and expressions. Accustomed to working out contradictions arising from the principle of liberty and the dictates of the economy, an increasingly powerful United States gradually entered a new global arena in which the rise and triumph of capitalism meant that the ideals of civilization and freedom would be increasingly defined by the race for maximum profit. Only a few decades after being feared and fought, Muslims were on the verge of entering the colonial and postcolonial periods as a backward people and exotic colonial subjects, not as mortal enemies or religious rivals. The Muslims' problem, like that of all other non-Western indigenous peoples, including Native Americans, would henceforth be their insufficient grasp of Euro-American political and economic ideals and their chronic inability to embrace the West's culture of progress.

CHAPTER 4

Liberties Undone

From liberties to liberty: that phrase encapsulates one of the fundamental thrusts in the history of Europe.
—Fernand Braudel, *A History of Civilizations*

One cannot talk about modern Islam without paying attention to the world-transforming activity of the eighteenth, nineteenth, and early twentieth centuries.
—Bruce Lawrence, *Shattering the Myth*

A few decades after the American Revolution, the United States and the few dominant powers in the West ushered in a new form of universalism that would sometimes accompany the primacy of Christian infallibility and Enlightenment ideals, sometimes undermine them, and sometimes even use them to advance its own ends. Beginning around 1848, when Marx and Engels published the *Communist Manifesto*, and going through a period lasting until roughly the mid-1870s, the consolidation of capitalism as the indisputable force of world affairs would create the background for the sort of Orientalism that Edward Said discusses in his work. The third part of the nineteenth century would be the prelude of modern imperialism and the era of colonialism, which later gave birth to what we have come to know as the postcolonial condition. The third great wave of post-1492 universalist ideologies began around this time and has never truly subsided—in fact, it is intensifying as I am writing this. Henceforth, it would be capitalism that would calibrate human attitudes and frame cultural relations across the globe. And Muslims, like all colonized peoples caught in their Otherness, would devise strategies of resistance that also continue to mark the global conflict today.

The epoch beginning around 1848 marks, in Hobsbawm's large time-lines of modern history, the advance of the Industrial Revolution and the retreat of the political one. (The Industrial Revolution "swallowed the (French) political revolution," in Hobsbawm's expression.) It was the age of progress, when the term "capitalism," although used earlier, entered the common lexicon, a time when the world's noncapitalist societies were confronted by the choice of accepting or rejecting Westernization, the two main strategies available to colonized people since then. In much of Europe, the period is marked by the abandonment of tradition, the dethroning of monarchies and their replacement with nations (with tricolor flags, inspired by the French model), and the politics of "public opinion." Free trade (except in the protectionist United States), facilitated by the revolution in transport and communication technologies (railway, steamships, telegraphy) and the exploitation of academic scientific research in industry, was the mantra of the age. And so with increasing standardization, history ceased to be a collection of local histories and became "world history."[1]

Such a history had its losers, of course, not the least of which were the non-Western peoples who, either through colonial educational policies or some other design, tried the limited options available to "catch up" with Euro-Americans but have failed consistently. Never had the world been so thoroughly dominated by the "white man." American Indians west of the Mississippi, caught between the Gold Rush and an expanding East, were mostly exterminated during this period, the surviving ones confined in reservations (established in 1867). As agriculture was increasingly incorporated into the capitalist economy, humans were unsettled and set out on what was to become "the beginning of the greatest migration of peoples in history," many of these uprooted choosing the United States as their preferred destination. Then, as now, the poor migrated as cattle, while the middle classes traveled on summer holidays, whether for cures in proliferating spas or simply as tourists. Theologically, Christian truths lost out to scientific conclusions, and although people still attended churches and missionary movements were still funded, it was Islam that expanded "without benefit of missionary organization, money or the support of great powers through the backlands of Africa and parts of Asia, assisted doubtless, not only by its egalitarianism, but also by a consciousness of superiority to the values of the conquering Europeans." Of course, Christian missionaries failed to conquer Muslim souls, while Japan created a new religion out of its traditions—Shintoism—to counter European influence.[2]

By the mid-1870s, this stable, liberal, bourgeois world was eclipsed by the growing consolidation of monopoly capital (a result of international competition) and the rise of working-class movements. This was also the era of full-scale imperialism.[3] By 1898, the *Washington Post* could write that "A new consciousness seems to have come upon us—the consciousness of strength, and with it a new appetite, a yearning to show our strength. . . . Ambition, interest, land-hunger, pride, the mere joy of fighting, whatever it may be, we are animated by a new sensation. . . . The taste of empire is in the mouth of the people, even as the taste of blood is in the jungle."[4] Eric Hobsbawm, whose own parents were brought together by "the economics and politics of the Age of Empire" in Egypt, defined the period as one in which "electoral democracies . . . liquidated bourgeois liberalism" and "the economic structures which sustain the world" were laid down.[5]

Technology widened the gap in living standards between "developed countries" and what would later be known as "Third World" in only a matter of approximately eighty years. (As late as 1800, standards were roughly equal.) Technology meant more efficient weaponry to defeat other peoples, and gunboat diplomacy was deployed to advance national economic and political interests. By 1875, there were relatively few nation-states, (and most of these were in Latin America), the liberal bourgeoisie was emerging as a political idea, and the spread of the secular university, still in its infancy, like the opera house, would be part of expanding "Western" civilization. Race was used to explain backwardness as whiteness was transformed into a social asset in Latin America. And except for small elites of collaborationists (Young Turks, *científicos*, etc.), "progress," which, among other things, implied that old ways and folk wisdom have little to say about the future, was resisted both outside and within the West.[6]

The word "imperialism," never mentioned once in Marx's writings, was a novel concept that was popularized in the 1890s as arguments over colonial conquests intensified. The emergence of a capitalist global economy, with its reliance on raw materials and mass consumption of new exotic foodstuffs in metropolitan centers, reduced the rest of the colonial or semi-colonial world into monocultures specializing in the production of one or two major export items. The competition and rivalries between industrialized powers, which are often invoked to explain the impulse for imperialism, simply cannot be isolated from this general economic integration, for "politics and economics cannot be separated in a capitalist society, any more than religion and society in an Islamic one." Imperialism served other purposes, as well. It not only "made good ideological cement" by uniting white social classes (even Christian missionaries and socialists paid scant attention to the plight of the colonized before 1914), but it also was a "cultural phenomenon." The most powerful and lasting cultural legacy was the process of "Westernization," initially limited to small elites.[7] To be sure, a few native ideas entered the Western vocabulary and imagination, but, more often than not, they helped to underscore the white man's superiority.

Europe's great imperial venture did not mute the class politics raging in metropolitan centers. The democratization of politics after 1870 encouraged "public political hypocrisy, or rather duplicity," since class differences remained, in practice, irreconcilable. In an attempt to forestall the pressure of mass politics, the ruling classes ventured into "programmes of social reform and welfare," which led to "the inevitable growth in the role and weight of the state apparatus," fostering nationalism through the "*invention*" of new political traditions (national holidays, coronation ceremonies), the control of the public school system, the playing of anthems, and the deployment of the flag as a national symbol. Through these devices, the ruling classes managed to adapt parliamentary democracy to capitalist interests.[8]

Formal education, organized sports, and the rise of feminist consciousness were part of this new social landscape. Medical research also responded to Europe's expansionist policies. Imperialism spurred new developments in bacteriology and immunology, while the racist and pseudofascist sciences of eugenics and genetics permitted the ideologization of biology by providing "biological solutions" to social problems, partly to undermine socialist alternatives. While mass public education, founded on the edification of reason, on science, on the idea of progress, and on the ideology of modernization, together with expanding urbanization and a strong anticlerical movement (especially in Catholic countries), forced "traditional religion" to the margins in "the European heartlands of bourgeois society," most of the nonwhite world sought inspiration in religion to counter colonialism. Belief in progress almost inevitably required a secular outlook. But such transformations and the emergence of mass societies also provoked skepticism in the deified notion of reason, as psychology, especially in its Freudian vein, began to attribute motives to irrational forces, while sociology sought to find ways to preserve the embattled bourgeois system.[9]

Capitalism destabilized the periphery "by undermining the old structures of its economies and the balance of its societies, and by destroying the viability of its established political regimes and institutions." The answer was often the rush to modernize by small Westernized elites from the colonies or semicolonies without the benefit of a necessary, dynamic bourgeois class. In Turkey, this led to the forced assimilation of minorities into a new Turkish ethnos, while Mexico and other Latin American countries— whose elites were self-consciously European, but whose countries were marginal—opted for a form of progress that meant economic integration with and dependency on the global economy. It was this dependency (on the United States) that ultimately led to a depression that ignited the revolution (blessed by the United States) against Porfirio Díaz in Mexico. But no revolution would match the one that would take place in Czarist Russia, a country that "exemplified all the contradictions of the globe in the Age of Empire."[10]

The rise and effects of Westernization have been scrupulously assessed by Theodore Von Laue in *The Revolution of Westernization*. The ascendancy of the West and its institutions had the effect of discrediting all non-Western ways of life, forcing "reculturation" on non-Westerners, a situation that resulted in chaos, alienation, and an ever brewing anger among the colonized.[11] At the height of European imperialism, the British consciously sought to impose an Anglo-Saxon culture on their subjects in India and other parts of the world. "We have to remember," stated the British statesman Lord Rosebery in 1893, "that it is part of our responsibility and heritage to take care that the world, so far as it can be moulded by us, shall receive the Anglo-Saxon, and not another character."[12] While 85 percent of the world's surface was controlled by Europe and America, other people's histories and memories were downgraded as non-Western cultures were left with the defeating options of ethnocide through Westernization, cultural orthodoxy, or falling into a paralyzing and deadly inaction.[13] In 1909, Mohandas Gandhi preached against the adoption of the British capitalist system, saying that "if India copies England, it is my firm conviction that she will be ruined."[14] His was an idea that had been shared by the British Sir T. Erskine May in the nineteenth century when he predicted that "in the hands of Eastern rulers, the civilisation of the West is unfruitful; and, instead of restoring a tottering state, appears to threaten it with speedier ruin."[15]

But the march of capital was unstoppable, spawning counterrevolutions against Westernization in Europe itself, let alone in old bastions of civilization such as China and the Islamic world. Such counterrevolutions, mostly inspired by Marxist and Communist ideologies, could not stem the tide of Westernization and in fact strengthened it. The choices were tragically clear to non-Westerners, as one Chinese intellectual, Chen Duxiu, stated in his "Call to Youth" in 1915:

> Considered in the light of the evolution of human affairs, it is plain that those races that cling to antiquated ways are declining, or disappearing, day by day, and the people who seek progress and advancement are just beginning to ascend in power and strength. It is possible to predict which of these will survive and which will not. . . . Our people will be turned out of this 20th century world and be lodged in the dark ditches fit only for slaves, cattle, and horses. . . . I would much rather see the past culture of our nation disappear than see our race die out . . . because of its unfitness for living in the modern world.[16]

A decade and a half later (1931), Stalin echoed the same warning when he said his country was fifty or a hundred years behind the West and had no option but to catch up in ten years. "Either we do it or we shall be crushed."[17] Mao Tse-tung, fusing Marxist-Leninist philosophy into Chinese traditions, also managed to build, through will and discipline, "the most effective state in Chinese history."[18]

Since 1914, the word "catastrophe" came to be applied to a new, horrifying world in which victims of war and aggression are counted by the millions. The optimism of the Age of Empire—despite undeniable progress in many areas—would be forever eclipsed by the specter of an even more devastating apocalypse. It gave way, in Hobsbawm's account, to the Age of Catastrophe (roughly "from the outbreak of the First World War to the aftermath of the Second"), followed by the relatively brief and momentous "Golden Age of 1947–73" that witnessed "the greatest, most rapid and most fundamental" "economic, social and cultural transformation[s]" in "recorded history," followed by what appears to be a permanent crisis in the global order. Although the world is no longer Eurocentric, and anxiety over the decline of the West is rising, wealth and power are still mostly concentrated in the hands of the same colonial powers that dominated the world at the end of the nineteenth century. In fact, the map of the postcolonial world is, except in a few cases, "almost entirely divided by the frontiers of imperialism."[19]

Fuelled by capital-intensive technological developments, during the decades following World War II and until the early 1970s, the "mixed economies" of the advanced capitalist states grew at an "explosive rate." Mechanization and the "impressive achievements of agricultural chemistry, selective breeding and bio-technology" led to a "massive and silent exodus from the land." As "the relation between the sexes" underwent a severe crisis (which shattered the structure of traditional nuclear families), the rise of a global youth culture further severed the links between generations—in fact, reversed their roles. "Youth culture became the matrix of the cultural revolution," which was promptly exploited by the cosmetics, fashion, music, and other industries. Rebelliously antitraditional, this culture espoused no serious alternative except for the stubborn insistence on elevating "private feelings and desires" as legitimate goals for radical political militancy. Yet the struggle for "unlimited autonomy of individual desire" was, coincidentally, the very psychological motivation that sustained consumer societies.[20]

This "triumph of the individual over society, or rather, the breaking of the threads which in the past had woven human beings into social textures" generated the now familiar neuroses afflicting anomic cultures. Traditional values were reduced to abstract rights and individual preferences, providing the context for the ideologies of "extreme free-market liberalism," postmodernism, and the "militantly nostalgic," but clearly anguished cries of "identity politics" movements.[21] The simultaneous (re)appearance of a new "underclass" inhabiting the "Hobbesian jungles" of housing projects and operating outside legal structures, together with the mounting calls for punishing the "antisocial," are all symptoms of the fin-de-siècle depression.

Meanwhile, the world's poor continue to live mostly in postcolonial states lacking any "traditional legitimacy," relying on "political systems derived from their old imperial masters or those who had conquered them." Their impoverished economies are further assaulted by international organizations and unelected supranational authorities whose only goal is to further spread the reigning "neo-liberal theology."[22]

The foregoing excessively abridged historical sketch forms the background to literary and cultural shifts from the mid-nineteenth century (The Age of Capital) through the postcolonial period that still characterize the present. The universalism of the American Revolution endowed Americans with proprietary rights over the Orient. Convinced that Protestantism expresses the true spirit of Christ and the early Christian Church, inspired by a "sense of divine mission," encouraged by the confidence in their unique political system and great natural and human resources, energized by religious revivals, Americans set out to spread the Protestant light in the lands of Biblical prophets, although efforts to convert Muslims—with minor exceptions—turned out to be mostly fruitless. Herman Melville, traveling in the Levant, wrote: "Might as well attempt to convert bricks into brick-cakes as the Orientals into Christians. It is against the will of God that the East should be Christianized."[23] Local Christian churches were also resistant to the American Protestants' proselytizing. Only Beirut, according to J. V. C. Smith, was considered an exception.[24]

The U.S. government would eventually coordinate its efforts with missionary activity as part of its larger expansionist ideology of Manifest Destiny. "Nineteenth-century politicians and evangelists looked to the frontiers—Western and Oriental—within the context of that sacred mission. The former called their effort 'Manifest Destiny,' the latter, the 'Great Commission.' Both politicians and missionaries offered realistic justifications of their expansion—on economic as well as geographical grounds. The ultimate aim was to appropriate more territory." Guided by a biblical geography of the Orient, Christians felt entitled to the ownership of Arab lands and sought to reclaim the Promised Land from decadent local religions. Travelers and pilgrims were disappointed to find their sacred geography populated by Muslims and non-Protestants. The lifelong missionary Henry Jessup had no doubt that "*in the conflict between civilization and barbarism Islam must be the loser*," because Islam, he wrote in *The Mohammedan Missionary Problem*, is "in direct conflict with" modern civilization.[25] For many travelers, as for the early Puritans, biblical Israel was preferred over ancient Greece, just as a Christian theocracy was preferred over Athenian democracy. Hadn't America, as one passage in Melville's *Redburn* states, been made in the image of Israel?

We Americans are the peculiar, chosen people—the Israel of our time; we bear the ark of the liberties of the world. Seventy years ago we escaped from thrall; and, besides our first birthright—embracing one continent of earth—God has given to us, for a future inheritance, the broad domains of the political pagans, that shall yet come and lie down under the shade of our ark, without bloody hands being lifted. God has predestinated, mankind expects, great things from our race; and great things we feel in our souls. The rest of the nations must soon be in our rear. We are the pioneers of the world; the advance guard, sent on through the wilderness of untried things to break a new path in the New World that is ours.[26]

The American intellectual tradition, with its biblical metaphors and spirit of covenant, its new sense of mission and its growing commercial and military interests, its proliferating millennial religious movements, and its religious revivalism in general, converged with its growing interest in the Orient to compel "a national commitment to rebuild the New Jerusalem, i.e., *the* City on a Hill."[27] Thus, imperialism and Orientalism merged into one indistinguishable ideology. Bedouins, with their simple and austere lifestyles, inspired many travelers and writers, including Emerson and Thoreau, but they were also seen as the Eastern counterparts of Native Americans at home. In his *Niles Notes of a Howadiji,* George William Curtis made such an analogy clear:

Strangely and slowly gathers in your mind the conviction that the last inhabitants of the oldest land have thus a mysterious sympathy of similarity with the aborigines of the youngest. For what more are these orientals that sumptuous savages?

As the Indian dwells in primeval forests . . . so lives the Oriental, the pet of natural luxury, in a golden air, at the foundations of History, and Art, and Religions; and yet the thinnest gleanings of stripped fields would surpass his harvest. . . .

Nor does the Oriental fail in dignity and repose. His appearance satisfies your imagination no less than your eye. No other race has his beauty of countenance, and grace and costume; nowhere else is poetry the language of trade.[28]

But the Bedouin, like the Native American, had been surpassed by history, now embodied in liberty-loving and world-saving Americans, or, at least, in other major European powers. Mocure Conway expressed this sentiment well in his "East and West," published in 1859: "The East had given its message to the World, and must retire."[29] This is the essence of American Orientalism, expressed succinctly as early as 1853 in an edition of the *Knickerbocker* aptly titled "Orientalism."[30] Muslims may be exotic, ancient, wise, free, and fascinating, but in the Western universalist imaginary, sustained by solid economic imperatives, only enlightened Euro-American colonialism could uproot the wretchedness that had afflicted the hapless subalterns for so long. When such an icon of women's freedom as Edith Wharton championed French colonial rule in Morocco in the early twentieth century, there is no other way to explain her attitude. Both Orientalism and racism appear as secondary side effects of this imaginary, but neither one of them motivated Wharton's reading of Morocco. One would seriously lose perspective and misdiagnose the problem by projecting present sensibilities backward to a time and place where meaning was determined by a different set of historical circumstances. My own experience with Edith Wharton's *In Morocco* (1919) convinced me of this.

In 1997, I devised and started teaching a course on Moroccan literature and culture to mostly health-professional undergraduate students. It was around the time that I started leading groups of faculty and students on short cultural tours of Morocco and thinking about writing my own travel book on that country. I had read some standard accounts of Moroccan history, a lot of travel books, and colorful accounts of Morocco before the protectorate, including the memoirs of an English woman who married and lived in Morocco several decades before Wharton's visit. So the reissuing of Wharton's book was quite an exciting event, especially because I knew of no major American writer since Mark Twain who had written this expressly on Morocco. As professors often tend to do, I quickly assigned the book in my class.

The session on Wharton's book turned out to be a disastrous teaching episode. The students hated it, labeled Wharton a "racist," and wanted to hear no more. As a Moroccan writing critically on Orientalism, Eurocentrism, and capitalism, I was rather perplexed and taken aback by this unanimous condemnation and did my best to defend Wharton's views. No one wanted to hear my rationalizations. I then reexamined my own reading, wondering about how I turned out to be more accepting of Wharton's descriptions than my students. My students' response to Wharton's was echoed in all sorts of critical studies, ranging from Amazon.com customer reviews to published essays and books. Of all the critics whose works I consulted, only Elizabeth Simmons seems to have discerned some positive value in Wharton's book, especially her descriptions of the harem, since this supposedly "most sexy of all male-oriented systems" turns out to be one of the most extreme and depressing form of the "patriarchal sex" that Wharton consistently criticizes throughout her work. Otherwise, Mary Suzanne Schirber does a good job highlighting Orientalist tropes in Wharton's narrative, particularly the latter's erasure of the Moroccan present and her depiction of Moroccan civilization as an unchanging Oriental specimen. Of course, what gives Orientalism its insidious connotations is the writer's (implied) triumphalist attitude about a progressive and benevolent West (even though at the time of her trip to Morocco, in the fall of 1917, western Europe was in the grip of what was probably the most barbaric and savage war in history), and so it is not surprising to find Wharton decorated by the French and Belgians for her propaganda and charitable work during the war. Judith Sensibar's superb essay shows that Wharton was not merely a propagandist for France's war efforts, but also a champion of French imperialism who deployed an equally masculinist attitude toward the natives. In a way that complements Stephanie Batcos's cautious remark that outsiders' readings of Morocco must always be questioned, since the subject position of the writer may well be traversed with cultural dissonances that simply cannot be bridged, Sensibar brings to light indigenous views that are typically repressed in most Eurocentric narratives and quotes the much admired Moroccan activist Aicha Belarbi on the evils of colonialism. Wharton, as we know, was invited to Morocco not only because she was a supporter of French imperialism, but also because she was an "inveterate Francophile"—to use the words of Roger Asselineau—one who "preferred Racine to Shakespeare" and who was also highly connected in the world of letters and even finance. It is no wonder, then, as Frederick Wegener suggested in his introductory essay to Wharton's recently discovered essay on Madame Lyautey, that Wharton's sympathies and prejudices confront Wharton scholars with some painful issues that cannot be easily swept away.[31]

One of these issues is Wharton's fascination with France's resident general in Morocco, General (and later Marshal) Louis-Hubert Lyautey. Presumably the model for the character Ménalque in André Gide's 1902 novel *L'immoraliste* (which was one of the books Wharton read before her three-week tour), Wharton had met Lyautey in Paris, had an affinity with his homosexuality, and like many historians and contemporaries, thought that he could do no harm. In many ways the embodiment of a certain aristocratic, royalist France, Lyautey conducted France's colonial policies like a grand maestro, relying on a mixture of European arrogance and universal values that, at times, seemed to transcend France's own colonial interests. Credited with single-handedly catapulting Morocco out of the medieval world in which it had been locked for centuries and into the modern, capitalist one, Lyautey was the rare soldier/administrator who relished the company of writers and expressed disdain for technical formalities that diminished creativity and stifled talent.

Long interested in theories of colonialism, he had published on the subject and was elected to the prestigious Académie Française the very year he assumed his residential post in Morocco, 1912. A man of contradictions, he exhibited the familiar sense of French superiority, yet had mostly contempt for the common French and seems to have preferred the nobler Moroccans. Muslims fought him, but also prayed for him when he fell sick in 1923. This grand colonial lord of the Third Republic with an epic style and Napoleonic gestures ultimately made his name interchangeable with Morocco's. Indeed, so dedicated was he to the concept of the protectorate that he prohibited Christian access to mosques (a policy that he steadfastly upheld even when he was invited by the '*ulama* [religious scholars] in 1923 for a healing prayer), preserved and restored Morocco's crumbling monuments, and, at times, insisted on walking on foot and proudly holding the sultan's stirrup (*étrier*). His was a colonialism of love, based on winning the affections and trust of the natives, even though critical studies have shown that his elitism prevented him from implementing much of what he believed philosophically.

In the 1930s, Britain's famed prime minister David Lloyd George stated that the story of French colonization in Morocco is inseparable from Lyautey's, "that Prince of Pro-Consuls, one of the finest sons ever born to France, rich as her story is in great men. His achievements would be hard to match in the records of conquest and colonization of any land," for "far greater and more decisive [than the successful conquest of fiercely independent native warriors] were his wise planning, his deep understanding and sympathy for the Moors with whom he had to deal, and his passionate sense of a mission to heal, to pacify, to spread order and prosperity under the aegis of his fatherland in the tortured darkness of Morocco" (14).[32]

Understandably, such statements are profoundly troubling to a generation of scholars influenced by a critique of Orientalism and to a cohort of students raised on a diet of values whose primary goal is to avoid making negative judgments about anything. Quite obviously, my students knew nothing about Orientalism, the history of the French occupation, or Lyautey, and many, in fact, espouse views that may seem antiliberal. They just instinctively knew that Wharton was a racist who looked down on the natives.

My colleagues' defense of indigenous traditions and the natives' response to colonialism are admirable correctives to Wharton's prejudices. John Maier has done a remarkable job by placing Wharton in historical context and showing the ways in which her account of the Sufi rituals at Moulay Idriss would have been appreciated differently by her Western predecessors, such as Nietzsche, and by later writers such as Paul Bowles. The natives, after all, are engaged in trance-inducing and self-mutilating rituals that antedate Islam and whose function is healing and communal peace. As such, one might add, they are the reverse image of French rational, but truly violent colonialist policies. From Wharton's description of Lyauety's balance sheet, it would seem that colonialism clearly benefited Moroccans, including women. But as Alison Baker has shown in her anthropological account and interviews with women resistance fighters, French policies (after Lyautey's demise, one must note) were universally rejected as divisive. Such women occasionally refused liberation into an un-Moroccan modernity (such as wearing Western clothes and not staying home) and sometimes even defeated large colonial armies. From Maier and Baker's critical accounts, it would appear that Wharton had nothing good to say about Morocco, and the only people who seem to fascinate her, Maier points out, are despots and feudal lords working on behalf of colonial interests.[33]

All this is indisputably true and needs no further emphasis, but as someone who has spent some time thinking about Orientalist attitudes, reads regularly on aspects of Moroccan history and culture, and acts as a tour guide to most monuments mentioned in Wharton's book, I am wondering whether our present sensibilities have made it nearly impossible to appreciate unadulterated Western views of Morocco. Wharton was a woman of strong opinions who much preferred France to her own country, and it is only logical to expect her to agree with Lyautey's presumably enlightened approach to the colonies. Like him, she may have been nurtured by nineteenth-century Orientalist fables (evident early in Lyautey's career at least) and espoused a contradictory universalist ideology that ascribed all sorts of benevolent attributes to an unexamined notion of progress, even while (echoing Lyautey's own prejudices again) she lamented the passing away of old Morocco and hated the financial parvenus in her own native city.[34] And as with Lyautey's legacy, one is called upon to make a balance sheet of Wharton's own narrative and examine the extent to which she has in effect managed to produce a book for the ordinary "happy wanderers who may be planning a Moroccan journey, " as she states in her preface and following note.

In addition to presenting Lyautey's sophisticated talents and creative policies (including "the policy of the smile") in much the same terms they were described in the period's literature, she concludes her account with an almost flawlessly executed summary of Morocco's impossibly complex history. To be sure, she uses curious comparisons, as when she likens the racially mixed Berbers to modern Americans. "For centuries, for ages,

North Africa has been what America now is: the clearing-house of the world."[35] Morocco's history is generally a tumultuous, chaotic, and unstable one, punctuated with exceptional moments of high civilization, usually ushered in by a remarkable sultan of one of the major dynasties. Astute enough to decipher the Khaldounian notion of cycles in Maghrebian history, she states that the death of a powerful leader is "followed by the downward curve to which all Oriental rule seems destined" (244). It is a wonder that places of high culture, art, and learning, such as the ones in Fez, were ever built (246–47). She also reminds readers that prior to the Cherifian empires of the Saadians, relations between Morocco and Christians were rather friendly, and Moroccan armies were assisted by Christian mercenaries, not by renegades, as is often assumed. "War in those days was regarded as a lucrative and legitimate form of business, exactly as it was when the earlier heroes started out to take the rich robber-town of Troy" (249). Indeed, Christian assistance persisted well into the fanatical and isolationist reigns of Saadians and what she calls the Hassanities (due to Spanish and Portuguese threats and incursions), especially in the piracy sector, for "Moroccans being very poor seamen," she writes in a footnote, their "corsair-vessels were usually commanded and manned by Christian renegadoes and Turks" (250). She ends the section on the Saadians by describing them as "ambitious and luxury-loving princes, who invaded the wealthy kingdom of the Soudan, conquered the Sultan of Timbuctoo, and came back laden with slaves and gold to embellish Marrakesh and spend their treasure in the usual demoralizing orgies. Their exquisite tombs at Marrakesh commemorate in courtly language the superhuman virtues of a series of rulers whose debaucheries and vices were usually cut short by assassination" (252). The infamous Moulay Ismail (to whom she devotes an entire section of the book) did a good job unifying the country and making it secure, but according to Wharton, since his death, with the exception of a few decent attempts here and there, it is Lyautey who brings much needed stability and peace to such a disorderly polity.

She classifies Moroccan architecture into two main (but overlapping) categories: defensive and religious. Indeed, because of the prevailing Muslim patriarchal culture, the private house "is a fortress, a convent and a temple" all at once (266). And several times throughout her narrative, she declares Merinid art, the best of Morocco's architectural design, to be influenced mostly by "European civilization," although she is referring to Moorish Spain (104–5).

Her description of Fez is superb, one of the best I have read. Upon entering this ageless, quintessential Moroccan city (with no traces of a pre-Islamic past), a city of culture, wealth, and trade, she immediately notices the "pale faces ringed in curling beards" listening intently to storytellers, in an unmistakably Oriental scene (78) and feels a sense of "overripeness" pervading the atmosphere: "Buildings, people, customs, seem all about to crumble and fall of their own weight: the present is a perpetually prolonged past. To touch the past with one's hands is realized only in dreams; and in Morocco the dream-feeling envelopes one at every step." Again and again, Wharton is struck by the Moroccans' indifference to buildings and their preservation. "'Dust to dust' should have been the motto of the Moroccan palace-builders," she almost laments in exasperation, especially because such an attitude is also to blame for the disappearance of all furniture—with one or two exceptions—that must have adorned Morocco's old palatial dwellings (86–87).

She also marvels at the mixture of races and classes in the Fez Elbali, "this land of perpetual contradictions" (90), and offers what is probably one of the greatest descriptions of a Fassi making his way through this chaotic scene:

The slippered Fazi merchant, wrapped in white muslins and securely mounted on a broad velvet saddle-cloth anchored to the back of a broad mule, is unlike the Arab horseman of the desert as Mr. Tracy Tupman was unlike the Musketeers of Dumas. Ease, music, money-making, the affairs of his harem and the bringing-up of his children, are his chief interests, and his plump face with long-lashed hazel eyes, his curling beard and fat womanish hands, recall the portly potentates of Hindu miniatures, dreaming among houris beside lotus-tanks. (90)

Marrakesh also fascinates her. With its population of mixed races, its "dark, fierce and fanatical" souks filled with "incessantly moving throngs" that seem to be "the central organ of a native life that extends far beyond the city walls into secret clefts of the mountains and far-off oases where plots are hatched and holy wars fomented—farther still, to yellow deserts whence Negroes are brought across the Atlas to that inmost recess of the bazaar where the ancient traffic in flesh and blood still surreptitiously goes on," this city on the edge of civilization nevertheless boasts great works of art, magnificent gardens that host sumptuous and decadent picnics, the penultimate Oriental site of the Square of the Dead, circumcision processions, and miraculously preserved Saadian tombs that point to a refinement and beauty radically opposed to the menacing atmosphere of the souk. How such juxtapositions manage to coexist in the same place is, for Edith Wharton, the "central riddle" of Morocco.

Her descriptions of Rabat, Sale, Meknes, Moualy Idriss, and Marrakesh can be equally insightful. Even her famous portrayal of harem women as melancholy creatures devoid of life is not necessarily an essentialist gesture. Moroccan women, especially the unveiled, bare-legged Berbers, are often described as mysterious, as intriguing, and, in one case, as superior merchants. In fact, the harem women of Rabat "but for the vacuity of their faces . . . might have been that of a Professor's family in an English or American university town, decently costumed for an Arabian Nights' pageant in the college grounds." Such sights remind Wharton that "human nature, from one pole to the other, falls naturally into certain categories, and that Respectability wears the same face in an Oriental harem as in England or America" (184–85). Lower-class women in Morocco, moreover, she makes sure to note, enjoy more public freedoms than their pampered sisters.

The book, quite frankly, is full of great insights and brilliantly crafted passages that, in my opinion, evoke Morocco's intangible cultural practices more successfully than any Delacroix or Matisse. In some cases, it captures Morocco better than the growing volume of scholarly monographs on Moroccan culture. And the comments that often appear insultingly Orientalist (and which may very well correspond to reality)—such as the Moroccan's indifference to preserving monuments, the cycle of destruction that follows the inauguration of a new dynasty, the lack of seduction (in the Western sense) in the traditional harem, the dreamlike quality of social life, the caricaturish figure of the patriarch, and the sense of fatalism that envelopes everything—could, in the hand of a travel guide, turn into intriguing accounts that ultimately make the discerning tourist more curious about differences and more skeptical about his or her own certainties. There is, after all, a lot to be said for allowing human constructions and ambitions to return to dust.

Yet as justified and even as convincing as Wharton's universalist ideals may be, the experience of colonialism in Morocco and the rest of the Muslim world was a traumatic one, one that mixed up guiding epistemologies and threw the native populations into disarray, failure, and violent refusals. In this sense, the Muslim predicament is similar to that of the Native Americans, since both cultures—Europe's Other in the post-Andalusian period—have continued to resist Westernization, although Native

Americans are still colonized, and their numbers are vastly smaller than those of Muslims. As is the case with Muslims, the tragedy of forced assimilation into the white man's world continues to haunt Native Americans and to spawn resistance.

In Mexico, the first modern European state in the Americas, nothing has ameliorated the lot of Native Americans since the conquest—not independence from Spain, not the Mexican Revolution, and not a series of economic policies ranging from import substitution to the North American Free Trade Agreement. Mexico remains dependent on the goodwill of its northern neighbor, and Mexican indigenous peoples fare the worst among Mexico's social strata.

Mexican literature reflects the indigenous peoples' infernal situation quite eloquently. In *El Indio* (1937),[36] Gregorio Lopez y Fuentes, the novelist of campesinos who is remarkably familiar with their languages and traditions, the Mexican Revolution appears mostly a white men's affair. Four centuries have already passed since the conquest, and the fiesta (the *volador*) celebrated by the Indians recapitulates "four centuries of painful history: first, the dancing, the music and the volador—the ancient ways; then, alcohol and disorder"(127). While the *gente de la razon*, who are called that because they always seem to have a "reason" for what they do, and who are also known as *coyotl* or *coyome*, are engaged in fighting, Indians are mostly unconcerned, untouched, and indifferent. The fact that the chapter in *El Indio* on the Revolution is only two and a half pages long (197–99, the second-shortest chapter in the book) indicates that the intellectual and ideological issues of the revolution are meaningless to Indians. Although the second half of the book situates the events unfolding in the novel during the revolution, the main goal of the novel is to highlight the marginality of Indians throughout post-1942 Mexican history and to emphasize that all the major wars and revolutionary movements that define Mexican history are ultimately oblivious to the Indians' dispossession and only exploit them for economic and/or political gain. The Indian is the permanent loser, whether change is implemented in the name of a liberal or conservative, religious or secular, capitalist or socialist programs. It is ultimately a clash of cultures—in the most profound meaning of the word "clash"—that has resulted from the conquest. The indigenous cosmology cannot be contained within any Eurocentric model of society, which is why the pre-Hispanic past is used only decoratively and for purposes of differentiation crucial to the construction of a national identity.

The symbolic significance of the title of the first chapter, "Gold," sums up the motives of the conquest, the resulting clash of cultures, and the long-term defeat and partial ethnocide of indigenous civilizations. Three white men (interestingly referred to as "traders") appear in an Indian "rancheria nailed high in the sierra," a village consisting of "one long alley of drab thatch houses grimed with smoke"(13–14). The whites, equipped with a map and pretending to be selling glass beads and looking for medicinal plants, are, in fact, looking for gold. The weakened Indians, already displaced by previous conquests, know that white men usually look for gold, or *teocuitatl,* "God's dirt" (20). When the Indians produce no gold, the whites settle for the night, and "thus begins the sad evening of an Indian village"(22).

Troubles begin the following day when the youngest of the three white men manages to attack an Indian girl. Desperate, the white men threaten the *huehues* (council of elders) with a paper they display as a "signed order" from higher authorities. Indians, frightened by the mere sight of the paper, desist from avenging their girl and provide the white men with a guide to the mountains, presumably in search of medicinal herbs. And so, "the paper won"(38).

The three white men ask the young, muscular Indian to guide them to the alleged location of a gold mine on their map—whites always use and trust paper (43, 45). Despairing, the head *coyotl* threatens to kill the Indian if he doesn't reveal the secret. The smiling and serene Indian is tortured before, hands tied, he plunges down a slope. The white men return to the village, pack, and leave.

Told of what happened, the village men rush to avenge their man and fight the mounted white men's firearms with rocks and by dislodging boulders and sending them rolling down the slope toward the white men. But fearing that they killed one of them, and that the white men's papers meant sure reprisals, "annihilation and pillage"(63), the *huehues* decide to seek refuge in the mountains and keep their lips sealed.

A punitive expedition led by the municipal president turns into a discussion about the fate of Indians after the conquest (the rancheria is already burned down). The schoolmaster, explaining why Indians don't trust whites, suggests alternatives to genocide and slavery: assimilation through the construction of roads to connect rancherias and a culturally sensitive education. Eventually the *gente de razon* (87) seek peace because labor is in short supply. The fugitive Indians return to their rancheria. Many contemplate migration, despite the *huehues'* decree to the contrary, but a good harvest persuades them to stay.

Unbeknownst to Indians, the revolution is taking place, while small-pox—a white man's disease (203)—ravages the rancheria and kills a cripple's only love and her daughter. The "deputy" arrives in the village to inform the Indians that the revolution has liberated them by choosing to introduce them to commerce and assimilate them into the white man's culture through education. This is considered progress (206–7). But given the lack of funds, Indians must contribute two days of labor to build the highway, although, according to the new constitution, they cannot be exploited (208–9). Building highways for automobiles and praying to an alien god, however, desacralizes Indian ancient sites (archaeological mounds) and leads the Indians to abandon their fields of maize, even as the specter of famine is never entirely absent (225). And when they finish building the school, it is named after the deputy (227–28).

Eventually, a young Indian, educated by his former master, comes to replace a white teacher. He is immediately struck by the oppression of Indians through illegal taxation and the maldistribution of lands. With the approval of the elders, he asks the authorities to improve the condition of Indians (connecting rancherias to other places through roads, supplying new teachers to teach new agricultural methods, etc.), and thus a young man becomes the leader and ends the very ancient tradition of elder rule because he is literate (241). The Indians, caught up in the world of modern politics, are reduced to holding mass demonstrations to further the educated Indian's idealist political ambitions. The constant participation in mass political demonstrations means that the fields will remain abandoned, and land distribution will be "pushed to the background of politics"(254). Now they have to fight the White Guards and suffer ambushes for no benefit at all. The novel ends with the cripple, posted as a sentinel, still watching out for the attack by the *gente de razon,* while their new leader is "well taken care of" in the city (256).

The condition of Mexican Indians is, of course, shared by Indians north of the border. Peter Nabokov's superb chronicle of the Yaqui Indians of Arizona from 1492 to the end of the twentieth century provides ample illustration of how Indians continue to be America's Other.[37] They, too, called (Spanish) whites *gente de razones* (xxi), particularly because of their relentless quest for money. As the great North American Indian leader Sitting Bull put it, "The love of money is a disease among them" (xvii). Charles Alexander

Eastman, a Santee Indian from Minnesota, recalled his uncle telling him that whites are "a heartless nation" for enslaving people and that "the greatest object of their lives seems to be acquire possessions—to be rich." Thus, "they measure everything" and divide everything into units (22).

Such harsh verdicts were not without reason: Between 1848 and 1870, during Hobsbawm's "Age of Capital," over fifty thousand natives died in California as a result of the Gold Rush (7). The Indians living on their native lands were so often seen as enemies of the expanding commercial empire of the United States that "in 1789 the United States War Department was created, in part to handle all Indian matters. When a separate Bureau of Indian Affairs was established in 1824, it remained under War Department control" before it was transferred, twenty-five years later, to the Department of the Interior (93).

The white man's treaties with the Indians were a remarkable act of European legality designed to disguise the dispossession of natives, for these treaties were "thinly disguised bills of sale transferring ancient tribal lands into white hands" (118). By 1865, General William Tecumseh Sherman was describing an Indian reservation as "a parcel of land set aside for Indians surrounded by thieves" (189). In March 1867, Maine Senator Justin Morrill noted rather rhetorically that "we have come to this point in the history of this country that there is no place beyond the population to which you can remove the Indian . . . and the precise question is, will you exterminate him, or will you fix an abiding place for him?" (172). "On March 3, 1871, Congress formally ended what Andrew Jackson had dismissed as 'the farce of treating with Indian tribes.'" The Indian Appropriation Act stipulated that "no Indian nation or tribe within the territory of the United States shall be acknowledged and recognized as an independent nation, tribe, or power with whom the United States may contract by treaty" (119). Under such schemes, Indians were reduced to a wretchedness they had never experienced before. Indian women often prostituted themselves to white men for money, got infected, and passed their infections on to their own men.

Almost from the very start of the occupation, Europeans tried to assimilate Indians into their culture, even as they assiduously maintained their inferior status. But the Indians could never fully assimilate to a culture that is not their own. Pedro Naranjo, an Indian prisoner, responding to interrogations after the Pueblo Rebellion of 1680 against the Church's oppression of the baptized Indians of the Southwest, related that after rebelling, the Indians tried to cleanse themselves from their earlier Christian baptism and built their own traditional altars, for the "devil had given them to understand that living thus in accordance with the law of their ancestors, they would harvest a great deal of maize, many beans, a great abundance of cotton, calabashes, and very large watermelons and cantaloupes; and that they could erect their houses and enjoy abundant health and leisure" (56). Becoming Christian didn't help, either. The Fox, or Mesquakie Indians of the southern Great Lakes region have an anecdote about the "good Indian's dilemma":

Once there was an Indian who became a Christian. He became a very good Christian; he went to church, and he didn't smoke or drink, and he was good to everyone. He was a very good man. Then he died. First he went to the Indian hereafter, but they wouldn't take him because he was a Christian. Then he went to heaven, but they wouldn't let him in—because he was an Indian. Then he went to Hell, but they wouldn't let him there either, because he was so good. So he came alive again, and he went to the Buffalo Dance and the other dances and taught his children to do the same thing. (57)

As Indians fought over which way to pursue, the pro-whites became known as "Breeches" (i.e., they wore pants) and traditionalists became known as "blankets" (71). They simply couldn't understand why their way of life was not respected. Petalesharo, a Pawnee leader, told President James Monroe in 1822 that the Great Spirit "made my skin red and yours white; he placed us on earth and intended that we should live differently from each other" (71). In fact, many Indians reassured themselves with the prophecy of the end of the white race on their land (93). On 4 November 1873, Big Bear, an Otoe chief from Nebraska told a U.S. commissioner in Washington, D.C. that he "cannot make white men of us. That is one thing you can't do" (139).

Part of the war against the Indians in the post–Civil War period included their assimilation into white society through education. Previously, the conversion to Christianity was thought to define the degree of the natives' integration. When Dartmouth College was founded in 1769, its purpose was to offer "all parts of learning which shall appear necessary and expedient for civilizing and Christianizing children of pagans" (214). But now the terms of civilization were redefined to uphold the capitalist doctrine. The Indian "must be imbued with the exalting egotism of American civilization so that he will say 'I' instead of 'We,' and 'This is mine' instead of 'This is ours,'" a Commissioner of Indians affairs said in 1886, as Indian territory was broken up into private individual allotments. Even Indian protectors upheld this capitalist view. In 1916, the president of Amherst College told a gathering that "we must make the Indian more intelligently selfish. . . . By acquiring property, man puts forth his personality and lays hold of matter by his own thought and will" (235).

Of course, Indians saw the matter differently. The Sioux sang death songs upon approaching schools. No wonder, for among the many trans-formations they were expected to undergo is the acquisition of a new name. The Omaha writer Francis La Flesche recalled in his memoir that "the aboriginal names were considered by the missionaries heathenish . . . in the place of Tae-noo-ga-wa-zhe, came Philip Sheridan; in that of Wa-pah-dae . . . Jonathan." These educated, half-assimilated people were called "the lost people" by the Stony Indians of Canada, which may explain why some preferred death to such schooling for their children. These In-dians knew that white education spelled the death of their culture. Al-though Indians were taught to believe in the backwardness of their culture, a Blackfoot preferred to kidnap his son rather than surrender him to the white school system. Sun Elk, of Taos, New Mexico, recalled this part of his education:

They told us that Indian ways were bad. They said we must get civilized. I re-member that word too. It means "be like the white man." I am willing to be like the white man, but I did not believe Indian ways were wrong. But they kept teach-ing us for seven years. And the books told how bad the Indians had been to the white men—burning their towns and killing their women and children. But I had seen white men do that to Indians. We all wore white man's clothes and ate white man's food and went to white man's churches and spoke white man's talk. And so after a while we also began to say Indians were bad. We laughed at our own peo-ple and their blankets and cooking pots and sacred societies and dances. (222)

Indeed, U.S. and Canadian authorities banned Sun Dances and the pot-latch ritual—to the protest of Indians. A Blackfoot, puzzled by the white man's objection to the Sun Dance, said "I do not understand why the white men desire to put an end to our religious ceremonials. What harm can they do to our people? If they deprive us of our religion, we will have nothing left, for we know of no other that can take its place" (225). A Kwakiutl Indian added that "it is a strict law that bids us dance. It is a strict law that bids us distribute property among our friends and neighbors. It is a good law. Let the white man observe his law, we shall observe ours" (227). But no matter: "the flood has come," lamented an old warrior, and the only dance left was the Ghost Dance that emerged in the American plains as an attempt to revive embattled Indian cultures. As John Mohawk explained, "People believed that through ritual they could revive the buffalo herds and bring departed ancestors back to life. They reportedly believed that bullets would not penetrate the spiritually purified shirts they wore."[38] But that dance, too, would come to an abrupt end in 1890, when U.S. soldiers killed a band of Ghost Dancers and their families (253).

Although they resisted the allotment policy, Indians gradually fell into poverty. Even those who adapted kept being pushed out of their lands. By 1900, there were about two hundred and thirty-seven thousand Indians left from an estimated 1.5 million during the time of contact. Outlawry replaced tribal uprisings. A new religion from the Southwest based on the consumption of the peyote cactus replaced the Ghost Dance. The Native American Church was incorporated in 1911 (296).

Every Indian had to deal with the traumatizing decision of how white to become (256–61). So agonizing was the decision that in September 1906, one tribe, the Hopi Oraibi Pueblo, split into "Friendlies" (those favoring white education) and "Hostiles" (those against it) and erupted in violence, forcing the Hostiles to migrate and establish their own settlement at Hotevilla (271–74). By the end of the twentieth century, the Creek Bill Bray still thought that the white man's academic community to be a poor substitute for a real community and refused to believe that "education must be painful and cruel" (458). Rose Johnson/Tsosie, a Navajo Indian who had succeeded in white culture and returned to native ways, reflected that "many white people have been given so much—possessions, land, money—that they have forgotten what the real world is" (462).

By the middle of the twentieth century, Earl Old Person, a Blackfoot tribal leader asked: "What is the 'mainstream of American life?' I would not know how to interpret the phrase to my people in our language. The closest I would be able to come to 'mainstream' would be to say, in Indian, 'a big, wide river.' Am I then to tell my people that they will be 'thrown into the Big Wide River of the United States'?" (336). A student who succeeded in his education at the Institute of American Indian Arts at Santa Fe reflected on his education thus:

I set out to prove that I was White. I believed in good grades, popularity, etc. Now I am tired of that, although these expectations still haunt me. Unfortunately many traditionalists are turning to these same shallow values. Many Whites are turning to Indians for an alternative to these values. Where are the Indians who still have an answer and are willing to share their wisdom with those who listen sincerely?

Probably most Indians will adopt materialistic values. But an alternative should be available for those who want it. (412)

The search for a survival strategy or a coping mechanism has informed the classics of modern Native American fiction. N. Scott Momaday's *House Made of Dawn* (1968)[39] relates the story of the "longhair" Abel, who is orphaned at an early age, loses his older brother, and grows up an Indian before he goes to war, defies death, and survives World War II. (At his later trial, Bowker testifies that Abel survived a massacre of his unit and defied a tank with his Indian dance [102–3] before trekking down to a city [110–111], and finally returning to his grandfather's house in Walatowa, Cañon de San Diego, weighed down by that experience.) Angela (Mrs. Martin) St. John, the wife of a physician who has just moved in town, hires him to chop wood and ends up seducing him for his muscular strength, stoicism, and sadness. Later, after a religious festival on a dark, rainy day, Abel walks out of a bar with a white man with blue lips and a horrible laugh (72), and, when out sight, stabs him to death.

After prison, Abel is released on parole and finds work in a factory with Benally, another "longhair" Indian. Abel still doesn't know how to adapt to white culture, although he knows there is no hope on the reservation. Careful not to violate his parole terms (he doesn't fight back insults), he begins to drink, loses his job, and runs out of money. Milly, a social worker, seen by Benally as kind and vulnerable, gives him money to drink. She is fond of Abel, but he is too sick to reciprocate her kindness, even though they make love. Things deteriorate further for Abel. He leaves Benally's apartment for three days and comes back almost dead, having lost a lot of blood. Benally takes him to a hospital and calls Angela, his older white lover from home. After two days, she comes to visit with her son Peter, who has grown to like Indian stories. Throughout their wretchedness, Abel and Benally plan on going back to a beautiful place, a "house made of dawn" (129). But they know that although the reservation is a site of beauty and nostalgia, it is empty, compared with the busy city, with its throngs of people and ritzy stores (158–59).

In the end, however, Abel returns to be with his dying grandfather, and after he buries him, Abel undresses, rubs his hands and chest with ashes, and joins his village dawn runners. He runs beyond pain to the words "*house made of pollen, house made of dawn. Qtsedaba*" (185).

Similarly, Leslie Marmon Silko's celebrated novel *Ceremony* (1977)[40] chronicles a Laguna Indian's quest for survival and healing in white America. A mestizo with hazel eyes, the light-brown-skinned Tayo returns from the Philippines, where he had been fighting the Japanese, a profoundly scarred man. Not only has his brotherlike cousin Rocky died before his eyes, but he also has refused to execute lined-up Japanese prisoners, because he sees his own uncle in them. His comrades attribute his attitude to malaria contracted in the wet, thick jungles of the Philippines. Once back in the United States, he is assigned to the mental unit of veterans' hospital in Los Angeles.

Tayo cannot shake his demons and memories (26). The army doctors are baffled by Tayo's symptoms (31), so his grandmother suggests the intervention of the medicine man Ku'oosh (33–34). Tayo, who spent much of his early childhood up with his itinerant, single, prostitute mother, who, like his caring Christian aunt (Rocky's mother), is ashamed of being Indian and is ultimately repudiated by her own people (51, 111, 68, 77, 71), protests to Ku'oosh that despite his guilt, he has never killed or even touched an enemy. This proves the unbelievable monstrosity of "white warfare—killing across great distances without knowing who or how many had died" (36). Ku'oosh admits that with the advent of white culture, his medicine has not been as effective (38) and seems to have no power to confront this new "witchery." Like many displaced postcolonials, the only advantage he gets from his service is attracting white women (40–41). Without his uniform, however, the Indian hero returns to his old subhuman status on the reservation.

Tayo vomits constantly, drinks a lot, and stabs his buddy Emo with a broken bottle when the latter insults him as half-breed (52–63). He visits Old Betonie, a mestizo, educated, well-traveled medicine man. Old Betonie tells Tayo that the reason he saw his uncle Josiah in Japanese soldiers is because Indians and the Japanese are related (124). Tayo now realizes that his "sickness was only part of something larger, and his cure would be found only in some thing great and inclusive of everything" (125–26). Betonie's new ceremonies are attempts to address the Indians' new reality, for without adaptation, the culture won't survive (126). Tayo continues to vomit, as if he were "trying to vomit out everything—all the past, all his life" (168). As he embarks on his arduous journey of healing and breaks into Floyd Lee's fenced ranch in search of his cattle, Tayo begins to realize white man's alienation, hollowness, thievery, fear, and lies. The "lies devoured white hearts, and for more than two hundred years white people had worked to fill their emptiness; they tried to glut the hollowness with patriotic wars and with great technology and the wealth it brought. And always they had been fooling themselves, and they knew it" (191). He is captured by white patrolmen looking for trespassers, but is let go when they hear about a mountain lion and set out to hunt him. This only intensifies Tayo's hatred of whites. "He wanted to kick the soft white bodies into the Atlantic; he wanted to scream to all of them that they were trespassers and thieves. He wanted to follow them as they hunted the mountain lion, to shoot them and their howling dogs with their own guns" (203–4). He despises the "sterility of their art, which continued to feed off the vitality of other cultures, and the dissolution of their consciousness into dead objects: the plastic and neon, the concrete and steel" (204).

Yet although whites have destroyed everything in sight, the Fifth World, the earth on which we live, has endured, and his love for Rocky and Josiah is still as intense as it had been when they were alive (219–20). White culture couldn't reach his inner core, now deeply moved by his hunter-gatherer lover, Ts'eh, a Montaño. Ts'eh confirms his views of whites as murderous destroyers of all life, including their own (229), and no weapon is more symbolic of this destruction, unifying all the world's non-Euro-American peoples as in the primeval time of the birth of humans from corn, than the atomic bomb, ironically conceived on the ancient mesas of New Mexico:

From the jungles of his dreaming he recognized why the Japanese voices had merged with the Laguna voices, with Josiah's voice and Rocky's voice; the lines of cultures and worlds were drawn in flat dark lines on fine light sand, converging in the middle of witchery's final ceremonial sand painting [of white corn, the life force of native cultures, 141]. From that time on, human beings were one clan again, united by the fate the destroyers planned for all of them, for all living things; united by a circle of death that devoured people in cities twelve thousand miles away, victims who had never known these mesas, who had never seen the delicate colors of the rocks which boiled up their slaughter. (246)

Constantly fleeing from arrest—whether by patrolmen chasing trespassers or by doctors chasing crazy Indians—he survives the deaths of his war comrades Harley, Elroy, and Pinkie and the exile of Emo, killer of Pinkie, to California. His ceremony eventually takes him back to Ku'oosh's kiva, back to undiluted tradition (256). The novel, which starts and ends at sunrise, as if what happens in between, in the course of Tayo's quest for healing, seems to be a break in an otherwise triumphant march of nature—associated here with the natives—suggests that the time of the whites may be of briefer duration, although this time will be characterized by great suffering and destruction. So frequent are the denunciations of white culture that they appear as a dark refrain set against the regenerating chorus of native myths.

Long persevering in the face of massive injuries, Indians in the United States and Mexico have begun to seek refuge in doomsday prophecies or in rebellion. *Almanac of the Dead*, Silko's historic novel about the uprising of indigenous people, echoes Zuñi and Apache prophecies about the end of white reign.[41] Unlike *Ceremony*'s rather quietist approach to the natives' plight, *Almanac of the Dead* forcefully blames the destruction of the world and its indigenous people on the genocidal policies of white Europeans, a culture from which only Marx and Engels, despite their limited knowledge of Indian ways, are exonerated. The Cuban Angelita—known as Comrade La Escapía—a colonel in the Army of Justice and Redistribution, or the People's Army (309–10), who is set on retaking Indian land, is shocked by the discovery of Marx, the first white man to ever make sense (311), who gives her more insight into the tragedy of modern Mexico (312, 313). Although inspired by Marx, Angelita is original enough to realize the Eurocentric dimensions of traditional Marxism and so sets out to salvage Marx from his misguided followers, including Stalin, Mao, the "locos" of the Shining Path, and the Cubans (312–17). In her reading, Marx appears as a dangerous Jewish tribal leader who tells stories to workers (521–22). By the end of the book, Angelita La Escapía credits Marx and Engels with being far ahead of their time and people—with understanding everything except the power of spirits and that the earth is "mother to all beings" (744).

But at least Engels and Marx had understood the earth belongs to no one. No human, individuals or corporation, no cartel of nations, could "own" the earth; it was the earth who possessed the humans and it was the earth who disposed of them.

Now it was up to the poorest tribal people and survivors of European genocide to show the remaining humans how all could share and live together on earth, ravished as she was. Angelita La Escapía was confident. All hell was going to break loose. The best was yet to come. (749)

Such an outcome would be the fulfillment of a prophecy encoded in the almanac, a bundle of notebooks with notes in Latin and Spanish and drawings of snakes, entrusted by Old Yoeme to her twin granddaughters,

Lecha—a TV psychic with powers to locate the missing dead who moves to Tuscon (which means "fresh water" in Papago [190])—and her sister Zeta, a drug dealer. The almanac, translated by the 60-year-old sisters, prophecies the reign of the Death-Eye Dog, now seated on the throne for 500 years, whose "influence has been established across the entire world," ushering in an age of chaos, destruction, and voraciousness (251, 252).

As Mexico disintegrates into chaos and civil war, and as poor Indians rise in rebellion against their long oppression, the macaw spirits choose as their servant Tacho (or Wacah), who hates whites and remembers village stories about how white men would disappear (511–12). Together with El Feo, who also knows that whites have no future in America because they have no past in it (313), Tacho promises the people that "ancient prophecies are about to be fulfilled" (709) and that they must walk north and give up all things European, for, despite any hardships they may encounter, all the world's tribal people are ready to retake their land from the whites (711–12).

Clearly, the whites and their religion are the scourge of the world's indigenous peoples. Lecha remembers her grandmother telling her that Christianity had died before the Spanish arrived: "Yoeme had delighted in describing the tortures and executions performed in the name of Jesus during the Inquisition. In a crude catechism book Yoeme had even showed them pictures, wood-block prints of churchmen burning 'heretics' and breaking Jews on the wheel. Yoeme said the mask had slipped at that time, and all over Europe, ordinary people had understood in the hearts the 'Mother Church' was a cannibal monster."

From her secret white rich seekers, Lecha knows that white people fear death, which is why they kill (718) and why they are desperate for healing, which is why they will buy anything from Indians (719). Wilson Weasel Tail, a Lakota law student who proclaims poetry to be the voice of the people, since the law serves the rich, condemns U.S. colonialism in a TV talk show (714–16). He chastises his people for abandoning the struggle and their ancestral spirits (by drinking and not fighting back) and announces that victory is approaching and that the buffalo are coming back. "Spirits! Ancestors!/we have been counting the days, watching the/signs" (722). The Barefoot Hopi strikes an alliance with "Green Vengeance Eco-Warriors," who explode the Glen Canyon Dam (727) and who have vowed to reclaim the earth's resources from the "biosphere tycoons" (728). A 300-pound Hopi (733) moves even affluent whites to contribute to his peaceful indigenous cause (734). Supported by Africans, he talks of the mass exodus of the poor to the north. "In Africa and in the Americas too," the Hopi says, "the giant snakes Damballah and Quetzalcoatl have returned to the people" (735). Or, as another character, Clinton, realizes, Africans and Indians have always been united by their attachment to "ancestor spirits." (742). But Lecha, unlike the Hopi, believes that only indigenous violence can save world from (white) destruction (739, 758).

Since the fear of white culture, with its incurably frightened people, is one of the main motifs of Native American literature, many Native Americans feel that only an indigenous comeback can save the planet from white destruction. After noting that humanity is "on the brink of disaster on my fronts," N. Scott Momaday has stated that only "native people can help us out of that, help push us back away from that brink." To be sure, it's not easy for him to know "how to change the future," but he is clear that part of the solution to humanity's apocalyptic crisis is "how to remain Indian" in the modern world, "how to assimilate without ceasing to be Indian."[42]

Momaday's views are widespread. Oren Lyons, an Onondaga "faith keeper," has warned that if nothing changes, the United States "will destroy both Indian and non-Indian people. If we destroy ourselves by our own folly, it is the working of natural law. When there are too many rabbits, they disappear. When lemmings overpopulate, they run into the sea. Human beings also may disappear. And it will mean nothing to the natural world, which is used to cries of anguish and pain. It is part of life."[43] Over and over again, Native Americans see no hope in the present system of Euro-American hegemony. The Apache see hope only in the reversal of roles in the next world, whereas the Zuñi prophecies see no hope at all, and claim that white rule simply heralds the end of the world.[44]

The outbreak of the Zapatista rebellion in Chiapas (supposedly prophesied by Silko's *Almanac of the Dead*)[45] on 1 January 1994—the day NAFTA went into effect—sent a powerful signal that trade treaties are a continuation of the dispossession of Native Americans. Inhabiting a state described as "rich land" with "poor people," the Zapatistas came to believe that armed rebellion is the only way to disengage peasant demands from "corrupt Mexican law and politics." The economic crisis of the 1980s, following the collapse of oil prices, dried up federal funds, the policies of President Carlos Salinas de Gotari reflected a deliberate reversal of the still largely unfulfilled promises of the Mexican Revolution. Indigenous peasant economies (not counted in GDP calculations) were devastated by the oil economy, which severely upset traditional patterns of work and production. NAFTA was the proverbial straw that broke the camel's back.[46]

The Zapatistas are in fact symptomatic of the larger challenges facing all Mexicans, a mostly mestizo and Oriental people who, like Jim Loney, refuse to accept their *mestizaje*, or crossbreeding, and are endlessly searching for their identity. Despite centuries of desperate attempts to become "white" or join the "developed" world, Mexico has not been able to resolve the legacy of its violent *mestizaje* of the sixteenth century and remains, in the view of Alan Riding, a new Western head on an old, Oriental body. (The inability to negotiate indigenous ways with white culture is what makes the predicament of the half-breeds particularly poignant in the novels described above.) Without recognizing their strong native identity, the "distant neighbors" of the United States, as Riding put it, will probably never be able to solve their problems. Mimicking Western democracies will not work for Mexico, Riding concludes, and Mexico has no option but to accept and rely on its ancient Mexican culture to move ahead.[47]

The violence that ensues from the breakdown of indigenous systems in postcolonial societies is also one of the main themes of modern African literature. Chinua Achebe's novels, for instance, are a chronicle of the dissolution of traditional customs and their replacement by a corrupt postcolonial order that is bound to fail Africans, much as the modernization schemes have failed Mexicans. Even in Mediterranean societies such as Morocco, the West often appears as deceptive and cruel, particularly when the authors or their protagonists reject Islamic patriarchal fundamentalism at home, only to find the West, with its Enlightenment ideals, exploitative and violent. In Moroccan novelist Driss Chraibi's *The Butts* (originally published as *Les Boucs* in 1955),[48] Yalaan Waldik, the protagonist who leaves Algeria for the promise of the West, turns into an "open wound," tortured and alienated by the West, and so grows more hateful, cruel, and destructive, becoming the self-appointed spokesman for the "Butts," other marginal Arabs in France. In such a role, he accepts his inevitable schizophrenic state of mind:

I'll never live except in the absurd. For ten years now my brain, my Arab thinking in Arabic, has been grinding away at European concepts, in such absurd way it transforms them into gall and even the brain gets sick from it. And if it goes on thinking, it is not by theorem of adaptation but because through all of its pulverizing, it is overwhelmed with proliferating membranes—the only part that has adapted to the occidental world. (39)

In a Cartesian—and racist—environment where the senses are dismissed, Waldik grows proud of his violent, sadistic inclinations (41) and spends more and more time in prison. He now realizes that Europe is a "mirage" and that is far better for Africans to "send their shoes [to Europe] instead of themselves" (60). As he looks at Mac O'Mac, with

eyes full of perspiration, of tears and of mist, there hangs a face: perhaps Mac's, or perhaps the numberless faces of Europe seen through his distress, a series of masks cut out of cardboard, colorful and vengeful, one dizzily substituting for another: Descartes, Kant, Bergson, William James, the masks of bridges and of pylons, of pioneers and of men who cut rivers into quarters, ratiocinations and powers, missionaries of materialism and of the machine gun, those who solicit and those who lay claim, specialists in everything from zero to human dignity, and later on those who discovered that all discoveries still have to be rediscovered, all because they had been found through the "Know Thyself" of Aristotle that seemed an invitation to explore the ego and as such made a fool of the whole Occident—while its frenetic and desperate search for reality lured it on, not wanting to awaken in its being what is carefully called the conscience—other labyrinths of his soul, choked shut since childhood, that suddenly were illuminated. (55)

Tellingly, Yalaan Waldik (whose name itself, "Curse Your Parents," fighting words in North African societies, suggests both anger and the repudiation of the West's heritage) throws away his black shoes when he gets on a plane bound for Algeria (65), a journey however, that will be as disappointing as the first one was.

The struggles of Muslims and Native Americans in a Western-dominated world show that the Islamic difference is only a question of degree and scale and that much of Islamic extremism, terrorism, and even stifling fundamentalism is a reaction to the West's domination in the colonial and postcolonial periods. Although the United States and much of the West dealt with Islam as Other throughout most of Islamic history, as many have argued, the current image of Islam in the West, and the West's image among Arabs and Muslims, are largely the effect of modern "world" history. The Muslims' plight is basically the same as Native Americans'—both are engaged in various forms of resistance to repeated colonial incursions and policies of dispossession—but what distinguishes Islam is its size and control of vast territories across the globe. Had it been a smaller religion, it might not have made a bigger impact than the Native Americans'. The

Saudis, who were heavily scrutinized after the events of September 11, have spent close to a century trying to come to terms with the radical transformation of their society within a global order dominated by the United States, a situation that has been brilliantly illustrated by Abdelrahman Munif's first three volumes of his quintet epic *Cities of Salt*, which, in effect, chronicle the birth of an Arab "nation" under the auspices of a secular Western modernity.

Munif's long, sprawling narrative aspires to be nothing less than a fictional account of an unnamed country, Bedouin and eventually oil-rich, governed by a corrupt royal family with the complicity of the sycophants who surround them. The tone of indignation that underlies much of the narrative is a manifestation of the egalitarian impulse that has erupted regularly in Arabia, whose spirit has been encoded in the Shariʿa itself, but now, as in the past, approximation to or distance from the ideals of social justice have never been entirely matters of will or moral strength only. Personal rectitude in a ruler, combined with genuine compassion for the people, should normally lead to political stability, social tranquility, and cultural florescence. But in the context of Western imperialism, followed by an aggressive neocolonial hegemony, it is hard to apply the time-honored standards of good and evil to influential leaders (whether Arab or from the Third World generally) caught in the maelstrom of global events. That is why I tend to see this novel as an account of the painful birth of a fragile Arab kingdom that is destined to become rich almost overnight and over whose destiny the West never ceases to conspire. And an account of how, in the process, *fitnah* (chaos) ensues.

Munif duly warns, retrospectively in the second volume of the trilogy, *Variations on Night and Day*,[49] first published in Arabic in 1989, that we are entering the century where everything is open for "reevaluation" and "reapportionment": "ideas, regions, countries, kings, sultans and little princes"(3). As the world is undergoing "great convulsions and transformations" (7) and is being hastily remapped, Mooran, Sultan Khureybit's reconquered domain, will also be ineluctably affected.

Meanwhile, Sultan Khureybit's ambitions in the region have no end. He banishes advisors who counsel restraint and annexes surrounding kingdoms. Through strict discipline, he grooms and initiates his sons, Khazael and Fanar, into the world of power and political intrigue. He persuades his people to join him in wars of conquest and annexation. Always careful to gather a consensus, he appeals to several constituencies at once, using astute diplomacy—not always successfully—with his capricious and untrustworthy patrons, the British, emotional appeals to the glory of Islam with pious heroes, and the promise of wealth with the merely ambitious profiteers. He juggles these interests throughout his turbulent career until he finally succeeds in conquering and imposing Mooran's puritanical mores and tyrannical regime on Awali, a "more sophisticated and civilized" region (138). To counter the claim of Awali's defeated leader Ibn Madi, that Khureybit has sold the country to the infidel British, the sultan consolidates his power by attending to long-neglected domestic issues and by mobilizing the religious establishment. Hamilton, the sultan's intimate British advisor, informs Khureybit that he must stop his wars of conquest and annexation, since, although Britain has selected him as the best prospect for an ally, she still is a power with complex interests and other friends in the region.

As is the case throughout the trilogy, Arabs are continually shocked by the amorality of British politics. The sultan, disappointed, painfully comes to the realization that the British cannot be trusted, because with them, one doesn't deal with people, but with replaceable clerks who work for impersonal organizations. Those who make commitments do not stay long enough to fulfill them and to be accountable for their own words. Yet Ibn Mayyah rebels against the sultan precisely because the latter is perceived to have capitulated to the British and abandoned the greater glory of Islam for which the people have fought (288–89). Caught in this dilemma, the sultan nevertheless moves to action, and after a series of carefully and strategically planned maneuvers, he launches an attack on the rebels and defeats them. The ruthlessly opportunistic and powerful British who drive him to tears and threaten him with intervention accept the outcome. No wonder Hamilton sees Machiavellian qualities in the Bedouin sultan.

Political woes are not the only ones on the sultan's mind. His palace, "a veritable beehive" populated by countless wives and children, is a nest of intrigue, malice, blackmail, and murder, all of which intensify when the sultan is away on military or political expeditions. Khureybit has so many children that he not only doesn't remember their names, but is forced to hold meetings with them in separate *majalis*, one for the boys and the other for the girls, in order to see them all (160–61, 182). Not all of the Sultan's marriages are for pleasure. Again, as has long been customary among Arab leaders, his marriages are sometimes purely political. He marries

Sheikh al-Ajrami's daughter Najma in order to co-opt the religious leader and get his support during the trying episodes of conquest. (This, however, ignites yet another fire in the already dark and grotesque world of the palace.) He even finds a teenage wife for Sheikh al-Ajrami. His political skills are tested against the worst of circumstances: While Mooran's dominion keeps expanding, his people suffer disorienting changes, droughts, famine, and plagues. There is no respite for the sultan. On one occasion, when he hears what goes on in the palace during his absence, he sighs: "What confusion for a man: both here and there. With his enemies and among his own friends and household" (268). The sultan, surrounded by scheming and opportunistic friends and sons competing for favors is indeed alone. Inexhaustible, resourceful, shrewd, and sometimes just plain helpless, he epitomizes the fate of Mooran—indeed, of all Arabs—emerging into the profoundly traumatic century of the West. Granted, one can scold the sultan for not living more ascetically or for leading an unnecessarily complicated life at the palace, but that would reduce the sultan to a mere politician, which he certainly is not.

Slowly developing under his wings, but not totally under his control, is Prince Fanar. The orphaned, delicate, humble, and intelligent Fanar, unlike both his father and his siblings, is simple, quiet, austere, and manly (16). He spends most of his early childhood, together with his sister Mudi, with his maternal family at Ain Faddan. When he moves to Rawdh Palace in Mooran to be with his father, he adjusts badly to the wanton brutality on the premises, where mock battles are staged and actual people killed for the sake of the prince's training. The shrewd and worldly Hamilton, perhaps seeing in Fanar the mark of leadership, likes him and takes him on visits to England. There, Fanar meets and is impressed by Hamilton's aunt, Miss Margot, a "magnificent woman" who "had spent twenty years in Ceylon" and seven years in "southern Africa"(78–79). She gives Fanar one of her books, and despite a hopelessly romantic Orientalist outlook (168–77), she fascinates Fanar and leaves a lasting impression on him. She would be the first woman Fanar has really known—for women in Mooran are only a background presence. But Fanar also learns a great deal about British political culture from his other encounters with government officials and scholars. Fanar's image of a rather otherworldly figure, reserved and pensive, is reinforced when Zaina, his wife, suddenly dies.

The days and lives of Mooran during the early decades of the twentieth century are recorded and reflected upon by Hamilton (Sahib), a

British civil servant who, despite his sympathetic understanding of Arab culture, never forgets who he is or why he is there. An adventurer and romantic who speaks the language and wears Arab clothes—he has been inspired by his aunt, Miss Margot—he maps the "northern borders," travels across the entire country, and recommends that Britain support Khureybit as the chieftain most likely to prevail over his rivals. He becomes an intimate and trusted friend of the sultan and even asks for the opportunity to join the sultan's troops in their campaign against al-Huweiza (70). The perfect illustration of the cultured Orientalist, Hamilton has nothing in common with crude civil servants such as Dennis Eagleton, the newly appointed consul, who shows no sensitivity to Bedouin ethics, or with William Butler, the hardened military man who brings the sultan to his knees before he allows him to save face at Ain Nabat. But despite his contempt for sterile academics at home, appreciation for Arab culture, and genuine affection for Khureybit and, particularly, Prince Fanar, Hamilton remains committed to the larger glory of the West (51). He does object to Britain's moral laxity (especially its unacceptable change of policy at the "Oriental Conference") and, as if to demonstrate his disapproval, converts to Islam, grows a beard, and renames himself Abdelsamad (51, 293–296). This transformation is rather surprising, for Hamilton is the seasoned voice of realpolitik in the novel, constantly reminding the betrayed sultan that empires have only interests, not morals. Still, Hamilton, eager to keep the West in Arabia, decides to support the "more daring and farsighted" Americans to obtain permission to explore Mooran's resources (295). Little does the sultan know that this seemingly insignificant decision would launch his new and fragile kingdom into yet another era of turmoil and confusion.

Cities of Salt,[50] the first volume of the trilogy, published in the original Arabic in 1984, is the novel that explores the sudden arrival of the American mechanized caravan to the sleepy, but dynamic oasis of Wadi al-Uyoun, a historically strategic point in the Arabs' battle against (Turkish) colonialism (10). Of the three novels in the trilogy, *Cities* is the one that most successfully examines the dramatic culture clashes, the political realignments, and the imploding of an entire Bedouin society. In fact, one has the impression that *Cities* was not designed to have any sequels and that the other two novels are last-minute decisions to expand on a successful venture. To the extent that *Cities* examines the genesis of an Arab people's traumatic insertion into a world economy where they are condemned to live in dependency, it can be fruitfully compared Chinua Achebe's de-

piction of the end of a traditional era and the beginning of a Western-dominated one in *Things Fall Apart.* And because Achebe's novel is shorter and
no less effective, I don't think Munif needed an additional 887 pages to finish his story. The third volume, *The Trench* and, especially *Variations,* strike
me as afterthoughts, attempts to fill in the gaps that may have been left
unanswered in *Cities.* As a result, much of their narrative is devoted to inconsequential details. While highlighting the whimsical behavior of the
kings and the delirious scheming of the opportunistic profiteers who are incessantly preying on them may be important themes to explore, Munif
could have woven them into *Cities* and avoided the many inconsequential
details that unnecessarily slow down the reading or even burden the narrative. In short, even without *Variations* and *The Trench,* and despite much
repetition in all three novels, *Cities* still succinctly depicts the awakening of
an Arab community into the turbulent era of Western hegemony and
global capitalism.

The arrival of Arabic-speaking Americans confounds local Bedouins,
especially Miteb al-Hathal, a descendant of valiant resistance fighters, who
suspiciously senses that "something terrible was about to happen," for
"those [American] devils are incapable of any good"(30–31). The tranquility and self-sufficiency of the village in the plentiful season of winter is upset by the digging of monstrous machines, an event apocalyptically described by Miteb al-Hathal as "resurrection day"(71). The Bedouins'
sudden, unannounced encounter with the West creates an irremediable anguish, for the Americans go about their business offending long-held traditions and customs. Their behavior unleashes endless suspicions and a
barrage of criticism, but their coming and their eventual destruction of the
wadi under the tearful eye of Miteb can no longer be averted. "It was the
end of the world, or perhaps the end of the long ages in the life of this distant, forgotten desert"(100). As the capitalist ethic slowly invades the
neighboring town of Ujra (124), and children such as Fawaz are forced into
instant manhood (122), the people predict bewildering changes and
tyranny before they rise to end it (164–65).

Like Wadi-al-Uyoun, the fate of Harran, a "forgotten community"
(195), will also be sealed the moment foreign ships, especially the one labeled by Arabs "King Solomon," unload their cargo—new "calamities,"
including seminaked women shipped to entertain their isolated male
compatriots. Arab men are so perplexed by the sight of these "nymphs of
paradise" (226), who awaken in them a disturbing desire, that they date

the history of Harran from the day these women arrived on the ship (215). Meanwhile, American men proceed to transform this once sleepy community into a new city, divided into the luxury quarters of American Harran and the lowly barracks for Arab workers—hired and overseen by the opportunist Ibn Rashed—which is known as Arab Harran. The Americans' manners and business habits (such as conducting interviews and requiring the filling out of questionnaires) are profoundly upsetting to local moral standards.

At this point, Ibn Naffeh, like most Arabs in Harran, begins to denounce this new cultural imperialism (331, 335). He becomes the oracle of doom in an ever growing environment of despair (387). Ibn Rashed, the Americans' agent, who initially thwarts attempts to get compensation for a worker's death is haunted to death by the fear of retaliation, but when he dies, the Arabs, out of compassion, attribute his regrettable fate to his association with the Americans (variously referred to as "wolves," "locusts," etc.) who have "no friends" (414).

Meanwhile, the emir of Harran is increasingly seduced by the West by means of gadgetry such as the telescope and the radio. He succumbs to the same desires first unleashed by the seminaked women on "the ship of King Solomon" (221) and is thrown into a delirious confusion when a new shipload of women arrives (424–25). No sooner does he recover than he is presented with a radio, whose powers turn out to be truly unfathomable. The newcomer Hassan Rezzae suggests to the bewildered emir that through this new technology, London knows more about Harran than does the emir (459). The radio thus undermines the Arabs' authority—as Ibn Naffeh suggests—over their own destiny and culture.

With the linking of Harran with Wadi al-Uyoun through an oil pipeline, both communities are integrated into the new logic of world capitalism, and as all sorts of gadgets flood Harran, the culture is gradually transformed into a consumer society: "Every Harrani wanted at least one thing" (469). Competitive capitalism leads to larger monopolies, displacing small, but endearing entrepreneurs such as the truck drivers, Akoub and Raji, whose tragic downfall exacerbates the already tense and explosive relations between Arab workers and their American supervisors.

Although Harran is still an unfinished town, it has grown in significance enough to attract Dr. Subhi al-Mahmilji, whose arrival would later be considered "one of the most momentous events in Harran" (523). With no friends, he relies on his assistant, Muhammad Eid, for public relations

(527–30). He manages to impress Crown Prince Khazael, when the latter visits Harran to inaugurate the oil pipeline, with his elegance, rhetorical powers, a typically inflated tribute, and the carpet he gives him as a gift (543–45). As he quickly expands and deliberately marginalizes the stubborn town healer, Mufaddi al-Jeddan, he gets help from an increasingly repressive political system. Things deteriorate quickly: Mufaddi is found dead, and twenty-three Arab workers are fired. A new hierarchical regime emerges, with the Americans controlling the oil business and the emir and the newly created military maintaining order. The telephone further connects the Americans with members of the indigenous elite acting as their agents, and their fate will be entangled in a growing conspiracy against the working people (598–9).

But the workers are not entirely docile. They are inspired by Ibn Naffeh's Friday *khutbah* reminding the workers that Islam calls on Muslims to resist oppression (603–4). When the workers respond and proceed to defy the government's tyranny, many are killed, and more confusion ensues. The emir falls sick and accuses Dr. Mahmilji and the Americans of plotting his death, while the dead Mufaddi reappears to heal the wounded. When the dust settles, and the emir, before leaving Harran for medical treatment, calls for the reinstatement of the dismissed workers and a general investigation of these bloody events, people begin to speculate as to who is ultimately responsible for all this chaos. Ibn Naffeh's answer is unambiguous: "The Americans are the source of the illness and the root of the problem"(627). Hamilton, nicknamed Abu Lahab by the Harranis (392), is by now certainly one of them.

In *The Trench*,[51] Munif introduces us to the last days of Khureybit, who becomes blind and probably delirious before he dies in suspicious circumstances (62). Here, again, the doctor, who has decided to leave Harran, plays a "momentous role"(11). Prince Khazael succeeds in arrogating power to himself, while three of his brothers, including Fanar, leave on extended travel. Doctor Mahmilji threatens to confiscate Sheikh Shamran's land if he doesn't agree to sell (14) and then builds a new residence, which he names Qasr al-Hir, or Garden Palace (15). Mooran is still a desolate, but resilient town "in those years following midcentury"(19), but the doctor tries to prevail—using the same eloquent flattery—on the superstitious sultan to use the oil bonanza and transform Mooran. In his pursuit of power and grandeur, the doctor gradually abandons his medical practice and neglects the needs of his wife. He enters into various business arrangements and begins to oversee the establishment of the Intelligence and Security Agency, to be directed by Hammad al-Mutawa, whose goals and operations are defined by Americans (123). Mooran continues to be modernized, while the Sultan's favors are increasingly coveted by opportunists. Muhammad Eid, disappointed by Dr. Mahmilji, returns to Harran only to find a cold, unrecognizable city where brutal repression has become the official means of controlling a disgruntled population. Eventually, Muhammad flees the city in a cab driven by another outsider, who also believes that not only Harran, but the whole world has fallen under the deadly grip of capitalism (182).

Dr. Mahmilji, always shrewdly anticipating new developments, especially the growing social disparities, decides to use the medium of journalism to contain and prevent social discontent (210–11). He decides that the state needs a philosophy and proceeds to conceptualize one that he calls the "Square Theory," based on maintaining a balance among the forces that control humans, which, in descending order, are the mind, the heart, the stomach, and the sexual drive (214–15). He even proposes the establishment of a Shari'a college to neutralize his enemies (232), but he becomes increasingly absorbed by visions of his own grandeur, endlessly meditating on his new philosophy while unconsciously letting events overtake him. His projects, however, keep expanding. He still manages to persuade an associate, Rateb Fattal, a onetime secret lover of his wife, Widad, to move to Mooran, and he visits his son, Ghazwan, in San Francisco. His wife, meanwhile, has an ongoing affair with Samir Caesar, an Egyptian journalist initially hired to help create a press in Mooran (chapter 43), because she feels alienated by her husband, who lives "in another world" collecting "elegant leather notebooks" in a room he calls the "*mihrab*"(374), dreaming of giving himself the more appropriate title of *al-Hakim*, instead of the rather mundane one of doctor (375).

Hammad, whom the doctor once selected for the security agency, changes during this period. Having been trained in the United States and having been totally impressed by that country and its women, he wonders why the doctor seems to be too harsh on other fellow expatriates, differs with him as to what is the most effective way to contain the danger of the "red winds" of communism, and in fact considers the doctor a fool, or as the Americans tell Hammad, a "chatterbox" (400). The doctor's ramblings about his theories are reported to him, and the doctor's access to inside information is curtailed. The latter begins to feel increasingly isolated and despondent as huge lucrative contracts are offered to business rivals (425). Even his son Ghazwan refuses to stay in Mooran upon completing his education, and instead chooses to become the first Arab to work for an American company that does business with Mooran.

Unlike during the reign of Khureybit, a general atmosphere of prosperity and opulence now prevails in Mooran. Both Sultan Khazael and his security man, Hammad, prefer to use the tested method of bribery before resorting to force to contain any perceived threat against the regime. By the time Prince Fanar returns from his travels, Mooran has become obscenely wealthy, and there are even plans for the city itself to be demolished and rebuilt. Sultan Khazael is suspicious of Fanar's austere ways, but when Fanar "suddenly and unexpectedly" moves into the Saad Palace (436), the sultan's fears seem to be temporarily assuaged. Even the shrewd doctor assesses the well-loved Fanar to be simple and harmless.

The tempo of events suddenly accelerates. Ghazwan returns with an important delegation from "the largest arms manufacturer in America" (473), and an arms deal with Mooran is sealed, despite popular opposition to it and to American hegemony in the region (481–82). While Widad, the doctor's wife, fantasizes about the sultan, hoping to attract his attention, the sultan sends Hammad to ask for her daughter's hand (chapter 82). In an atmosphere of popular discontent and suspicion, the sultan marries Dr. Mahmilji's daughter and, with his entourage, leaves for a honeymoon in Europe. On that same day, the people of Mooran learn that Khazael has been deposed and is now replaced by Prince Fanar. The following day, the doctor is forced out of the country as yet another era of repression and political reshuffling begins. "And still," the novel concludes, "Mooran listened expectantly and waited" (554).

The meditations on royal eccentricities and the lives of fortune-seeking expatriates and other opportunists in *The Trench* and *Variations* can be quite interesting if one considers the political pressure under which most Arab writers labor, but, as I suggested, it is *Cities of Salt* that finally highlights the major issues confronting Arabs in the modern period. Munif's novels are of immeasurable political and cultural significance, for they recount the now familiar saga of a scattered people that, under the compulsion of inexplicable forces, is forced to come together under one nation to be controlled by a family that has, so far, managed to placate its critics and enemies through lavish spending and patient diplomacy.

The founding of Saudi Arabia also signaled the end of the oasis cultures that had existed in Arabia since the early days of the caravan trade. Visited by sudden and massive wealth in what Daniel Yergen called the "hydrocarbon" age,[52] the country helplessly opened up to all sorts of opportunists and speculators, while the cultural foundations of the people were left to wither away. The journalist Sandra Mackey, author of *The Saudis*, once reported that the Bedouins still describe the erosion of their indigenous social system as *waqt-al-takhreeb* ("the period of destruction").[53] In light of September 11 and the tensions that ensued with the United States over security issues, Munif's novels appear like the chronicle of a clash foretold (to use Gabriel Garcia Marquez's expression).

In fact, the Saudi responses to forced assimilation into modernity is only one facet of the larger Arab and Islamic response to Western hegemony in the modern period. One brilliant and concise attempt to examine the West in the Arab Muslim imaginary is Moroccan Noureddine Afaya's *L'Occident dans l'imaginaire arabo-musulman*.[54] The book is set up as a response to the Lebanese René Habachi's question in 1969 (in his book by the same title), "Orient, quel est ton Occident?" (Orient, what is your West?). After some basic reflections on Self and Other and cautionary remarks against generalizations—one needs to speak about the West in the plural, since it has multiple identities—Afaya reminds us that for Arab-Muslims, the West is, paradoxically, an object of fascination and suspicion and that periods of "détente" between the two civilizations are rare. However, both Arabs and Muslims, with the exception of some historical chronicles, travel narratives, and diplomatic reports, did not produce the equivalent of the West's Orientalist literature, perhaps because alterity is conceived differently across the two Mediterranean (and now Atlantic?) shores.

Unlike the European Renaissance, which came out of the Muslim defeat in Spain, what is now known as the Arab Renaissance (alternatively called "awakening," "development," etc.) appeared as an effect of Napoleon's invasion of Egypt in 1789 and the colonization of Muslim lands beginning in the 1840s and 1850s and constitutes a turning point in Arab and Muslim thought, henceforth preoccupied by the search for effective ways of resistance through reform and a reassessment of both West and Islam. The two major trends of conservative salafism (idolization of the early generations of Muslims, or, more simply, fundamentalism) and modernist liberalism (what the West calls "moderate") that define Muslim responses to the West emerged at this moment. The present and the Self are now seen through the prism of the Other. "This is how the psychic state of the Arab intellectual, whether salafi or liberal, Muslim or Christian, advances and avoids dealing with (*escamote*) objective reality." [55]

Napoleon's introduction of the values of modern, secular Europe and, later, the doctrines of the French Revolution made Arabs and Muslims aware of their backwardness. Mohammed Ali, the governor of Egypt, opted for openness and the modernizing of institutions. Jamal Eddine al-Afghani was more skeptical of European intentions and the dangers of copying Europe's model because he saw Europe as an imperialist power driven by its own self-interests and believed that Muslims must recuperate their scientific heritage—the source of Europe's power anyway.

Mohammed Abdu, his partner, sought a synthesis of the two responses—reforming Islam by modernizing it by trying to reconcile salafism and liberalism. The two tendencies diverged after Abdu's death, forever entrapping the Arab and Muslim worlds in this dichotomy.

The legendary Egyptian intellectual Taha Hussein, initially influenced by liberal thinkers at home (Rafaa Tahtaoui, Chobli Chmaïl, Farah Antoine, Georgy Zaïdane, Qasem Amin, Lotfi Assayad, and others), then by the French culture he discovered and fell in love with, was a lifelong believer in the powers of science and rationalism and seems to have adopted Europe's myth of its undiluted origins and to have accepted the myth of ancient Greece's cultural superiority, whose legacy was now supposedly carried on by thinkers such as Voltaire, Descartes, Comte, Spencer, Saint Simon, and so on. Compromising with conservative forces in his own society, Hussein nevertheless labored all his life to impress on his compatriots the virtues of reason and critical thinking. He insisted on their Mediterranean—and thus European—origins (through its Hellenistic heritage) and that Islamic decadence was, in fact, caused by the Turks.[56] His imagined Egypt, achieved through a rationalist philosophy, was utopian, an "ideal city" that surpassed Europe itself by its humaneness.[57] And yet, the protagonist in his novel *Adib* goes mad in the end, unable to reconcile the cultures or to choose one.[58]

The introduction of modernity into the Arab and Muslim worlds was a profoundly disruptive event, as Roxanne Euben and others would argue, and when later adopted by (badly) Westernized postcolonial elites who reduced Islam to mere empty rituals, simply strengthened the Muslims' conviction that the only solution is in recuperating their Islamic traditions. Believing that the past determines the future, these Islamists' reaction against the West is a statement that Islam defiantly refuses its relegation to a museum. The failure of nationalism and socialism, the defeat in 1976 of Arabs and Muslims by a Jewish state, and the uprooting of peasants and the spread of urban poverty were all factors that gave this new movement increasing momentum. Islamism, which, one must remember, is a very heterogeneous movement with multiple manifestations, ranging for the quietism of mystics to terrorism, is thus, ironically, the fulfillment of the West's Orientalist fantasy.[59]

Egypt, the crossroads of ideas and the initial place of this clash of cultures, is crucial in the emergence of Islamism. On 2 March 1924, Kemal Ataturk abolished the caliphate, decreed secularism in Turkey, and under the threat of repression, abolished everything Islamic, from courts and dress to alphabets, through repression. This elicited a major reaction everywhere, but in his *Al-Islam wa usul al-hukm* (Islam and governance), Ali Abderrazik, an Egyptian sheikh, found nothing fundamentally wrong in such an act and thus elicited a strong response, leading to the fall of King Fuad's government. In this volatile climate grew Hassan al-Banna (who had once rejected Taha Hussein's thesis on pre-Islamic poetry), who founded the Muslim Brethren organization in 1927. Al Banna was assassinated on 12 February 1949, but the Muslim Brethren had already established clandestine relations with the Free Officers and went underground when the latter found out about a plot to assassinate Gamal Abdel Nasser in 1954. Repression and the imprisonment of Muslim Brethren members followed. So many followers of al-Banna were in prison that a "literature of prisons" emerged as a new genre. One imprisoned member, Sayyid Qutb, wrote *Ma'alim fi attariq*, a major reference for Islamists and a real manual for life and death in such a setting. Qutb was influenced not just by his own brutal treatment in prison (the product of "ignorance" or even "barbarism"—al-Jahiliyya— the state in which people lived before Mohammed), but by Abul 'ala Mawdudi, who during a transitional period for those Muslims on the Indian subcontinent founded the Jama'at Islami party in 1941 and divided the world between the realm of "al-Jahiliyya" and that of "al-Hakimiyya"—divine sovereignty based on Allah as the sole Lawgiver. Thus Islamism in the Arab world appeared in Egypt, a society undergoing traumatic changes and confusions, afflicted by severe social disparities and illegitimate regimes, and torn between modernity and tradition.[60]

Whereas the French and Bolshevik Revolutions were violent coups engineered by a committed leadership for the transformation of a corrupt order, Islamists plan a gentler, less traumatic transition. Thus, Hassan al-Banna rejected both capitalism and communism and insisted on social justice derived from a political concept of unity (one that excludes a multi-party system and a trans-Islamic concept of freedom of expression, for instance). Also, Sayyid Qutb's strict Manichean view led to the creation of Islamist groups that were committed to cleansing the world of impurities and that, through a new jihad, aimed at the overthrow of impious governments. They would tolerate no compromises, since divine instruction is nonnegotiable, but their violence ironically has legitimized state repression, which only hardens the Islamists' resolve—and so on, in a deadly cycle of ever mounting violence.[61]

Such movements, however, have been opposed by scholars such as Ahmad Kamal Abu al-Majd (also a member of the Muslim Brotherhood), the Tunisian Rachid al-Ghannouchi, founder of the Annahda, and Sa'id al-'Ashmawy, all of whom see no necessary correlation between a clerical government and Islam. Although such scholars suggest that reconciling Islam with secularism is not impossible, the question of how to reconcile it with secularism without "confronting the West's own history"[62] remains a daunting one.

Although the Arab/Muslim view of the West varies from Christian to crusader to colonialist or to Zionist, for the Islamist, there is only one West, which contains all these separate categories. It is a West characterized by extreme ignorance, as Qutb would have it, since the successive phases of its history (ancient Greece, Rome, the medieval Church, and secular modernity) have always been distant from the divine and, in various ways, corrupt and materialistic. Mounir Chafiq, author of *Al-islam fi m'araqat al hadhara*, has surveyed the West's history and charged it with hypocrisy, for its Renaissance, glorious revolutions, Enlightenment, and modernity were all founded on different genocidal acts and exclusions. So the West's rule, in Qutb's expression, is one of *taghut* (tyranny), a sick entity that is not worthy of imitation—hence the necessity of finding solutions elsewhere. Since the middle ground of *dar assulh* (the realm of truth) is excluded, jihad will not only save Muslims from their impending apocalyptic fate, but it will also to save the whole of humanity from the West's crass, soulless materialism. Thus, the West remains the Other against which the Muslim Renaissance is to be forged and renewed. Produced by the effects of colonialist incursions in the East, and using the West's own secular methodologies against it, Islamists, much like Yalaan Waldik in *The Butts*, see the West as an empty entity whose entire destiny and goal in life is determined and constrained by blind market forces. With few exceptions, the West is read through these adversarial lenses.[63]

Many Muslims and Arabs have multiple, contradictory images of a complex West which is far from being unified, homogeneous, or the same. But when they have a monolithic view of it, Arabs and Muslims refuse to adopt modern Western ideas not because of the West's difference (Arabs had incorporated Greek and Far Eastern philosophies in the tenth century), but because of the humiliating defeats brought by colonialism and the occupation of every facet of the Arab's and Muslim's life, including the attempt to master his or her will. Moreover, the ethnocentric West is seen as racist, exploitative, uninterested in justice and equity, driven by crude interests, applying the worst form of violence on others by forcing them to give up their histories and memories (and thus their identities), and as imposing secular fundamentalism by preaching it as the only way to progress, forgetting that both fundamentalism and secularism are themselves Western practices and ideologies born out of the West's own internal contradictions and tensions. And among Western nations, the United States probably fares the worst.

Thanks to its powerful commercial mechanisms, the United States is seen to have homogenized everything from beverages to laughter and sadness and to have developed a bulimic appetite that is shocking. The country is vast and never stops, although it has no clue where it is going or how to stop. Americans have no language to express basic emotional situations, and most conversations are characterized by banality. The American is born immoderate, and his discourse is often centered on numbers and budgets. Worse still, the government's unconditional support of Israel against the Palestinians adds more injury. Yet in the country's rural areas and universities, people's friendliness is also acknowledged with admiration, so there is no simple, pure view, even of the United States.[64]

In such a world, which includes rich Arab Gulf states that also live the contradiction of being bulimic consumers of Western products and lifestyles while financing the Islamist movements that fight the West, Arabs and Muslims suffer from the double despotism of the capitalist West and their own governments. How, then, do Muslims (and others) rethink the West without adopting an illusory hybridity and seek a mending of wounds ("ébranlement existentiel de la coupure").[65] How does one undo misperceptions and the false assignment of blame when the world is constantly being pushed into the dark corners of orthodoxy, driven there by seemingly universalist convictions and blind economic forces that ultimately undermine the anti-Orientalist legacy and ideals of the American Revolution? The three ages of Capital, Empire, and Extremes have failed to integrate non-Western cultures into secular progress's elusive promise of abundance, freedom, and tranquility and have in fact brought us back to the brink of yet another age of "apocalypse," one that is rife with crusading and jihadic violence. Secular modernity, with its mixture of political ideals and the relentless pursuit of profit and economic domination, has delayed the envisioning of a more harmonious, multicultural civilization, a form of coexistence that could accommodate differences without blurring our common humanity. There is no doubt, as my next chapter will show, that, unless we radically alter our imaginaries through Herculean acts of political will, humanity will continue to be passively pushed into a future of worse perils.

CHAPTER 5

Perils of *Empire*

That corporations have taken the spotlight as latter-day English-speaking conquistadores—Magellans of technology. Cortéses of consumer goods, and Pizarros of entertainment—reflected the cosmoplitanizing of their profits, a cousinship to earlier Dutch and then British cosmopolitanizing of investment. By the late 1900s, many of the Fortune 500 companies were one-third, one-half, or two-third tied to international sales, earnings, plants, and employees. Some managements hoped to no longer process or manufacture anything in the United States, but merely to import and distribute goods, much like the ill-fated Enron transformation, from producing company to financial trader.

—Kevin Phillips, *Wealth and Democracy*

It has become a truism to say that 9/11 changed everything. Muslims and Americans were suddenly thrown into a confusing world of suspicion and war, with the Muslims appearing ever more extremist and Americans draping themselves in their symbolically powerful flag. The bearded, top-hatted Uncle Sam was determined to extract revenge from the bearded, turbaned Osama bin Laden, and for good reason. Innocent Americans had been gratuitously attacked by Muslim men, all of whom connected to bin Laden and to his nebulous terrorist organization, whose nucleus lay hidden in the distant mountains of Afghanistan. The Muslims reacted quickly, defending their faith against the atrocious acts committed in its name. The United States introduced and enacted a series of legal measures to control its borders and protect its citizens and nation. A flood of denunciations, apologies, editorials, articles, and books hastily attempted to explain the situation. Everyone became an expert on Islam. Words, once exotic, proliferated in the media.[1] The United States had become a bewildering place.

It was a disorienting place for Muslims and Arabs, too. Hunted down, psychologically embattled, subjected to stringent inspections everywhere, sometimes even killed, they protested their innocence and condemned Bin Laden even while their nonimmigrant coreligionists elevated the hunted terrorist to the status of Che Guevara. Posters of the Jesus look-alike Saudi were sold in Arab streets.[2] Middle-class men and women wished him well and cursed America for its long list of grievances against them, even while Muslim and Arab governments committed themselves to the antiterrorist cause.[3] Then conspiracy theories spun out of control, and Arabs embraced them with gusto—when they chose not to believe that al-Qaʻeda played a role in the deadly attacks on Americans.

Islam was, once again, back into the limelight with a vengeance. Every American by now knows the word "jihad." What is Islam? People bought books and found the same stories, repeated over and over again—the life of the Prophet Mohammed, how Islam was born and expanded, the rise of Islamic civilization and its fall and humiliation in the modern period. The tone ranged from sympathetic to indifferent to sometimes just condescending. Some, like Silvio Berlusconi, Italy's conservative prime minister, unrestrained by the ways of polite diplomacy, and known for his harsh measures against antiglobalization protesters, simply spoke his (and many other people's) mind by expressing pride in the superiority of Western civilization, which, according to him, "consists of a value system that has given people widespread prosperity in those countries that embrace it" and which, unlike in Islamic ones, "guarantees respect for human rights and religion." And Berlusconi didn't stop here. He added that the West, as it did with Communism, "is bound to occidentalize and conquer new people," although he expects Islam to be rather unyielding.[4] Needless to say, he didn't echo any of the goodwill expressed by major scholars, journalists, politicians, and other Western commentators.

Bernard Lewis, the doyen of Orientalist studies, in characteristic form, produced essay after essay, followed by a book on what went wrong with Islam.[5] Fareed Zakaria of *Newsweek* asked the same questions, as did, of course, Thomas Friedman of the *New York Times* and many others. Eschewing automatic vilification of Muslims, authors such as these three blamed the proliferation of fundamentalism to a devil's brew of poverty, medieval academic curricula, the absence of democracy and women's rights, and the stifling of capitalist entrepreneurship in the Arab and Muslim worlds. Bernard Lewis readily says that Islam once flourished without these modern institutions, but that was then, and this is now. No nation can be peaceful without adopting capitalism. As Zakaria put it in a long article "How to Save the Arab World," Marx was wrong about everything except when he said that a business class is indispensable for liberal democracy. Margaret Thatcher would have had no problem agreeing: As others have done since the end of the Cold War, she equated Islamic extremism with Bolshevik Communism.[6] The Red menace has turned green, and the working-class hammer and sickle are replaced by a crescent whose stubbornly undimmed light has long hovered over America's consciousness, as we have seen in an earlier chapter.

Obviously, if that is so, the solution is to open up Islamic countries to capitalism in order to reduce poverty. George Tenet, director of the CIA said as much in a congressional testimony. Poverty, exploding populations, and unstable states produce terror and terrorists.[7] Despite this almost insurmountable challenge, Jeffery Sachs, the development and economic shock-therapy expert, optimistically declared that "we need to resist the idea that the Islamic world is somehow culturally incapable of development." No, Islam is not necessarily hostile to globalization. Some even suggested a "new Marshall Plan" to "promote modernization and economic opportunity" in Islamic countries. "Islam Inc.," as one *New York Times* headline put it, is what might bring Muslims to their senses and make them moderate.[8]

While some commentators promoted the virtues of capitalism and globalization, other columnists, such as Peter Steifels, wondered whether there are any courageous Muslim scholars willing to reconcile Islam with "individual freedom, political democracy, pluralism, equal rights for minorities and women and other values that have emerged as the better part of modern civilization."[9] Writing on 29 September 2001 in the *New York Times*, Steifels announced that secularization, long believed to be the magical solution to fundamentalism in the Muslim world, is now practically dead. Can Islam be itself while becoming more Western? The scholar Lamin Sanneh asked for compromises on both sides, including tolerance for nonsecular forms of nationalism. Later, Thomas Cahill wrote to reaffirm what many of us believe, namely, that "each religion, because of its metaphorical ambiguity and intellectual subtlety, holds within it marvelous potential for development and adaptation." Forget the much vaunted example of secular Turkey: Without a top-heavy military command protecting the state's secular ideology, secularism would probably wither away under mounting pressure from a resilient Muslim population willing to re-connect with its roots.[10]

We have come a long way from the initial outbursts of demonization and hate crimes. Islam is now taken seriously, scrupulously examined for clues of flexibility. The big question now is whether Muslims and Arabs can embrace modernity, give up their fixation on past glories (a theme re-peatedly emphasized by Bernard Lewis), accept the superiority of the West at this stage in history, and do the best they can to make up for lost time. The various periodicals and books honestly looking for answers and solu-tions to the "clash" of values between Islam and the West—and I am not talking about boastful culturalists who think that one culture is better than another— have all postulated that the only way for Islam to become a good, acceptable religion is if Muslim societies choose to operate by capi-talist rules and use a political system that is modeled on the West's—such as free elections, freedom of speech, human rights, and a civil society. Many of these writers generously acknowledge Islam's difference, but they also ungenerously want the latter not to devise political and economic sys-tems based on its own traditions and worldviews. They want a difference that is cleansed of its mystery, folklorized, and relegated to a museum, one that is not truly alive and that does not challenge the iron laws of "global-ization" or contest the hegemony of European cultural traditions.[11] One can admire many civilizations—Chinese, Egyptian, Indian, Maya, African, and even Islamic—but these civilizations must remain properly ancient. They can exist only as relics of the past. The right to do things that make cultural sense is not really extended to them. The Maori scholar Linda Tuhiwai Smith expressed this eloquently when she objected to the ways in which "white" research works to undermine indigenous cultures and traditions. "It appals us that the West can desire, extract and claim ownership of our ways of knowing, our imagery, the things we create and produce, and then simultaneously reject the people who created and de-veloped those ideas and seek to deny them further opportunities to be cre-ators of their own culture and own nations."[12]

As in scholarship and research, real business—international politics and economics—must be conducted in Western terms only. The wisdom of others must be confined in museums or appreciated in documentaries. Just as the conquering Spaniards subjected natives to genocidal policies be-cause they were non-Christian, and their English neighbors to the north defined themselves against both natives and Islam, today's Muslims are still deemed atavistically attached to archaic, non-Eurocentric ways. In all cases, Euro-American universalism does not include difference in any meaningful way. And Islam, as it did during the colonial and Revolutionary eras, continues to help remake and renew American nationalism and to justify restrictions on civil rights and mounting expenditures on defense.

Yet associating Islam with terrorism had been a staple of U.S. political discourse since at least the 1970s, even before the outbreak of the Iranian Revolution. In 1977, historian Gaddis Smith published an article titled "The U.S. vs. International Terrorists: A Chapter from Our Past," arguing that modern terrorism would not have surprised Americans of the late eighteenth and early nineteenth centuries because Americans had fought Muslim sea pirates long before the latter extended their reach into the skies.[13] As I have already indicated, Barbary corsairs seriously affected U.S. vital commercial interests and consumed the best minds of the new nation. Adams, Franklin, and Jefferson were authorized by Congress under the Articles of Confederation to deal with the Muslim "terrorists," as Gaddis Smith recalls the episode. While Congress allocated a small budget for ransom and concluded treaties with deys and sultans, pressure was mounting to establish a navy. This was a controversial issue. Not only were there no tax revenues to finance such a project, but people were still wary of a strong central government. Still, Jefferson, hawkish and incensed by such an affront to U.S. dignity, pushed hard against skeptics. And who could argue with the popular Federalist slogan, "Millions for defense, but not one cent for tribute!" after Tripoli and Algiers violated their treaties and declared war on the United States in 1801 and 1802 for not receiving enough tribute?

In a letter written earlier to John Adams, Jefferson had outlined six reasons why a navy is in the best national interests. One that resonates today was that the navy "will arm the federal head with the safest of all instruments of coercion over their delinquent members and prevent them from using what would be less safe." Meanwhile, the Federalist John Jay, Secretary to Congress for Foreign Affairs, quickly realized that the war with Muslim corsairs would cement American nationalism. He told Congress that "this war does not strike me as a great evil. The more we are ill-treated abroad the more we shall unite and consolidate at home." A Senate resolution in favor of establishing a navy passed in 1791, leading Senator William Maclay of Pennsylvania, suspicious of Federalist designs on state sovereignty, to comment that "war is often entered into to answer domestic, not foreign purposes," and that American freedom is imperiled by such legislation.[14]

Despite their distance in time, the Barbary Wars and the 9/11 attacks provoked similar reactions and debates. In fact, soon after 9/11, when Senator Evan Bayh of the Select Intelligence Committee was asked by National Public Radio's Neal Conan about signing a declaration of war— Bayh's father, former chairman of the same committee, was an opponent of the Vietnam war—Bayh replied that the United States was fighting a stateless entity and the only other time in U.S. history this happened was with the Barbary pirates, during the age of Jefferson.[15] Echoing Gaddis's article published 24 years earlier, the *Washington Post* published a long article on 15 October 2001 with the title "Terrorists by Another Name: The Barbary Pirates."[16] Stephen Wrage wrote for the *Washington Post* recalling the same Barbary episode and suggesting that Muslim pirates once were declared enemies of the human race (*hostis humani generis*) and were fought out of existence, and modern-day terrorists should be treated the same way.[17] The historian Paul Johnson, meanwhile, wrote for the *Wall Street Journal* recalling that the solution to Barbary pirates and other Oriental outlaws was colonialism, an idea he had suggested for Africans almost a decade earlier. Some of the countries on Johnson's list are Iraq, Sudan, Libya, Iran, and Syria.[18] The *Boston Globe* published a reader's letter that reaffirms the role of Islam in consolidating and strengthening America. Titled "Two Hundred Years Ago Islam Bullied U.S.," the letter argues that Muslim pirates forced the United States to become the power that is now being fought: "Can it not truly be said," the writer says, "that the 'American bully,' so despised by modern Islamic extremists, was largely the creation of their own ancestors?"[19]

There is yet another parallel between the aftermath of 9/11 and another historical event that seems to have gone unnoticed by the media and experts so far. In 1904, Theodore Roosevelt dispatched seven U.S. warships to intimidate another Muslim "terrorist." A Moroccan dissident and troublemaker by the name of Raisuli had kidnapped a wealthy American in Tangier, and the U.S. media, once again recalling the Barbary episode, thought Morocco should be taught a lesson. "We Should Deal with Morocco As We Dealt with Other Barbary Powers," wrote *Harper's Weekly*. On 29 May 1904, the *New York Times* published this headline: "American Marines May Invade Morocco." Roosevelt, whose presidential nomination had been opposed by most Republican Party leaders, used the occasion to jumpstart his lackluster campaign by declaring that he wanted "either Perdicaris alive or Raisuli dead." With this single statement, Roosevelt reversed his political fortunes and won the election "with the largest popular majority heretofore bestowed on a sitting president." Meanwhile, the wealthy American was released after an acceptable settlement, and Raisuli rode in the northern hills and mountains of his native Morocco. It was later discovered that Roosevelt had known that the kidnapped American was in fact a Greek citizen.[20]

The point to remember is how the modern West—both in Europe and in the colonies they settled—continues to define itself against the Muslim Other. Anyone who does not shed his or her history and embrace European ways becomes, in effect, a (Muslim) fundamentalist and anti-American. Yet a single way of life, upheld by massive policing power, is bound to generate more forms of extremism—unless diversity is totally stamped out of existence.[21] Modern history, particularly in the twentieth century, is strewn with many strains of extremism—most, if not all, of the isms, really—because such isms were almost all produced *in reaction*—this is the key word—to the stress of *perceived* indignities. Nativism—which, as David Bennett showed in his masterly treatise *The Party of Fear*, has a long history in the United States—is a natural reaction against such perceptions,[22] and yet we are surprised to see colonized peoples in Africa, Asia, and the Americas retreat into violent orthodoxies that mutilate their own traditions.

Writing from Tokyo in January 2002, the *New York Times* columnist Nicholas D. Kristoff reminded his readers how Japan, China, and Korea, for instance, once developed their own anti-Western philosophies. He then explained that such ideologies reflected "frustration at the humiliating choice faced by once-great civilizations heartsick at the pressure to catch up with the nouveaux riches in the West."[23] Within the West itself, many Europeans, particularly the French, have repeatedly expressed undisguised anti-American sentiments, probably prompted by the same perceived threat to a European or French way of life. (Such divisions within the West reached an almost unprecedented level on the eve of the U.S. war in Iraq.) If we want peace and coexistence, we can no longer afford to drive people to such extremes. We need to invite them out—and back—to a place of their own, one we share with them, and they with us.

The well-meaning journalists and scholars who think that capitalism is the solution to extremism are in fact prescribing the wrong medication.

Capitalism, or its dominant euphemism, globalization, *is* what produces extremism. This may sound rather odd to people who associate the ferocity of fundamentalism with the Muslims' rejection of modernity or to those who see Islam and globalization as violently at odds. The world has been accustomed to the image of a primitive, fanatical Islam unable to cope with modernity, just as it has been inundated with pictures of a process of globalization that is benevolent, but irresistible—as if propelled by some divine, transhistorical logic. To oppose globalization, it is often suggested, is to oppose some ineluctable force of nature, to stand in the way of progress. This is why antiglobalization protesters appear as unreasonable youth, misguided by some false idealism and an exaggerated sense of solidarity with the poor. They are supposed to be too young to grasp the complicated details of the global economy or the realities of Third World countries. Besides, what's the alternative anyway, particularly after the "evil" Communist regime collapsed of its own rotten weight? The post–Cold War terrain has been entirely monopolized by free-market doctrines, but to flesh out a solution or outline a blueprint for a new global economic model is to invite more trouble, for no one can plan out a system that is good for every human being and culture, in all places, at all times. This is why there has been no credible alternative to capitalism in the West since the collapse of Communism in the late 1980s, as Jean Ziegler noted even then.[24] Yet not to challenge "globalization" is to nourish the conditions for more violence and terror, not simply along the fault lines of cultures and religions, but across the entire globe and within all nations.

A quick reading of the global situation in the years following the publication of Hobsbawm's history of the twentieth century reinforces the now-incontrovertible fact that we live in a dystopian world horribly out of balance because of misplaced economic priorities. The white man's fear discussed in Silko's *Ceremony* has now become global, affecting both the poor and the rich although, as is the case in the Native American novels, the poor suffer disproportionately. We read about Bangladeshi children being kidnapped and sold to work as maids, prostitutes, or camel jockeys in rich Arab states,[25] while the number of (mostly unpunished) rapes and attempted rape cases in South Africa skyrocketed to 52,860 in 2000.[26] By choosing to go capitalist, uprooting millions of workers from their traditional state-sponsored jobs, Russia and China have aggravated class divisions and undermined the health of their populations. Market economies have made basic health care, the pride of both countries during Communist rule, inaccessible, even while private, tech-based medicine has become available to the rich. "In China," wrote a *New York Times* reporter in 2000, "treatment is often an economic rather than a medical decision." In Russia, life expectancy is tumbling down, while the number of disabled people and the rates of alcoholism and accidents continue to go up.[27]

The woes of former Communist countries are troubling the world community. A report titled "The Silent Crisis," issued in 2000 by the European Children's Trust, a group active in ten eastern European countries, found that more than fifty million children were living in "genuine poverty" and in societies increasingly ravaged by the spread of tuberculosis. "Since the breakup of the Communist system," the report commented, "conditions have become much worse—in some cases catastrophically so," and observed that "for all its many faults, the old system provided most people with a reasonable standard of living and a certain security."[28]

Eastern European women are also vulnerable and trafficked across the globe, particularly to Western Europe, in ever growing numbers. (Sixty percent of Russia's unemployed are women, and children as young as nine are used as prostitutes.) The International Organization for Migration estimates that about seven hundred thousand women are forced into the sex trade and trafficked worldwide. Even NATO and UN officials have been implicated in the exploitation and abuse of these vulnerable women. Both the CIA and the UN have issued reports on this disturbing trend, the latter organization calling the traffic in women the "biggest human rights violation in the world."[29] Some have referred to human trafficking as part of a "dark" global diversified industry of organized crime, one in which even UN and U.S. for-hire military personnel (contracted by the government) were found to be implicated,[30] yet the exploitation of human desire is not a shady business at all. Prostitution, including sexual tourism, is a lucrative business, generating more than $7 billion annually,[31] while pornography in the United States is a 10–billion-dollar industry, its "products" beamed into hotel room TVs and streamed into computers by major corporations such as Marriott and AT&T. According to Eric Schlosser's eye-opening examination of vice industries, Americans spend as much on "adult entertainment" as they do on all Hollywood releases and spend more "at strip clubs than at Broadway theatres, regional and nonprofit theatres, and symphony orchestra performances—combined." (In 2001, Schlosser further reveals, "about 11, 000 hard-core videos were released, some costing as little as little as $5,000 to produce.")[32]

Despite tighter security measures in the aftermath of 9/11, the heroin industry is flourishing as never before, penetrating new markets and posting revenues in excess of $400 billion a year. Despite a long-standing war on drugs and draconian punitive measures, the cultivation of marijuana, worth anywhere between $4 billion and $25 billion a year, is possibly America's largest cash crop, outpacing even the heavily subsidized corn (valued at $19 billion in 2001).[33] Piracy on the high seas is also on the rise (with 285 cases reported in 1999). As ships sail through oceans of "poverty, envy, and desperation," they are targeted by pirates ranging from "desperate fishermen" to "highly organized syndicates slaughtering crews to steal multimillion-dollar vessels." Jack Hitt, the author of a long article on this subject, writes: "Today's pirates are a troubling symptom of a new world order, one shaped by a fierce Darwinian struggle in the feral markets of modern international trade." Meanwhile, underground economies, money laundering, and tax evasion schemes have become an integral part of the global economic structure. The International Monetary Fund (IMF) estimates that "the annual revenues from money laundering are now about 2 to 5 percent of the world's GDP—about $800 billion to 2 trillion a year." Underground economic activity—partly fuelled by alienation and class disparities—now constitutes almost a third (between 9 and 29 percent) of economic activity in Los Angeles and is even bigger in Europe and other parts of the world.[34]

The present climate of fear has affected poor and rich countries alike as violence has become a global epidemic affecting all countries and layers of society. In its first comprehensive study of the subject, released in October 2002, the World Health Organization displayed a chilling picture of a world rampant with conflict, murder, and suicide (more than half of the estimated 191 million dead in the twentieth century were civilians), and reported "that in some countries, health care expenditures due to violence account for up to 5% of GDP."[35] In 2002, for the first time in history, the number of inmates in U.S. prisons and jails exceeded 2 million, although violent crime in that same year was "lower than it [had been] in 1974." And of the incarcerated people, African American males continued to bear the most onerous burden: 12 percent of men between the ages of twenty and thirty-four were behind bars. (The disproportionate number of incarcerated blacks in U.S. prisons means that the recent enfranchisement of blacks is already being reversed, because about 14 percent of African American males convicted of felonies are prevented from voting.)[36] In 2002, when the fear of terrorism was affecting the civil rights of citizens, the U.S.

State Department registered the lowest incidence of terrorist attacks since 1969, with not a single attack taking place in the United States. In a study of rampage killers that spans more than fifty years and covers "102 killers in 100 rampage attacks," the *New York Times* found a consistent motive for this socially heterogeneous group of mostly white men. "By far the most common precipitator was the loss of a job" (47 percent of cases). Excluding the victims of the 9/11 attacks, there were 15,980 homicides in the United States in 2001. And fear is rampant all across Western societies. In October 2002, the French cabinet approved the so-called, "Sarkozy law," named after the interior minister, Nicolas Sarkozy, a set of new legislative measures criminalizing begging, "vagabondery," prostitution, and squatting, among other offenses of the poor and the marginalized. In such a Hobbesian society, new architectures and structures, including prison and security industries, gated communities, surveillance technologies, and even menacing-looking SUVs and cars (such as the "Al Capone" model) have turned Americans into a besieged people inhabiting an increasingly militarized universe. Yet bigger vehicles are not making the roads safer: A preliminary National Highway Traffic Safety Administration's statistic, released in April 2003, showed that 42,850 people died in traffic-related accidents in the United States in 2002.[37]

While the poor die from curable diseases and cannot find basic medicines for simple ills or have access to health coverage (about one-quarter of "nonelderly Americans" were without coverage at some point in 1998), the rich are increasingly medicalizing their social problems through the use of lifestyle drugs such as Viagra, steroids, and diet pills. (About two hundred thousand prescriptions for Viagra are written every week in the United States.) And yet such remedies offer little relief: "About 170 million children in poor countries are underweight because of lack of food," but the amount of obesity in the United States has increased since 1990, leading from 15 to 35 percent of American adults to spend between "$30 to 50 billion a year trying to lose weight." Even children in Asia and other parts of the "developing" world are getting obese as urban populations adopt Western lifestyles and dietary habits that threaten an entire generation with a life of chronic illnesses and premature deaths that are likely to strain the already ill-equipped medical infrastructure of these societies—even while malnutrition is still rampant in rural areas and in the countryside and the Western ideal of extreme slimness is being adopted in fashion circles. So severe and global is the problem that scientists are now concluding that humans are undergoing another evolutionary change, with obesity becoming the norm, a change that is likely to cause an untold amount of misery. Given this state, is it any wonder that the number of bariatric operations reducing the size of stomachs in the United States" reached forty thousand by 2000, 80 percent of which were performed on women?[38]

The *New York Times* ran two articles in September 2001 showing how life in a capitalist system has endangered the lives of children. Junk (corporate) food in schools has turned students' diets into a menu of soda and chips and other snack foods, while the "per capita consumption of food increased about 8 percent from 1990 to 2000, according to the Department of Agriculture," which translates into "something like 140 extra pounds of food a year . . . per person." (Even as obesity is developing into a national and global epidemic, food and beverage producers have introduced more than one hundred and sixteen thousand new products since 1990 and spent about eleven billion dollars in 2002 alone on marketing them.)[39] So many American teenagers are getting in trouble with the law or at school and are suffering from serious, debilitating psychological problems that well-to-do parents are sending them to "wilderness therapy" schools and programs costing from fifty thousand to eighty thousand dollars a year, part of a "multibillion-dollar industry," as the *New York Times* put it on the eve of 9/11, "that has surged in the last 10 years to satisfy what many say is a booming market in parental desperation." The headmaster of one such school described some of his students as "emotional terrorists" who have turned their homes into war zones.[40] Another article published on the same day reported on a study by University of Pennsylvania researchers who estimated that a staggering "325,000 children a year were subjected to sexual exploitation, including prostitution, use in pornography and molestation" in the United States.[41] The troubles of American children seem to have no end: The United States ranks thirty-third in infant mortality rates in the world, while 14.8 percent of American children live in poverty. The Census Bureau's 2002 report on income and poverty not only reveals that poverty is increasing among all social groups (a family of four that made less than $18,104 was considered poor), but it also showed that out of the 32.9 million American poor, 11.7 million—or about 16 percent—are children under the age of eighteen. (Since the overhaul of welfare during the Clinton presidency, about a million black children have fallen into deep poverty and more women have been incarcerated.) One year after 9/11, the U.S. Department of Health and Human Services released its 2001 National Household Survey showing that 10.8 percent of youths between the ages of twelve and seventeen were drug users in 2001. Children were also consuming prescription drugs in larger numbers than they had done five years earlier.[42]

This clearly shows that there are no beneficiaries in this reigning global economic order. Despite the statistical affluence of many people in the West, life in these "advanced" societies has turned into a desperate attempt not to fall behind and to guard against any number of potential disasters lurking right behind the corner, as Teresa Brennan's recent account makes absolutely clear. By adopting capitalism as a regulatory system of human relations, Westerners have alienated themselves from the natural rhythms of life, including those of their own bodies, and succumbed to a series of illnesses that seem to have no end. Commuting for hours on end to work, polluting their natural environment, jeopardizing the health and education of children, suffering from a host of nearly debilitating chronic and mental illnesses, eating dangerous foods, and living in permanent fear and exhaustion, members of these societies seem to have become literally insane. As Brennan puts it:

> Constituting a physical danger to oneself, let alone others, is intrinsic to the legal definition of insanity, when the body is at risk from the mind. And if the well-off mind knows, however unconsciously, that it is endangering the body, this would only increase its anxiety, depression, and, for that matter, paranoia. It knows it is under attack from somewhere, it knows life is at stake, but it looks for the source of its fears anywhere but in its own conduct.[43]

While people are thus abandoned to their dismal fate, corporations have amassed so much power that they operate largely out of control. In 2000, twenty-nine of the world's largest economies were, by a conservative estimate, corporations.[44] In the aftermath of the accounting scandals that rocked the United States in 2002, Kate Jennings, a writer who spent much of the 1990s working as a speechwriter for major Wall Street financial firms, described the corporate environment—with its rampant paranoia, surveillance, and fear—as Stalinist. Free-market "fundamentalists . . . roamed the globe preaching a triumphant gospel of deregulation from which all freedoms would flow," Jennings wrote, then return "to a bureaucratic roost perfectly Soviet in its rigidity." Not only that, but some of the globe's most powerful entrepreneurs are impoverishing democratic cultures by seeking to control information and limit people's access to alternative views. While many Americans supported President Bush in his war for freedom in Iraq, they scarcely paid attention to how businessmen were diminishing their freedoms at home. On the same day that *New York Times* displayed the dramatic picture of the statue of Saddam Hussein being toppled amid jubilant Iraqi crowds on its front page, the front page of the business section featured an even more powerful and poignant story about Rupert Murdoch's acquisition of DirecTV and the effect of his media empire on Americans. "The deal," wrote the *Times*, "will give Mr. Murdoch [who owns, among other media outlets in the United States, the Fox TV network and film studio] even more power in determining what programs are beamed to television sets across the United States and how much consumers pay for them."[45]

Although corporations may dispense a few social services and do some occasional good, they are not agents of benevolent change. Ted Fishman, a former currency trader, estimated that offshore companies, sheltered from taxation and regulation, attract nearly $5 trillion in deposits, and that money derived from crime and war has become part of the global financial structure. "The estimates of how much criminal money is entering the world financial system from all sources range between $500 billion and $1 trillion a year," wrote Fishman. "The midpoint of the estimates tops the GDP of Canada. That number does not include the unknown hundreds of billions of dollars in illegal flight capital—money from government bribes, looting, privatization schemes and mineral licenses—that flow from corrupt regimes. Offshore banking centers have the infrastructure to wash it all."[46] And this system is making many people fantastically rich. *Forbes*'s 2002 list of the world's top billionaires shows that the combined wealth of 497 people (mostly men) is, in the analysis of John Cavanagh and Sarah Anderson, "greater than the combined incomes of the poorest half of humanity."[47] A few of the world's superrich—people like George Soros, Ted Turner, Bill Gates, Ed Cohen, and others—do commit themselves to worthy social issues, but they cannot fix the world's unbalanced social structures.

Why, then, promote economic and cultural globalization when both undermine the very foundations of human civilization? Stanley Hoffmann, the Buttenwieser University Professor at Harvard, wrote that the "present form of capitalism, ironically seen by Karl Marx and Friedrich Engels, poses a central dilemma between efficiency and fairness" and that such a model "does not favor social justice. Economic globalization has thus be-

come a formidable cause of inequality among and within states," uprooting people and cultures and creating resentments that can be transformed
into apocalyptic events. "Insofar as globalization enriches some and up-
roots many," says Hoffman, "those who are both poor and uprooted may
seek revenge and self-esteem in terrorism," for terrorism "can also be a
product of globalization." To avoid such a stark fate, Hoffmann suggests a
"political philosophy that would be both just and acceptable even to those
whose values have other foundations."[48]

Objections to globalization have become more vociferous in the last
few years. In 1999, Edward Herman, professor emeritus of finance at the
Wharton School, described it as a dangerous "ideology" that must be
"fought at every level." After detailing the catastrophic economic and political effects of globalization, Herman warned against "an explosion if the
process is not contained and democracy is not rehabilitated.[49] In 2000,
Joseph Stiglitz, an economist with impeccable credentials who later won a
Nobel Prize, blamed the IMF and what is called the "Washington Consensus" for the ills that have befallen Russia and East Asia in the last
decade, and he has continued to make the same argument.[50] After 9/11,
John Gray, professor of European thought at the London School of Economics, announced the death of the false utopia of market liberalism,
since the rich can no longer "be insulated from the collapsed states and
new forms of war." The free-market ideology has failed miserably to uphold the basic vision of human civilization. "It is worth reminding ourselves how grandiose were the dreams of the globalisers," wrote Gray.
"The entire world was to be remade as a universal free market. No matter
how different their histories and values, however deep their differences or
bitter their conflicts, all cultures everywhere were to be corralled into a
universal civilization."

Gray compared the free-market ideology to Marxism, since both
have universalist aspirations and view human beings "primarily in economic terms." Those who preach market liberalism and want to force the
world's people into a "single mould" as the only way to achieve progress
are, in fact, inviting "unending conflict," since cultures would never agree
on what is best for everyone. Countries "should be free to find their own
version of modernity, or not to modernise at all. So long as they pose no
threat to others, even intolerable regimes should be tolerated. A looser,
more fragmented, partly de-globalised world would be a less tidy world. It
would also be a safer world." Thus "the lesson of 11 September is that the

go-go years of globalisation were an interregnum, a time of transition between two epochs of conflict. The task in front of us is to forge terms of
peace among peoples separated by unalterably divergent histories, beliefs
and values."[51]

Even the *New York Times Magazine* saw fit to publish a feature article
on the failure of globalization, with a list of suggestions to fix it. The
Times's editorial writer, Tina Rosenberg, wasted little time in noting that,
under the present rules of global trade, enunciated in the World Trade Organization's twenty-five-thousand-page agreement, the poor have virtually
no chance of benefiting from the system, so rigged it is in favor of the rich
and powerful countries and corporations. "No nation," Rosenberg writes,

has ever developed over the long term under the rules being imposed today on
third-world countries by the institutions controlling globalization. The United
States, Germany, France and Japan all became wealthy and powerful nations behind the barriers of protectionism. East Asia built its export industry by protecting its markets and banks from foreign competition and requiring investors to buy
local products and build local know-how. These are all practices discouraged or
made illegal by the rules of trade today.[52]

Rosenberg says economists are undecided about whether globalization
creates poverty or not, but it clear that the model she describes—and rejects—is not likely to go away. In late September 2002, rich nations refused to dismantle their subsidies to farmers while forcing poor nations to
open their economies and privatize their assets. So bad was the situation
that Nicholas Stern, the World Bank's chief economist, estimated that European and Japanese cows receive sometimes receive almost triple the
amount in daily subsidies of what 75 percent of sub-Saharan Africans
make in a day.[53]

Globalization, as Mark Weisbrot, the codirector of the Center for
Economic and Policy Research in Washington D.C. writes, has failed to
deliver in places like Latin America and Africa, for "the last 20 years have
also seen a significant slowdown in progress on the major social indicators
in most low and middle-income countries: life expectancy, infant and child
mortality, literacy and education." The dogma of globalization, with its unfettered capital flows, has meant disaster to the world's disadvantaged.
"None of today's high-income countries tried this experiment when they
were developing countries," says Weisbrot. "The United States had an average tariff on manufactured goods of 44 percent as late as 1913. Yet, for
more than 20 years protectionism has been condemned by the IMF and
World Bank as a grave impediment to growth."[54]

Questions of equity and cultural diversity are not, however, the only reasons to reject the present model of globalization, for the world's natural resources are also in danger of being permanently depleted. The environment has become so exhausted and imperiled by the wasteful ways promoted by capitalism that the colonization of new planets by 2050 is now seriously contemplated as an exit option (for the rich, of course).[55] On 20 March 2002, the *New York Times* published shocking images of the disintegration of a massive chunk of the Antarctic Peninsula, the first time an event of this magnitude happened in about twelve thousand years, according to scientists.[56]

The world's freshwater supply, a finite resource that makes up less than one percent of the world's water, is also shrinking through massive consumption and industrial pollution, raising fears of impending conflicts among nations sharing the same rivers, for instance. The U.S. National Intelligence Council, which advises the CIA, has warned against such prospects while sources in both the United Nations and the United States estimate "at least 40 percent of the world's population, or about three billion people, will live in countries where it is difficult or impossible to get enough water to satisfy basic needs." Five billion people are expected to suffer from inadequate water supplies in 2025. And yet, as the global crisis over water is intensifying, conglomerates such as Vivendi and Suez, encouraged by the neoliberal creed, are jumping into a $200 billion market that is growing at a steady pace of 6 percent annually. "According to *Fortune* magazine," Maude Barlow and Tony Clarke wrote in the *Nation*,

the annual profits of the water industry now amount to about 40 percent of those of the oil sector and are already substantially higher than the pharmaceutical sector, now close to $1 trillion. But only about 5 percent of the world's water is currently in private hands, so it is clear that we are talking about huge profit potential as the water crisis worsens. In 1999 there were more than $15 billion worth of water acquisitions in the U.S. water industry alone, and all the big water companies are now listed on the stock exchanges.

The bottled-water industry, "one of the fastest-growing and least regulated industries in the world, expanding at an annual rate of 20 percent," is also one of the least regulated and most polluting businesses. In 2001, "close to 90 billion liters of bottled water were sold around the world—most of it in nonreusable plastic containers," while "in rural communities all over the world, corporate interests [such as Nestlé, Coca-Cola, and Pepsi] are buying up farmlands, indigenous lands, wilderness tracts and whole water systems, then moving on when sources are depleted." Described as either a "good," "service," or "investment" in various trade agreements such as the WTO and NAFTA, water, the very source of life, has been placed out of range for many of the world's poor, sparking resistance movements in places such as Argentina and Bolivia to reclaim water as a public good.[57]

The world's poor, to be sure, are fighting against the false promises of globalization (the privatization of national assets and resources) since they have fared worse under such schemes. In Latin America, foreign debt, unemployment, and poverty have become worse in the last decade, and so "a popular and political ground swell is building from the Andes to Argentina against the decade-old experiment with [a] free-market capitalism" that has benefited only corrupt officials and "faceless multinationals." By the end of 2002, Venezuela, Brazil, and Ecuador had elected militant leftists to the presidency (called by U.S. Representative Henry J. Hyde the "axis of evil"), and Bolivia (which, like many poor countries, pays more on servicing debt obligations to the rich than it does for health care) developed a strong socialist/indigenous movement headed by Evo Morales, described by the *New York Times* as a "coca-chewing Aymara Indian" guided by the "goddess Pachamama, the mother of the earth for the Aymara," who doesn't exclude "the possibility of violent revolt" to wrest the country's autonomy from the control of multinational corporations.[58]

Capital flight from poor countries and payment of interest on debts incurred by Third World officials who often reinvested their loans back in lender countries, combined with the growing trade deficit in countries like the United States, means that the rich are getting more out of the poor, even though the poor need more resources than ever.[59] Even as the U.S. defense budget has grown to about the size of the rest of the world's countries combined, the U.S. economy is registering a growing trade deficit, mounting personal debt, and dependency on foreign investment that endangers its long-term security. Thus, while Americans are living well beyond their means, poor nations are denied the opportunity to use their resources (undercut by rich states' subsidies to their farmers).[60] And just as the world's poor are rising against globalization, apologies for imperialism are mounting, one senior British diplomat going as far to advocate a "postmodern imperialism" to restore order in mostly ravaged postcolonial societies, an imperialism that is "acceptable to a world of human rights and cosmopolitan values" whose major feature is the "voluntary" submission to the international financial institutions such as IMF and the World Bank.[61]

The U.S. intelligence community, which had been faulted for not preventing the 9/11 tragedy, has been aware of this apocalyptic future since late 2000, when it published *Global Trends 2015*, a 70–page report predicting trends in the first fifteen years of this century. The report estimated that more than three billion people will not have enough water or other resources, that the traditional concept of identity will be eroded, that governments will have less control over information, human movement, and illegal businesses, that more conflicts will erupt in weak states, and that the gulf between the haves and have-nots will widen even more. The tide of globalization, the report concluded, "will not lift all boats."[62]

Though globalization is driven by the profit motive, economic behavior is informed by cultural and religious values and cannot be assumed to be otherwise. Because human identities are primarily cultural and religious, globalization must also be considered a cultural phenomenon in the sense that it upsets global cultural balances.[63] In fact, cultures themselves, under the Midas touch of corporate planning, end up being exploited as commodities. Janet Wasko has made the astute observation that by manipulating "innocence and dreams" and manufacturing "fantasy for profit," Disney not only exploits global labor, but continues "to plunder history, mythology, and folktales for its visual icons—and transforming these into new, fun-filtered, licensed products aimed mostly at children, who are taught to buy into both the visual images and the final licensed products."[64] Under the pressure of fashion and film industries, cultures are forced to reinvent themselves in the image of the West—sometimes literally. The "round face, arched eyebrows and small mouth of the classical Thai look," reported the *New York Times*, is now giving way to the "sharper and more pronounced features of the West." In sub-Saharan Africa, women willing to win in beauty contests are forced into upsetting local standards of feminine beauty, with traditional African robustness undermined by the cult of slimness. Even veiled Muslim women are trying to change visible parts of their bodies along more Western dimensions. One suspects that the booming market in cosmetics and cosmetic surgery in Iran, especially for women who opt for rhinoplasty (nose-change surgery), has something to do with these changing self-perceptions. [65] The galloping spread of American popular culture, considered to be the art form of democracies, irritates both pretentious aristocratic elites and Muslim fundamentalists. Edward Rothstein wondered if there is a way "both to promise liberty and the pursuit of happiness while preserving some discrimination among desires and differences among cultures? Or are disgust and desire doomed to be intertwined? Answers are not likely to appease Islamic totalitarianism," Rothstein concluded, "but they are increasingly important for the evolution of American democracy and culture."[66]

A better question would be whether the West can contain the globalizing impulse of profit and conquest that has girded its main ideologies in modern history and produce alternative visions that are conducive to a new world order, one governed by reciprocity and dialogue. With the passing away (at least temporarily) of Communism, Western progressives cannot envision philosophies of coexistence outside their familiar paradigms, as Franz Fanon knew long before then. They continue to think for the world, and the solutions they produce continue to be thoroughly Eurocentric. Partaking of the same social imaginary that influences the politics they oppose, constrained by professional demands, and operating out of hegemonic academic corporate structures, they postulate agendas in culturally familiar languages and never assume that such gestures are driven by the same universalist impulse that has defined the West's relations with Muslims and others in the last half millennium.

Thus, Antonio Negri's and Miachael Hardt's manifesto of liberation, *Empire*,[67] published at a symbolically auspicious moment, the very dawn of a new Christian millennium (or is it the year 2000 of our "common" era?), was immediately and eagerly heralded by many apostles of the academic Left as the new agenda for the future, replacing the obviously dated and spectral Marxist warnings to and about capitalism. However, they did so without paying much attention to the ways in which this volume is trapped in the West's Eurocentric unconscious and thus insidiously perpetuates the colonization of the world's non-European, or, perhaps, nonwhite masses.

In a sense, by objecting to *Empire*'s Eurocentrism, I am merely adding to the intractable debate about the nature of representation and power (or is it the power of representation?), an issue recently revisited by John Mowitt in *Cultural Critique*. Mowitt asks tough questions and quotes Said's double-edged remark, one designed to enable and perplex, perhaps even silence: "Without significant exception the universalizing discourses of Europe and the United States assume the silence, willing or otherwise, of the non-European world. There is incorporation, there is inclusion, there is direct rule, there is coercion. But there is only infrequently an acknowledgement that the colonized people should be heard from, their ideas known."[68] How could it ever be otherwise? Mowitt adroitly reminds us that even the most strident critiques of Eurocentrism (what Immanuel Wallerstein called "anti-Eurocentric Eurocentrism") cannot easily avoid the same sphere of objectionable European epistemologies (something that has bedeviled Said and Gayatri Spivak, for instance) and that an unexamined notion of U.S. multiculturalism may exacerbate, not attenuate, this tendency.[69] It is not without reason that Wallerstein called Eurocentrism a "hydra-headed monster." For instance, Wallerstein finds the suggestion that had the West not destroyed the structures of other civilizations, the latter would have reached the same stage of capitalist development paradoxically absolves Europe of its sins, and, in fact, universalizes the blame by making all of human history complicit in the violent enterprise of capitalism. Wallerstein argues that China, India, and the Arab world did not produce capitalism *because* they were "better immunized against the toxin" and could contain it through equally strong "cultural, religious, military [and] political" institutions. Therefore, "to turn their credit into something which they must explain away is to me the quintessential form of Eurocentrism."[70]

I mention Mowitt and Wallerstein's Sisyphean wrestlings with the ideology of Eurocentrism (and there are many others, particularly among anthropologists, who are engaged in the same processes of self-examination) to highlight the epistemological quandary confronting all committed progressives operating in and from the West. Yet *Empire* is so remarkably silent about this crucial issue and so unself-conscious about its privileged cultural location (never mind Negri's house arrest in Italy) that it could practically turn the worst form of culturalism into harmless nationalist bombast.

I may be exaggerating a bit, but the problem with the book is discernible at first sight: The authors' program of emancipation simply excludes non-Western visions and locates the world's problems and their solution squarely within Western traditions. The non-West is relegated to its historical emptiness—those outside the West are a people without history, in Eric Wolf's now historic phrase—or, as recent events have tragically shown, to an atavism that only quickens its demise.[71] The authors do mention the Iranian Revolution—a landmark event in recent history—but say nothing about Islam, with its vast corpus of writings on the issues that preoccupy them. This glaring omission, which is shared by "post-al" theories, can be explained only by the absence of a robust model of multicultural

education and by Western(ized) scholars' ignorance of non-interpolated indigenous traditions, is all the more remarkable because Islam continues to
be the only form of Otherness that challenges Western hegemony and
therefore the only non-Western ideology to be unscrupulously dismissed
in the familiar Orientalist vocabulary supposedly long gone into disuse in
leftist circles.[72] And what applies to Islam necessarily applies to all the
world's indigenous idioms. By choosing to draw exclusively from Western
philosophy, Negri and Hardt have, in fact, constructed a super metanarrative, or, perhaps, a hypernarrative, one so globally encompassing that its
ethnocentricity easily escapes attention. So, as a first step in interrogating
Empire, I will try to present the book's main argument, compare it with
other recent books trying to come to terms with Islam's difference, and
then introduce the alternative theory of Sophie Bessis, presented in her still
untranslated volume on the West's supremacist ideologies in the last half
millennium (*L'Occident et les autres: Histoire d'une suprématie*), coincidentally published in 2001, the year of all perils.

In Negri and Hardt's postulation, Empire (the name given to the
present global order), decentered and deterritorialized, brings together various forces and tendencies in innumerable variations of exchange, all informed by the one supreme logic of capitalism that fragments sovereignty
into multiple centers and reaches into the deepest recesses of nature to produce social life itself. Empire thus "presents the paradigmatic form of
biopower," and although always bathed in blood, it is always dedicated to
peace. The globalization of capital in the postcolonial, postimperialist (in
the classical sense of imperialism) and, perhaps, the post-Soviet order is a
new historical shift that aims at fusing the political (juridical) and economic into a "properly capitalist order." Under the moral ideology of "international right" and "perpetual peace," the concept of the "just war" has
been revived, permitting military action and the policing of noncompliants. Thus, the new imperial rulers aim at producing the universal values
of peace and upholding right by relying on an intense process of what
Foucault termed disciplinarity, a system of controls that reaches into the
"depths of consciousnesses and bodies of the population—and at the same
time across the entirety of social relations." While the absorption of the
"social bios" and civil society into this amorphous and flexible imperial
capitalist structure keeps resistance alive at the level of singularities, the
structures of Empire dissolve identity and history in the inexorable march

toward universal citizenship. Much as Marx saw "civil society" as a bour-geois ploy,[73] Hardt and Negri identify the seemingly benevolent non-governmental organizations (NGOs) as the "mendicant orders" of the new imperial system.[74]

For the authors, Empire is still better than the systems that precede it, just as capitalism was with Marx. In fact, for them, the sentimental and parochial calls for localism are more damaging and insidious, for such calls somehow assume that the local is not a notion produced out of the same tensions that give birth to globalism. Besides, the authors simply reject the claim "that we can (re)establish local identities that are in some sense *out-side* and protected against the global flows of capital and Empire." So, the authors ask, how does Empire create conditions for emancipation? "*How can productive labor dispersed in various networks find a center? How can the material and immaterial production of the brains and bodies of the many con-struct a common sense and direction, or rather, how can the endeavor to bridge the distance between the formation of the multitude as subject and the consti-tution of a democratic political apparatus find its prince?*" (authors' italics). The answer to such a question is a "*materialist teleology*" that fulfills the "*Spinozist prophetic function, the function of an immanent desire that organ-izes the multitude.*" [75]

To understand how the promising humanism of the Renaissance cul-ture gave birth to such an Orwellian Empire, the authors retrace their analysis back to show what went wrong at the birth of modernity. From its inception in the Renaissance, modernity has been a binary process. One fundamentally democratic moment of this process has involved imma-nence, in which being singularly human (*homohomo*, or doubly human, in the words of Carolus Bovillus) is the ultimate goal, a moment that finds its ultimate expression in Spinoza. Yet the liberatory moment at the Renais-sance gave simultaneous birth to its antithesis, the darker powers that seek to control and contain the humanist momentum in the name of peace and security. A great human experiment was cancelled and gave way to the pri-macy of a feudal, racist, divisive, plunderous, and Eurocentric *transcen-dence*, or sovereignty. Hobbes and Rousseau tried to theorize this crisis away by explaining sovereignty as a contractual process involving the sov-ereign and the consensually governed, but such a modern notion rests pri-marily on the assumption of "capitalist development and the affirmation of the market as the foundation of the values of social reproduction." Indeed, the authors reiterate the long-held view (and, to their credit, against many who are trying to claim otherwise these days) that "European modernity is inseparable from capitalism." This "sovereignty machine," relying on a "modern bureaucracy," gradually absorbs society into power and gives birth to "biopower," a "new from of transcendence." The bourgeois nation-state, with its imagined unities, strikes at and undermines the "multitude" of singularities operating freely on an open plane.

Hardt and Negri do realize that, notwithstanding its fundamental oppressiveness, the concept of the nation has been used for emancipatory battles, such as the ones conducted by the colonized in recent history. The problem is that once sovereignty is achieved, the progressive elements embedded in nationalist ideologies cede to the tyranny and totalitarianism of the state, whose primary function is to map out and control every detail of social life. Premised on the capitalist exploitation of labor, nation-states produce alterities that consolidate their Eurocentric base.[76] However, the boundaries of this indispensable dialectic cannot be securely contained and have, in fact, always been porous: Contagion, not hygiene, or probably both simultaneously, is what truly characterizes contact.[77]

How, then, does one resist the tyranny of nationalism? Hardt and Negri argue that postmodern and postcolonial theoretical calls for dismantling essentialist binaries to recognize hybridities and difference not only hark back to the first progressive phase of modernity (the immanence of the *homohomo* versus the transcendence of sovereignty), but they articulate such views at a time when the Enlightenment they oppose has already been superseded. Postmodern theories turn out to be naïve (if not conspiratorial) echoes of already established strategies of domination. "Perhaps," the authors write, "the discourses themselves are possible only when the regimes of modern sovereignty are already on the wane."[78]

In their attempt to account for everything, the authors argue that Islamic fundamentalism (based on static views) needs to be understood as a paradigmatic case of the postmodern refusal of modernity and that the Iranian Revolution is best seen as "the first postmodern revolution" (149).[79] To them, fundamentalism is the unprivileged poors' version of the cosmopolitan's academic and highly reified "post-al" theories, since both, in their reading, are designed to reject modernity. The glamour of postmodernity and the assumed pluralism of identity politics do not fool the authors, either. The politics of difference, they know, is part of the capitalist marketing strategy, and corporate culture for the world market has never been constrained by modernist binaries. In Empire, subjectivities are no longer produced within discretely delineated institutions, but are forged across "the entire social terrain."[80] Diversity is "an effective apparatus of command" that thwarts labor unity, just as it in early twentieth century America.[81] Yet the fabric of Empire is also paradoxically based on a corrupting system that could open the way for new possibilities.[82]

What, then, is the proposed solution to this Orwellian condition? For Hardt and Negri, a Counter-Empire cannot be achieved by delinking from the global system—a view that, following Samir Amin, I think is indispensable—but by means of a global republicanism that takes its cues from the philosophies of St. Augustine and the International Workers of the World (Wobblies). This republicanism is characterized by the "the will to be against" or simply a "being-against" that is expressed in "desertion, exodus, and nomadism."[83] To this forced mobility of the poor, the authors add that only a posthuman culture (premised on Foucault's call for "le travail de soi sur soi" and inspired by Donna Haraway's cyborgs, an updated version of Spinoza's project), a culture in which people reinvent themselves however they please in the nonplaces of Empire, can take the multitude to a new plateau of freedom.

Because capitalism is condemned to incorporate everything and everyone into its sphere, thereby necessarily erasing classical imperialist boundaries, Hardt and Negri reject the cycle-based interpretations of history and capitalist development, for such views tend to naturalize systems and practices and also to reduce humans to helpless subjects without agency. In such a view, decolonization effectively decentered the classical distributions of production as the masses of the Third World (a notion that no longer applies now), led by modernist elites, were brutally integrated into the global wage system. The rise of a postcolonial world forced the world market to rethink its assumptions, because older categories, born out of the obsolete imperialist model, are no longer applicable in a postmodern space in which the object of proletarianized labor is as immaterial as life itself. Despite the radically new environment of Empire, however, the authors remind us that capitalism still depends on the nation-state, although such a state appears in an altogether different guise.

The authors rely on Foucault's concepts of the *dispostif* and the diagram to move beyond a modern disciplinary regime of multiple, but discrete, subjectivities to a "society of control" in which modern institutions have collapsed and have produced mutating and hybrid subjectivities, and they apply the same principle to nation-states. Nation-states are no longer situated along a continuum of development, but within the smooth surface of Empire with its various degrees of development. (This is probably a rephrasing of what is commonly known as "uneven development.") An imperial world of similar social segmentations is thus administered through local autonomies and biopolitical control, for nations that cannot control their communication, cultural, and educational systems, and even worse, those that don't possess the nuclear bomb, cannot make serious claims to sovereignty. What, then, is to be done? The immediate strategy is to invert the conservative tirade against big government and use it for communist—not anarchist—ends.[84]

The authors state matter-of-factly that there is no subjectivity outside Empire (as if subjectivities had ever existed outside the world, whether conceived in material or immaterial terms). Empire is a nonplace where the political is beyond measure, immeasurable, as is (exploited) labor, a place where the "being-against" of the multitude is expressed only in "nomadism and miscegenation," the legal and clandestine crossings of boundaries. Thus migrants (and this is something with which Edward Said would probably agree) are the real postcolonial heroes, who help subvert the illusory claims of nation-states.[85] The solution for the crisis cannot be resolved outside one's being (the outer spaces of modern sovereignty no longer being available), but must be rethought as a solipsistic move, an "ontological human dimension that tends to become universal." Resistance takes place on the terrain of communication, linguistic articulations, and meanings—in other words, the struggle is over the shaping of subjectivities, as Foucault had repeatedly emphasized. Only the generative force of a hybrid, cyborgian biopower can demystify "the overbearing power of bourgeois metaphysics" and replace the corrupt institutions and psychopathologies of capitalism.[86]

Out of postmodernity's immanent labor will rise the "earthly city" (not to be confused with the "city of God") attesting to the multitude's (not the masses') "material mythology of reason." Yet the question remains: How does one mobilize a multitude of irreducible singularities into a single coherent political project? In a clever conceptual move that restates Marx's basic tenets in postmodernist terms, the authors identify the goal of this revolution as a global citizenship that allows the multitude to reexpropriate space and establish a "new cartography," together with a "social wage and guaranteed income" to all citizens. (Because in its postmodern, horizontal, and collective immateriality, labor can longer be individually measured or accurately quantified, it only makes sense to compensate the entire social body of workers.) At the same time, the multitude must also reappropriate its communication systems and liberate them from capitalist colonization. Having taken these steps, the multitude finally merges with machines in a system of self-regulation and control and, thus (re)constituted, is transformed into a "posse" of "social workers" (as distinct from professional and mass workers) bent on opposing capitalist exploitation. But again, how such ephemeral cyborgs unite is left answered. To conclude, the authors go back to praise the democratic and insurrectional spirit of the Wobblies and the joyous brand of early communism practiced by St. Francis of Assisi.[87]

Thus, this impressively researched and wide-ranging book ends with hypermodern speculations about the future, a *Matrix*-like vision that presents liberation in the elusive world of the virtual. It proposes a manifesto that seems to give radical content to computer technology (and the subjectivities that arise from this mode of communication) and loads the immature dreams of suburban computer wizards and Silicon Valley entrepreneurs with prophetic destiny. In tune with the times, the book does away with the old terminology of the Left, spends a great deal of time renaming the world ("multitude," "posse," etc.), but fails to live up to its claim of offering an interpretation of the real that supersedes the more solidly grounded theories of Marx or even Foucault's irreducible and nontransferable subversive practices. Dismissing the value and resiliency of communal traditions, the authors are totally incapacitated by their own brand of unreflective Eurocentrism and cannot imagine models of a human future outside the boundaries of the very cultures they accuse in the first place. Thus, rather incredibly, the United States Constitution (the outcome of a revolution dismissed by Hobsbawm and French revolutionaries as a local bourgeois dispute),[88] American radical workers, an American academic, and—to add some geographical representation—St. Francis of Assisi hold the keys to global human emancipation. Only a powerful Western institution could have marketed the book as a manifesto for all humanity without somehow feeling conscious about its claims.

Now I want to go back to question of Islamic fundamentalism partly because it is one of the rare instances (or is it the only one?) in which a non-Western movement is presented as an act of refusal of modernity. The authors could have spent more time on this issue, particularly because Islam—as I mentioned earlier—is still described in the same terms long applied to non-Europeans after 1492.[89] A few years before the publication of *Empire*, Bobby Sayyid made a similar argument, but he did it not to erase Islam by inserting it within a larger Eurocentric scheme, but to affirm its singularity and defend its difference.[90] Reflecting on the "hauntology" that conflates Muslims with ghosts in the Western imagination, and finding the recent voluminous scholarship on Islam and Islamic fundamentalist repetitively empirical, Sayyid sets out to articulate a "conceptual narrative" that would explain the persistent refusal of Islamists to accept the universality of the Eurocentric project.

For Sayyid, the need to "conceptualize fundamentalism, not just as journalistic slogan, but as an analytical category," is all the more urgent, since the dominant research identifying a series of structural deficiencies that opened up spaces for Islamism has failed to account for the specificity of the trend it seeks to understand. The control of women's bodies is used as a unifying metaphor for Islamic fundamentalism, but Sayyid uses Foucault's notion of "governmentality" to argue that the control of bodies, in one way or another, male or female, is what (modern?) governments are designed to do. Likewise, fundamentalism is invoked as a style that is specific to Islamists (and other religious groups), but Sayyid reminds the reader that what passes for fundamentalism is often "dogmatism," an attribute that is equally shared by the most radical liberals. The meaning of fundamentalism as a differentiated category in the sense implied in current literature collapses when it appears as part of what Richard Rorty termed "our final vocabulary." Like socialists, nationalists, and postmodern bourgeois liberals, Islamists simply place their identities at the center of their political practice.[91]

Pointing to what Leonard Binder refers to as the aporia in Said's work—specifically, the negation of Islam in his project of demystifying the discursive functions of Orientalism—and recognizing the well-intentioned attempts to pluralize the Muslim experience, Sayyid insists that an Islam that retains its singular universality still "needs to be theorized." Looking for usable theoretical models, he quickly tests Saussurean linguistics (the signifier/signified binary) and Barthes's notion of "polysemy" ("the possibility that a signifier can be reattached in different contexts") before he settles on Lacan's metaphor of the "quilting point," or "crucial nodal point," stretched by Islamists to the thin, but irreducible, function of the "master signifier" to which "other signifiers refer."[92]

The transformation of Islam from a "crucial nodal point" to a "master signifier" in Muslim societies is the result of the abrupt collapse of the institution of the caliphate (despite its political weakness) as "the nodal point around which a global Muslim identity was structured" and the triumph of Kemalism on 3 March 1924. An imagined community (Sayyid finds Anderson's concept useful, but not applicable in the case of [pre-colonial] Islam) was now replaced by a nationalism that necessitated first the Orientalization of Islam in order to dismiss and outlaw its manifestations in favor of a modernization that imposed the mimicking of European cultural traditions as the only national policy. Modernization and secularism meant that Islam had to be de-Orientalized, defined as a "religion," and privatized. Thus, a hegemonic Kemalism best describes the condition of the Muslim in the postcaliphal, postcolonial period. What Sayyid calls the "Pahlavist strategy"—the de-Islamizing and de-Semitizing of Iran into a glorious Aryan race—including Nasser Egyptianism after the 1967 defeat, Algeria's anti-FIS "Mediterraneanness," and the Baathist "Mesopotamianism" in Iraq, are different manifestations of this tendency. "The Kemalist construction of Islam turned it into a metaphor for primitivism, for tradition, for anti-modernity." Yet by decentering Islam, Kemalism unsettled and disseminated it into the general culture, "where it became available for reinscription" as a new political force. Among the various possibilities of contestation, only Islamism seems to have succeeded in posing a formidable challenge to this already exhausted ideological simulacrum.[93]

The failure of the discourses of liberalism and socialism to contest Kemalism successfully is that, like Kemalism, they, too, are organized around the principle of a modernity, which presupposes the superiority of Western cultural traditions. Since many scholars, using all sorts of empirical data, have argued that Islamism is a "modern" phenomenon (in the sense that its discourse has no antecedents in the precolonial period), Sayyid wonders why would Islamists who proclaim their opposition to the West adopt a cultural practice that is indissociably connected to Western history. One must remember that in Kemal Ataturk's nationalist project, modernity and Westernization were conflated and made practically indistinguishable. Relying on Stuart Hall and Agnes Heller, Sayyid shows that the project of modernity emerged from fragmented European entities to create a unified notion of Europeanness, which was later broadened into the West. Thus, the West, as a master signifier fixing "a variety of discursive chains," was differentiated and made unique by its modernity, against which the rest of the world looks hopelessly antimodern. "Modernity positions itself as a ruptural moment which divides history in two."[94]

Sayyid's analysis ventures into difficult terrain when he reads anti-Western Islamist discourses as part of the periphery's contribution to the project of postmodernism, whose goal, Sayyid thinks, is to decenter the West. One may agree that Islamists are interested in replacing a global, overreaching metanarrative with their own metanarratives, but that conclusion might suggest that Muslims and Islamists are aware of and reacting to the same cultural and symbolic effects that have led Western academics and philosophers to articulate a notion of and express the desirability for postmodernity as a social project. Like the limitations of Said's critique to which he alludes, Sayyid assumes the actual decentering of the West from a reading of theories and philosophies that have not displaced the global balance of power from its colonial centers. Although Sayyid's attempt to link Islamism with postmodernism is not entirely convincing, his observation that Khomeinism signals the final crisis of Kemalism is quite illuminating. It is significant that Khomeini is unique among the major Muslim reformers in not being anxious to legitimize his program by relying on "Western discourse." In fact, his remarkable disregard for Western citations is what may have turned him into a powerful force.[95]

If many scholars of Islamic fundamentalism have tried to discredit Islamism by dismissing it as a modernist project, it is because this self-serving verdict allows them to rearticulate the universality and unsurpassability of the West. From Sayyid's account, one realizes that by making "genealogical claims for elements of Islamic discourse" and then asserting copyrights over them, these scholars also paradoxically essentialize the West into the contradictory position of being both particular and universal.

Aside from this, I am not sure I agree with Sayyid's definition of Eurocentrism as "the project that seeks to recenter the West, a project that is only possible when the West and the center are no longer considered to be synonymous." Such a definition presupposes the gradual erosion of Western hegemony Sayyid believes to have taken place in the last two or three decades, an assessment that reflects the weakness of relying solely on discursive practices and not paying enough attention to the material conditions in which such discourses are generated. Still, Sayyid is right to assert that one of the effects of Khomeini's advent and the return of Islam(ism) is to (once again?) provincialize the West and finally to give substance to Fanon's (premature) statement that "the European game has finally ended" and that "we must find something different."[96]

Sayyid uses postmodern theory to insist on the irreducible difference of Islam. Roxanne Euber adopts the different strategy of showing that even the most fundamentalist Islamic texts could appear as part of a "transcultural" rejection of modernity.[97] Euber argues that the "antifoundationalist," rationalist, positivist explanations of Islamic fundamentalism suffer from an inevitable ethnocentricity that can be alleviated—and the term "alleviated" should be stressed—only by recourse to a dialogic approach that presupposes Islamic fundamentalism to be motivated by more than the predictable social determinants of economics and so on—that it represents and defends a worldview that disturbs the humanist traditions of Enlightenment narratives. She thus examines concepts of transcendence and sovereignty in early fundamentalist writings and finds that, despite diverse articulations or differences between Sunnism (best represented by the Egyptian scholar Sayyid Qutb, who, incidentally, also wrote his major work in prison) and Shi'ism (best exemplified in Khomeini), earlier Islamic revivalism and twentieth-century fundamentalism converge on their rejection of the West's humanist traditions, their critique of rationalist philosophy, and their insistence on the limits of human reason.[98] To the extent they do so, such movements can be seen as engaged in a project of "reenchanting" the world.[99] Even the hard-liner Qutb's preoccupations with and critiques of modernity—however unrigorous and inconsistent—are part of a Western intellectual movement that is anxious about the limitations of the Enlightenment and its ideology of reason, supposedly conceived to enlarge the sphere of freedom and fulfillment, only to undermine that project in the end by its refusal to pay any attention to the equally crucial need for divinity. Looked at from this perspective, Qutb's agenda doesn't look idiosyncratically Islamic, but appears to be part of a transcultural concern that blurs the rigid dichotomies of Islam and West.

Hannah Arendt's diagnosis of modernity as a state of crisis—a crisis of authority and meaning resulting from the disintegration of a common and shared social vision, historically made possible and sustained by religion—is shared by Qutb, too. Her ideal city of Athens is mirrored in Qutb's Medina. For Arendt, modernity is similar to Qutb's *al-Jahiliyya*, which can change only through political action. Alasdair MacIntyre also traces the shift from shared values to what he calls "emotivism," a condition that has reduced human virtue to a series of preferences, needs, and feelings. The result is a society of strangers whose quest for personal self-fulfillment is adjudicated by an ever expanding impersonal bureaucracy. This idea is further taken up by Charles Taylor in his *Ethics of Authenticity*.

In such a new world, where people do "their own thing," social relations are debased and reduced to utilitarian and manipulative moves. For Taylor, higher forms of authenticity can be retrieved only by embracing a dialogic approach.

Richard John Neuhaus, in *The Naked Public Square*, states that religion is, in fact, necessary for the protection of freedom and for keeping the ever lurking forces of extremism and totalitarianism at bay. In his view, secular humanists who refuse to acknowledge the pervasive religiosity of Americans are undemocratic. In secular liberal democratic systems, citizens are empty "ciphers" whose weakness strengthens the specter of totalitarianism. Thus, he argues, reclaiming biblical traditions as a source of identity is America's only protection against total alienation. Robert Bellah, in *Habits of the Heart*, unmasks America's poverty and makes a similar call for reviving biblical traditions. Even Daniel Bell in *The Cultural Contradictions of Capitalism* shows how secularization undermines the transcendence and shared meaning necessary for the successful operation of a bourgeois society. For him, religion is the answer, for "where religion ends, cults appear."[100]

Thus, Euber shows that Qutb and many prominent Western scholars agree that modernity entails a profound loss of meaning and authority, the decay of morality, and the annihilation of a sustaining and sustainable community and that such features, even in Max Weber's view, cancel the promises of the Enlightenment and threaten humanity with the prospect of a dark age, darker than has ever occurred. Islamic fundamentalism appears as part of a global attempt to address the failure of the Enlightenment and can be dismissed "at our own political peril."[101]

If we take the three books discussed above as different poles of thinking about Muslim Otherness, we realize how difficult it is to articulate a non-Eurocentric agenda that truly accounts for the Muslims' irreducible cultural differences. Negri and Hardt work out of a classic liberal tradition—notwithstanding their revolutionary thesis—collapsing all differences into a global hypernarrative of emancipation. The Muslim god—like all other gods—is excluded in their vision of the world's liberated "multitude." Sayyid comes close to overcoming this conceptual hurdle by repositioning Islamism as part of the postmodern retaliatory event, one that rejects European modernity by insisting on its own distinctness. Yet this version does not fully account for the fact that Islamism—like all modern isms—has been produced by the West. Islamism has no pure identity and makes sense only within the larger context of Eurocentric hegemony. A few months after 9/11, Avishai Margalit and Ian Buruma gave a hint about what might have caused violent reactions against the West throughout the twentieth century:

Oswald Spengler warned in 1933 (of all years) that the main threats to the Occident came from "colored peoples" (*Farbigen*). He prophesied, not entirely without reason, huge uprisings of enraged peoples in the European colonies. He also claimed that after 1918 the Russians had become "Asiatic" again, and that the Japanese Yellow Peril was about to engulf the civilized world. More interesting, however, was Spengler's view that the ruling white races (*Herrenvölker*) were losing their position in Europe. Soon, he said, true Frenchmen would no longer rule France, which was already awash with black soldiers, Polish businessmen, and Spanish farmers. The West, he concluded, would go under because white people had become soft, decadent, addicted to safety and comfort. As he put it: "Jazz music and nigger dances are the death march of a great civilization."[102]

The failure to account for the impact of capitalism and colonialism turns the entire "clash" of values into discursive contestations, and this doesn't explain much. Euber comes closer to an explanation by situating Islamic fundamentalism into a larger continuum of resistance to modernity, but this account also is silent on capitalism and its effects. Hardt and Negri take on capitalism, but erase the world's thick cultural diversities. What, then, is a Western(ized) academic/liberator to do?

The answer clearly is to question the West's irresistible penchant for universalist ideologies, mantras, and beliefs, whether couched in the language of Christianity, the philosophies of the Enlightenment, or the doctrines of free-market capitalism and democracy. But how does a Westerner step outside a social imaginary that has been made so fundamental to the construction of his or her own identity through the processes of education and acculturation? Perhaps minorities (i.e., historically oppressed peoples whose foundational narratives are different) who are tenuously situated in the Western magma could accomplish some of this rather extraordinary feat. For privileged Western whites to escape their dominant imaginary and write about others, they must have a different memory, one that would allow them to see through their own cultural complacencies. That is the case with Sophie Bessis. Indeed, I can think of no recent work that has captured the effect of modern globalizing trends since 1492 as has Bessis's book on the history of the West's supremacy.[103] Very few people are as ideally located to examine this almost treacherous subject.

A Jew born in Tunisia, Bessis experienced Otherness as a girl in the French colonial education system, which privileged French girls and constantly reminded Arabs and Jews of their lower social status. The French girls who took their superiority for granted have become, in Bessis's mind, emblematic of the general attitude of the West and of Westerners in general—their "tranquil certitude" reflected in even the most mundane of gestures. This certitude structures everything to the point one might speak of a supremacist culture.[104] To be sure, the West is not the only culture to use violence, nor are its nations the only ones to do so, but they are the only ones in history to have produced such elaborate theories of legitimation, and much of this process happens outside of religion—other cultures' classical excuse—and within a universal secularism. The author recognizes that she is part of this Western tradition, but she also knows that she carries other memories as well.

How did this consciousness of Europe's natural superiority that Bessis experienced as a schoolgirl in Tunis come about? Whence this division of West and East? Surely not with the emergence of Islam, for the Byzantine Empire maintained closer ties with the Muslim Ommayads and Abbassids than with the Christian kingdom of the West. Al-Andalus, with its Arab, Jewish, and Islamic mixtures, was too complex to allow for such clean-cut separations. Moreover, the cleavage between Christianity and Islam was not the only "religious caesura" of the Middle Ages—the schisms within Christianity were almost as serious as the differences between Islam and Christianity.

Bessis chooses 1492 as the founding date for a new era of European modernity and its emerging myths, myths all based on a series of convenient exclusions. While the Europeans were undertaking their genocidal conquest of the New World, European intellectuals were remaking history at home, tracing a direct genealogical line back to the Greco-Roman world, allowing them to forget and erase the manner in which Greek thought came into Spain, to forget how the rationalist approach of separating theology from philosophy was first worked out by Muslims and was best exemplified in the work of the great medieval scholar Ibn Rushd, or Averroes. Not only were Muslims and Jews expelled from Spain by a series of edicts, but, as Bessis recalls, Spain was the first country to introduce the deadly concept of *limpieza de sangre,* purity of blood, thereby making converts ineligible for Spanishness, the latter being the exclusive right of the elite race. Thus, Christianity was racialized, an act that paved the way for the world's first genocidal war against Indians. The whole of Europe followed Spain. Even Las Casas, a defender of Indians, inaugurated the notion of the white man's burden, since he saw the defenseless Indians as children in need of guidance from elders.

Having decimated the native populations, Europe turned to Africa for slave labor. To be sure, Europe didn't inaugurate slavery—the Arabs had done it before and would do it after (even today, in some places). Arabs also developed a crude racist mentality that saw blacks as inferior. But chattel slavery was more efficient, more intense, and affected Africa negatively for centuries. An antiblack discourse emerged, joining biblical myths and racist assumptions as legitimate reasons for the slavery of hapless blacks. The physical cleansing of Europe, the genocidal wars against Indians, and the enslavement of Africa would now be supported by an intellectual mission that sought to remove all traces of Otherness from the emerging purity of Europe. These are the founding principles of globalization still operating today.

Despite its claims, the Enlightenment, with its secular assumptions supposed to dispel the prejudices of religion, solidified Euro-American supremacy by inventing a universal being—male and white—who, although imbued with the egalitarian spirit of new philosophies, refused to extend it to blacks and Indians, since that would hamper the process of colonization so indispensable to the supremacy of the West. America's Indians had to be fought and expelled (even after their rights had been recognized by the likes of Jefferson) because they refused to surrender to a nation determined to execute its "manifest destiny." Almost without self-reflection, white Europeans were now deciding the fate of the entire human race, a situation that would change only after World War II and the decolonization of native peoples, when the Other erupted back into the West's consciousness.

By the end of the nineteenth century and the beginning of the twentieth, physical anthropology, philosophy (Hegel), sociology, and history had established a racial order in which the Caucasian occupies the central place, with other races being ranked according to their degree of separation from the white race. Egypt was "delocalized." Only in the mid-twentieth century was Cheikh Anta Diop able to force a debate on the Africanness of Egypt. By now, the medieval cult of *limpieza de sangre* had evolved into a new science of racism, allowing Europeans to embark on yet another semi-genocidal project of colonization, one in which all of Africa would suffer major population losses. This process of colonization was caused partly by the necessity to get rid of Europe's displaced rural populations. In a little more than a century (the nineteenth), more than sixty million Europeans, or about 14 percent of the population in 1914, left the continent. Once again, the Enlightenment's secular moral philosophy was superseded or cancelled by economic interests and Europe's colonial mission.[105]

Even after World War II, with its large-scale atrocities, European and American students continued to read textbooks in which the supremacy of European/Western culture was naturally assumed. Not even the revolutionary Communist movements—inspired by the tenets of the Enlightenment—were conscious enough to realize their paternalistic relations with others and deeply embedded belief in their own cultural superiority. Aimé Césaire knew this well when he tended his resignation to the French Communist party (PCF) in 1956, charging them with the same colonialist and racist tendencies they condemned in the bourgeoisie. By endowing the Western proletariat with a messianic role—and thus exonerating it from the West's historic culpability in the violent mission of colonialism, which benefited all layers of Western society, albeit differently—and by erasing the "cultural matrix" of Marxism and Leninism, Communism became, in effect, a reactionary cultural movement.[106]

The horrors of Nazism, universally repudiated, are the culmination of this long history of racism and the West's inability to forsake its violent doctrines. Bessis does not want to "banalize" evil, to use Hannah Arendt's famous expression, but to show that evil had long been banalized. After the war, racism was discredited, and such ideologies were left to right-wing movements. For the most part, Others became backward or primitive. But the process of decolonization upset the West's relationship with its Others and, for the first time since the Renaissance, the West's certainties were challenged (although the West's power remains, as Hobsbawm has shown, unchallenged). In light of these changes, Bessis finds the last quarter of the twentieth century hard to read: Is it a form of interregnum, after which the West will resume its full powers? Or does it augur the dawn of a chaotic future in which the West's powers will be diminished?[107]

Although many Westerners are sympathetic to Third World revolutions, as I have indicated—now that the poor are the only ones left carrying the torch of freedom, since the Western proletariat has by and large been bourgeoisified—Western progressives cannot conceive of revolutions outside of European/Enlightenment references, as the case of Latin America exemplifies. Very often, Western youth cherished their "doubles" in many Third World guerillas (such as Che Guevara), even as they believed they were embracing the Other.[108]

During this period, the dominant economic model was based on the notion of stages of development, hence the institution of foreign aid and the race to catch up with the only conceivable model of Western capitalist modernity. Unable to adopt a pluralistic perspective, of imagining different ways of entering modernity, alternative visions were "folklorized." In fact, Bessis sees the West's relegitimation of its history and universalism as a backlash against the Other's emancipation and quest for freedom and equality. As we have seen, in Europe, colonialism is now being exonerated and reconsidered as an option to solve intractable Third World problems.

Confronting the breakdown of order and occasional butcheries in poor countries, such renewed assessments begin to make even more sense to white Euro-Americans long accustomed to their benevolent universal mission. Colonialism is seen to have inaugurated order in precolonial societies and as a benign, largely unprofitable venture. Once again, a selective use of history is deployed to absolve the West and to renew its imperialist energies, badly needed in an unpredictable future. Within this climate, a new discourse of relativism is emerging to show that the West (paradoxically abjuring its loftier universalist humanism) is neither better nor worse than the Aztecs, Incas, or the various African, machete-wielding tribes. If anything, colonial humanism had emancipated and cured the indigenous people, even though the schooling rates and health conditions in postcolonial nations in Asia and Africa increased exponentially after independence. This backlash could be explained only by the West's anxiety in the postcolonial period, one in which Westerners themselves make up no more than 20 percent of the world's population (and that percentage is shrinking rapidly, as I mention in the Preface), an anxiety that transforms the nations outside its borders into potential hordes of immigrants or the "Yellow Peril" of old. Without direct political control, Western powers try to consolidate their hegemony in the economic sphere and, as always, the West continues to be incapable of imagining a world in which its culture is not central.[109]

Economically, with a few gray areas and exceptions, the World Bank has now divided the world into an industrialized North and an underdeveloped South. Former Communist states in Europe are quickly embraced as part of this North, as is the Russia of Peter the Great (not Ivan the Terrible), of Saint Petersburg, not Moscow, and not the Russia of Stalin, the last Oriental despot. Asia, however, continues to be problematic, and Japan often appears in the literature of development as an unnatural case that needs repeated explanations. Although anti-Americanism is real in many European quarters, it still doesn't change the perceived unity of this North. Only the South threatens and unites the sometimes disparate cultures of the North.[110]

Meanwhile, the South, with its mimetic postcolonial elites who have conflated development with civilization, continues to bet on catching up with the West. Despite the ravages of capitalism (or globalization), their goal remains "the emergence of an industrial society, salaried and urban, founded on systems of accumulation analogous to those Europe had experienced through its own industrial revolution." Yet such a model prescribed for the South occludes Europe's long phase of accumulation marked by two centuries of trade, an agricultural revolution, slow demographic growth (compared with that of today's sub-Saharan Africa, for instance), unlimited options for immigration, and Western power projected across the globe.[111]

Moreover, half a century of development policies hasn't altered the world's geography of wealth. To be sure, as heavy industries move south, the percentage of the world's commerce has grown and expected to grow further in a few select zones (China, Southeast Asia, India, Brazil). Indeed, South Korea ranks second (after Japan) in creativity in terms of registered patents per capita. But these delocalized industries, the cause of recurring anxieties in the North, have taken nothing from the North's supremacy, which has already moved to the third stage of industrialization (high tech) and a service economy that is more profitable and less labor intensive. Indeed, most factories in the South are owned by Western financiers, and their headquarters are still mainly located in the West. The global commercial architecture is still very much the same as it was in the nineteenth century, a fact noted by Hobsbawm. Europe is still the second exporter of textile products, and since the passage of NAFTA, Canada has received twice the amount invested in Mexico. Still, unemployment has become a structural feature of the North's economy. Although the North has opted for finance capitalism, labor is more expendable and more mobile. With capital fluctuations and declining rates of profit leading to cuts in labor costs, globalization has created pockets of poverty hitherto unknown. In any case, if the threat of cultural hegemony is left aside for now, globalization is reviled and critiqued by many for a variety of inconsistent reasons, and each nation, organization, or even politician has a different reason to blame it.[112]

The South, home to about 80 percent of humanity, continues to survive in mostly precarious conditions. The oil crises of the 1970s were unevenly felt in the North (U.S. oil companies supported high prices, but Europe and Japan were badly affected) and were devastating to the South (with the exception, of course, of oil producers). Oil revenues encouraged projects of industrialization and, in the case of Saudi Arabia and Kuwait, helped fund Islamist movements inspired by Wahhabism. Southern nations, investing mostly in "white elephant" projects and arms, were forced to borrow ever larger sums of money from oil money deposited in Western banks and promptly recycled them back in the form of contracts. Western financial structures were thus directly feeding "massive corruption" in poor countries, a situation that became untenable in the early 1980s, for example in 1982, when Mexico defaulted on its loans. The direct flows of money into the West in the form of debt financing (which surpassed two thousand billion dollars in 1998) and the imposition of structural adjustment policies on such nations meant that they were forever trapped in servile and totally dependent and hopeless conditions. This is what a liberal globalization means now, Bessis argues—merely a recipe for more disaster.[113]

The West's conquest continues through trade treaties and other economic policies. Coercing poor countries to sign and adhere to self-defeating treaties (such as the 1995 WTO agreement to protect intellectual property) while protecting its members with subtle protectionist measures, the rich North undermines the South's agricultural potential by dumping its surplus agricultural products, such as cereal, meat, and corn, on its markets. The entire planet, in effect, has turned into a supermarket for rich countries, while the North's consumer patterns have by now become scandalous and are perceived in the South as posing a mortal danger not just to their cultures, but also to the physical health of the planet. "We now know that none of the elements that guarantee life on earth has unlimited capacities for regeneration," comments Bessis. Yet the North continues to devour the planet's resources in shocking quantities: By the end of the twentieth century, the North was consuming 60 percent of the world's energy, 75 percent of its metals, 85 percent of its wood, and 60 percent of all agricultural products produced on earth. The North was home to three-quarters of the world's automobiles, produced three-quarters of the world's solid waste and unleashed 54 percent of the world's carbon dioxide. This situation has turned the West into a culture of banal opulence, one that is simultaneously a fascinating and horrifying spectacle. And yet, almost no will is left in the West to question this model of civilization. The health of nations is measured by levels of consumption, and to question this would make one look archaic, or perhaps, one might add, dangerous.[114]

The bill, Bessis warns, will be coming due, for unless we surrender to some impending catastrophe, we are forced to rethink the paradigms that have created this disastrous situation. The South, enduring all sorts of political and economic constraints imposed on it by an opportunist North (lack of to technology, dumping, the West's protectionist policies, etc.), is required to keep its people chained at home. Never have such draconian restrictions been imposed on human movement. While Europeans move to other countries without visas, as one Algerian woman wrote a French consulate, the poor are not even allowed the privilege of travel. (Because of visa restrictions, countries such as Morocco have become a vast prison house for most people. Only satellite TV and to some extent the Internet allow people to connect with the outside world.)[115] Those who used to be called "whites" can travel and live anywhere, whereas those who don't assimilate can barely leave their native countries. Although the number of non-European immigrants in the West is comparatively low and decreasing (everywhere less than 10 percent of the population),[116] the repeated alarms about the "browning" of Euro-American societies makes it sound as if the bastion of civilization is under siege. The West's ambivalence and contradictions are just startling: liberalism mixed with xenophobia, freedom with repression.

Is it surprising, then, that literalist approaches to religion are making a comeback, although world attention seems to have singled out Islam for this troubling trend? This resurgence of extremism allows barbarism to be located elsewhere and the West to dress itself in the familiar language of its unquestionable universalism, and hence its natural superiority; for the Other cannot exist unless he or she reflects back the West's assumptions. Even naturalization and citizenship haven't improved the lives of people with exotic names and different skin colors in Europe, and their status is more or less comparable to newly arrived immigrants. As Cornelius Castoriadis suggested, in such a climate, essential Otherness is simply nonconvertible.[117]

No, in such a confusing context, it is not surprising that Islam has emerged as the West's worst fear and main enemy. It is the only movement left to assert its difference. And despite all disclaimers to the contrary, a new syllogism equating Islamism with its larger cultural matrix of Islam has turned the latter into the ultimate threat to the West's hegemony in the future. What gives Islamism its fascistic dimensions is not necessarily the content of its ideology, but its internationalist scope, operating as it does throughout the world's Islamic communities (*Dar al-Islam*). Islam's universalist message puts it into direct conflict with Western ideology and thus seriously threatens its uncontested hegemony. Transnational, much as Communism was, Islamism has the added effect of turning every Muslim into a potential threat. And so Islam, once again, has been held responsible for underdevelopment, oppression, and all sorts of other evils, while writers who antagonize Muslims, such as Salman Rushdie, the Bangladeshi Taslima Nasreen, and V. S. Naipul have become household names.[118]

Bessis reassures Muslims that they are not the only ones to be thus essentialized. When things go wrong in Asia or Africa, some Oriental trait or ethnicity is used to explain it. Others are measured by their degree of closeness from the center, although their radical differences are happily ennobled and relegated to museums, as Claude Lévi-Strauss suggested in his *Tristes Tropiques*, only after their live cultures are annihilated. Looks count, too, and three-piece suits are more reassuring than traditional garbs. (After the defeat of the Taliban in Afghanistan, the new government convened in Berlin, took a picture in dark suits, and looked perfectly legitimate.) A de-Arabized and re-Berberized Maghreb, for instance, is a more desirable Other for France. This gesture of appropriation has taken on interesting dimensions in recent years. Saint Augustine is now considered a mere *pied noir*, a French settler in Algeria, not a Berber. Judaism, relentlessly persecuted over a period of two thousand years, has now been officially attached to the West in the common (but charged) denomination "Judeo-Christian." The vilification of Jews and their representation in a long literary tradition as an Oriental Other (even when inhabiting the metropolitan ghetto) has been rehabilitated at the expense of Muslims, who have now come to see both Jews and Christians as conspiring against their freedom and sovereignty. Meanwhile, many Jews themselves have embraced the West's supremacist ideology by seeing Israel as a Western country somehow (mis)placed in the Orient, which explains why Oriental Jews have been relegated to a lower social status in Israel.[119] In any case, Western ideology produces essentialist views of the Other, either by condemning different traditions to barbarism or by exonerating their offensive practices in the name of culturalism. Yet the West denies others the advantage of change, since only the West is capable of generating such a progressive process.[120]

Islam as difference is now being manifested in variety of cultural and religious practices. Peruvian guerilla fighters of the Shining Path, Afrocentric historians such as Cheikh Anta Diop, who want to reverse Eurocentrism by placing Africa at the heart of human civilization, Asianist philosophies of the last few decades, autarkic economic policies, name changes from Christian to African ones, and Islamism are all attempts by the South to resist Western domination (perhaps born out of an endemic fear of loss) and to fight back and restore their long-lost autonomy by rewriting history and reconstructing glorious pasts.

Yet this restoration of the past, particularly among Arab nationalists and Islamists, has largely obscured the goal of this undertaking. For every criticism leveled against Muslims, there is an answer from the past, a reference to some golden age of early caliphs or the dazzling culture of al-Andalus. As is the case with other cultures, these are all reactive reflexes justifying a paranoid style of politics that is ultimately paralyzing and counterproductive. If the West is suspected of plotting Malthusian policies in the Third World, people will adopt birthist (*nataliste*) ideologies and accuse the West of spreading the HIV virus—manufactured in U.S. labs— in their countries. Arab secular nationalists will suspect the West of implanting Islamist movements to undermine the Arab promise, while East Asians, responding to the crisis of 1997, accuse Jewish and Wall Street financiers of sabotaging their national economies. Meanwhile, school books in Arab countries exalt the past and vilify the West. It's almost as if by hating the West, the postcolonial poor affirm their existence.[121]

The question always is how to escape the tyranny of ancestors without Othering oneself. Bessis is right to find the answer for Arabs in the promise of a progressive Islam,[122] but could people move beyond their reactive reflexes if the West continues to cast its long shadow on the world? Three days after 9/11, Bessis explained in an interview that since the West's universal ideals have, in truth, benefited only the West's ruling classes, nonsecular Others are embracing their alternative forms of religion-based universalism, because they are now painfully realizing that the West will never allow them to be full partners in its own universalist agenda, which is at once utopian and discriminatory.[123]

In such circumstances, I would argue, it is not up to the Senegalese and Bolivians to provincialize the West, but for Westerners to resist their globalizing impulse or question it in others. A collective movement to freedom must emanate simultaneously across cultures in the process of deglobalizing economies and ideologies and reestablishing reciprocal dialogic relations based on the belief that our cultures and points of view are unalterably provincial or ethnocentric. As Peter McLaren puts it, "In a world of global capitalism we need counterhegemonic global alliances through cultural and political contact in the form of critical dialogue," for the kind of liberal pluralism often advocated by Western "democracies" is often "the politics of white supremacist patriarchal capitalism." Only a "postcolonial multiculturalism that moves beyond the ludic, metrocentric focus on identities as hybrid and hyphenated assemblages of subjectivity"[124] can reinvest human civilization with hope. Such a project, however, entails a vigorous notion of culture, one that accounts for genuine, inscrutable differences while totally committing the world's people to open and nonhegemonic interactions. In other words, the best antidote to all universalisms, particularly the ones that have marked world history in the post-Andalusian age, is a world of strong cultures and religions.

CHAPTER 6

Provincialisms Now

We need to find in "primitivism," whatever it may or may not be,
something other than the image of our fears.
   —Clifford Geertz, "The Last Humanist"

Indian religion appears to many of us as the only ultimate salvation
for the Indian people.
   —Vine Deloria, Jr., *Custer Died for Your Sins.*

None of the European universalist ideologies that shaped world history in the last half millennium had been conceived by or for non-European, non-Christian or Judeo-Christian peoples. Renaissance humanism,
whose figures counted the likes of Erasmus, Rabelais, Montaigne, and
Shakespeare, which fostered skepticism about one's own views and took
multiple rationalities and cultural pluralities for granted, was much closer
in spirit to the multicultural global civilization that many of us aspire to
than is the dogmatic culture of modernity that arose in the post-Andalusian period, characterized, as Stephen Toumlin explained in his insightful
study, by the search for general principles, abstractions, the privileging of
formal logic and rationality.[1] Renaissance humanists relied on argumenta-
tion, not proofs, on rhetoric, and on practical philosophy to make sense of
the world. Their narratives may have been secularized, especially when
knowledge of exotic cultures became available, but many Christians accepted the humanity of their conquered natives. These traditions, however, were eclipsed in the seventeenth century with the rise of Cartesian
philosophy and the application of scientific thinking to natural and social
life. Descartes's dogmatic, solipsistic rational thinking replaced Montaigne's skeptical humanism, severed emotion from reason, and fostered

"moral escapism."[2] As Fernand Braudel has noted, the freedoms available to the poor and the marginalized in the Middle Ages were simply criminalized or pathologized, and hence, persecuted and banished, in the early modern period:

A certain form of liberty, at least in the physical sense, was open to a peasant who fled from his lord to find another who was less oppressive, or to take refuge in the town. The same was true of a soldier in search of a recruiting officer, or of an immigrant leaving for better wages or for the New World and the illusion of a better life. There were also the unemployed, the inveterate vagrants, the beggars, the mental defectives, the handicapped and the thieves—kept alive without work by charity or crime, and therefore in some senses free.

All these people, protected hitherto under the shadow of the Almighty, became in the seventeenth century the enemies of a society that was urban, already capitalist, attached to order and efficiency, and shaping the State in the same spirit to the same ends.[3]

Although the emergence of rationality and scientific thinking was long attributed to the salutary effects of improving social conditions, Toumlin suggests that the opposite is true, that such intellectual trends appeared at a time of unending religious wars and political upheavals, profound economic crises, and natural disasters in European history. The citizen—the "atom" or "particle" of politics—became the new social unit in the state.[4] The Catholic Church, relying on the same intellectual methods popularized by the rationalists, hardened its stance into "dogmas" circulated in manuals. Toumlin's recontextualization of the rise of modernity in the seventeenth century and his insistence that it was no coincidence that Descartes wrote most of his work during the period of the Thirty Years' War (1618–48), shows that modernity had two "distinct beginnings," as was later suggested by Negri and Hardt in *Empire*: the spirit of inquiry, toleration, skepticism, and reasonableness that characterized the work of Renaissance humanists and the scientific methods, quest for certainty, and irrefutable proofs derived from abstract principles espoused by seventeenth-century rationalists.

Out of this emerged the modern world with its nation-states (consolidated by the Peace of Westphalia) and the reconfiguration of social classes along more horizontal lines. While the state's concern was now stability, intellectuals such as Descartes and Leibniz consumed their energies in search of universal principles that transcend history and cultural partic-

ularities. A new "common sense" based on the Cartesian dichotomy of separating reason from emotions emerged and, until very recently, was rarely
questioned. The rationalists' view, based on unproved assumptions and
half-truths, would become the "scaffolding of Modernity."[5] Scientific views
of nature were used to justify economic exploitation, racism, and sexism at
home and then to export these practices to other peoples in the course of
colonial conquests. A new rigid puritanical sexual code, well suited to
those who equated emotions with sex and distrusted both, was placed at
the heart of "values" wrongly deemed traditional.[6]

Max Horkheimer and Theodor W. Adorno had reached a similar
conclusion in their *Dialectic of Enlightenment*, written and published during World War II. As Toumlin also argues, the war helped erode the belief
in modern rationalism.[7] Horkheimer's and Adorno's task is to examine
why, despite the promises of the Enlightenment, humanity is "sinking into
a new kind of barbarism" and seems to be doomed to "self-destruction."
Noting that humans are devalued by capitalism even as they are being sat-
urated by goods and commodities, they conclude that "the Enlightenment
must reconsider itself, if men are not to be wholly betrayed."

Much like the twin legacies of the Renaissance and modernity, "the
Enlightenment has always aimed at liberating men from fear and establishing their sovereignty. Yet the fully enlightened earth radiates disaster triumphant. The program of the Enlightenment was the disenchantment of
the world." By leveling down everything to abstractions and calculable figures, however, Horkheimer and Adorno argue, the Enlightenment became
destructively rational and utilitarian. Consumed by bringing everything under its control, its main urge was to domesticate differences, "because the
mere idea of outsideness is the very source of fear." And since everything
must make rational sense and be objectified, "mathematical procedure became, so to speak, the ritual of thinking." Science, in such a context, "relates
to nature and man only as the insurance company in particular relates to life
and death. Whoever dies is unimportant: it is a question of ratio between
accidents and the company's liabilities." Religion and art (emotion) were
disinfected by the "cold rays" of this sunny order, while the "individual" (a
bourgeois creation who imagines friendships only as "social contact"), ham-
mered by the culture industry, is reduced to a set of abstract values and surface registers, often determined by commercial interests. In such an environment, personality "scarcely signifies anything more than shining white
teeth and freedom from body odor and emotions." The Nazi—the latest in-

carnation of the "burger"—thus becomes the perfect subject of this order, condemning to extinction all Others who embody "the negative principle" and thus obstruct the perfection of humanity.[8]

In a letter he jotted down to a friend in 1981 and published for the first time about a month after 9/11, the late prominent scholar of the Enlightenment Isaiah Berlin echoed some of these reservations about the Enlightenment and its legacy by saying that "the oceans of blood" that run through the veins of history are often caused by the unwillingness to extend truth to other beliefs and cultures. Yet it is this openness to differences that "makes people wiser, nicer, & more civilized" and "absence of it breeds irrational prejudice, hatreds, ghastly extermination of heretics and those who are different." Nothing is more destructive to human civilization than this form of intolerance. "Jesus, Socrates, John Hus of Bohemia, the great chemist Lavoisier, socialists and liberals (as well as conservatives) in Russia, Jews in Germany, all perished at the hands of 'infallible' ideologues." Berlin singles out nationalism, another feature of modern Enlightenment, as "the strongest & most dangerous force at large to-day," sustained by unexamined stereotypes of threatening Others.[9] In his cautionary message, Berlin reiterates again and again that coexisting with pluralism is the only way out of contemporary violence.

As we have seen, John Gray, whom Terry Eagleton derided as "once a swashbuckling free-marketer" who has recently "become increasingly despondent about the state of the world," extended Europe's cultural and political legacies into the realm of capitalism, particularly in its Anglo-American variety.[10] Reminding readers that prior to mid-nineteenth-century England, economic life was "embedded in society and subject to many kinds of regulation," the man who once championed Thatcherite reforms now says that free markets in the United States have contributed to social breakdown on a scale unknown in any other developed country, and only "mass incarceration" is now serving as a force of social control. The statistics are telling: The jail population of California "exceeds that of Britain and Germany combined." About 20 percent of Americans—poor and rich alike—live in gated communities. "Nearly three-quarters of all murders of children in the industrialized world occur in the U.S.," and the "U.S. has by far the highest rates of childhood suicide, homicide and firearms-related deaths of any of the world's twenty-six richest countries." No wonder the United States also has "at least one-third of the world's practising lawyers." Anglo-American free-market ideologies are not only destroying their social fabric at an accelerated pace, but they are also at odds with democratic ideals and continue to perpetuate Western imperialism under the same benevolent guise of progress:[11]

A reform of the world economy is needed that accepts a diversity of cultures, regimes and market economies as a permanent reality. A global free market belongs to a world in which western hegemony seems assured. Like all other variants of the Enlightenment Utopia of a universal civilization it presupposes western supremacy. It does not square with a pluralist world in which there is no power that can hope to exercise the hegemony that Britain, the United States and other western states possessed in the past. It does not meet the needs of a time in which western institutions and values are no longer universally authoritative. It does not allow the world's manifold cultures to achieve modernization that are adapted to their histories, circumstances and distinctive needs.[12]

Sounding like Marx, Gray argues that capitalism not only dissolves those institutions around which "social cohesion is preserved," but also "nullifies precedent, it snaps the threads of memory and scatters local knowledge. By privileging individual choice over common good it tends to make relationships revocable and provisional." This, in fact, is the paradox of the Right, which wants to "destroy what remains of the past in a vain attempt to recover it."[13]

Because the free market "has gone far towards establishing itself as the unofficial American civil religion"—represented by the Right as an extension of American values—the United States is, in fact, no longer a bourgeois society. Precariously wedged between an "underclass" and "overclass," the "anxious majority" of middle-class Americans, relying on debt and living from paycheck to paycheck, increasingly resembles "the class proletariat of nineteenth-century Europe." So different has the United States become from other Western societies that it might be more properly called a "post-western" society.[14] Indeed, barely a year after the shock of 9/11, such a vast chasm of cultural differences separated Europe and the United States that Charles Kupchan concluded an article on the "The End of the West" by stating that the "coming clash of civilizations will be not between the West and the rest but within a West divided against itself."[15]

As the most powerful legatee of the Enlightenment, Gray continues, the United States "threatens to render intractable the most difficult task of the age—that of contriving terms of peaceful and productive coexistence among peoples and regimes that will always be different." If, as Gray argues, Westernization has failed in Russia—a Eurasian state that is never-theless, more knowledgeable about the West than many Western na-tions—what hope, one might ask, is there for Muslims and others? Gray, whose book was attacked when first published, wants a "*modus vivendi* among species of capitalism that will always remain different,"[16] but not even Gray himself is willing to contemplate the notion that capitalism (not to be confused with truly balanced trade or commercial exchanges) tends toward monopolization and expansion, the sort of rigid "economic global-ization" Gray repeatedly condemns, and cannot be otherwise, as Lenin convincingly reasoned.[17]

In the end, it is an oxymoron to charge capitalism with excess, just as it would be to penalize a race car with too much speed, for the excess of profits is what drives all capitalists. To put a cap on profit is no longer to opt for capitalism. It is not merely the Anglo-American variety of capital-ism that is bad for the world's cultural diversity (as the French and many Europeans would have us believe)—capitalism *in any form* has the same ef-fect, for capitalism, born out of the same universalizing hegemonic Euro-pean modern history, is not merely an economic system, but a system of social relations, and cannot exist with precapitalist or noncapitalist forms of human relations without producing the debilitating tensions and paral-yses described in many postcolonial novels. This is why capitalism will al-ways undermine religious and cultural coexistence, since capitalism always comes charged with its European, secular origins. Capitalism, in other words, is a culture (however paradoxical this term may sound, and how-ever anticultural the system actually is), not a transcendental, transhistori-cal economic practice, and as such, it must be contained by other indige-nous or local cultural practices.

But the relationship between culture and globalization, as John Tom-linson deftly has shown, is not as easy to define as it first appears. The ef-fect of economic globalization is to produce a process of "*complex connec-tivity*" that increases "global-spatial *proximity*" by annihilating "space and time," as Marx postulated in the *Grundrisse*, or, at least, as David Harvey has suggested, by compressing them.[18] Globalization doesn't necessarily homogenize all spaces, but produces the experience of "dis-placement" and a "unicity" that accentuates social and cultural differences and protec-tionisms. Its real effect is deterritorialization,[19] the weakening of the "ties of culture to place," as new realities impinge on older habits. The clocking of time and its abstraction from space or locale, the technologization of the home, and the faith in ever more sophisticated and incomprehensible systems and technologies have turned generally self-contained premodern locales into "phantasmagoric" spaces "penetrated by the ghostly presences of distant influences," the whole eventually leading to "cultural disembedding." Tomlinson is careful to note that deterritorialization is not necessarily a bad thing, since it has the potential—at least theoretically—to unite people within a global cosmopolitan framework that can paradoxically resist the (negative) effects traditionally associated with globalization.[20]

Tomlinson traces back the globalizing impulse to the eighteenth and nineteenth centuries and rightly notes that the Eurocentric or even Orientalist view of the world implied a common humanity. "It is within this complex and often contradictory mixture of ethnocentric cultural projection, increasing awareness of, and interchange with, other cultures, 'cosmopolitan humanism,' and, importantly, the promise of the social impact of technological developments, that we can view the 'utopian' globalism of nineteenth-century radical thinkers such as Marx." He also rejects the homogenization thesis as too simplistic, one that doesn't take into account the diverse cultural responses to Western commodities, and he seems to be more comfortable with the view that cultures and cultural experiences are being reduced to shopping experiences and purchasable items and souvenirs. As the West has been deterritorialized, the provenance of commodities has become irrelevant, especially because Westerners feel no proprietary relations with what are perceived to be Western objects. This is yet another example of disembedding, which, in the West, is accompanied by a decline in self-confidence.[21]

Through the process of deterritorialization, globalization "fundamentally transforms the relationship between the *places* we inhabit and our cultural practices, experiences and identities." Although, in the expression of Marc Augé, "nonplaces" become ubiquitous sites in the globalized order (airports, hospitals, hotels, supermarkets, refugee camps, and other similar spaces), even though abstraction characterizes major aspects of this order (the case of food availability and consumption is one fascinating example), because globalization is an uneven process, reaching and affecting social classes and nations differently; deterritorialization is a "deeply ambiguous" process that entails a simultaneous process of a disembedding and reembedding, as in the case of Mexican towns (Tijuana and the small town Aguililla in Michoacán, studied by the Mexican cultural critic Néstor Garcia Canclini). Displaced traditions are replaced by the hybrid combinations

characteristic of all "border" cultures. "So deterritorialization cannot ultimately mean the end of locality, but its transformation into a more complex cultural space." Using John Thompson's notion of "mediated quasi-in-
teraction" (the feature of monological mass communication), Tomlinson
seems to argue that such media distanciate and disembody and thus rede-
fine the notion of "intimacy" while opening up "our lifeworlds to a larger
world" of moral demands as bad news inundates our living spaces.[22]

In what seems to be a promising final chapter, after stating that what
is needed is a cosmopolitan attitude, Tomlinson, arguing with John Gray
and Nicholas Garnham, concludes that "cosmopolitan people need to be
simultaneously universalists *and* pluralists." This disposition includes "an
awareness of the world as one of *many* cultural others." The cosmopolitan
"must have a grasp of the legitimate pluralism of cultures and an openness
to cultural difference. And this awareness must be reflexive—it must make
people open to questioning their *own* cultural assumptions, myths and so
on." It is an attitude that disposes us "towards an *ongoing dialogue* both
within ourselves and with distanciated cultural others." Tomlinson even
quotes Anthony Giddens's statement that "the cosmopolitan is not someone who renounces commitments—in the manner, say, of the dilettante—
but someone who is able to articulate the nature of those commitments,
and assess their implications for those whose values are different."[23]

Tomlinson likes Roland Robertson's notion of "glocalization," originally a Japanese marketing concept (*dochakuka*) designed to localize the
global, because, as he explains, "we cannot expect people to live their lives
within a moral horizon that is so distant as to become abstract." Cos-
mopolitans are thus conceived of as "ethical glocalists" inhabiting a world
without true cosmopolitan structures. How, then, to develop this cosmopolitan attitude? Urry's "aesthetic cosmopolitanism," premised on the expansion of the tourist industry and the willingness of (mostly Western)
travelers to take risks by stepping out of the tourist bubble, and his notion
of "indirect travel" through (tele)mediated experiences, is too restricted
and superficial to be practical. The first category also implies an education
that may not be available to many of the world's people or travelers. So, despairing of a world body such as the UN to foster a healthy cosmopolitanism, Tomlinson finds hope in American model of civic voluntarism and
redefines morality as *Bildung*.[24]

Trying to develop a modest optimistic view of the process of deterritorialization, Tomlinson eschews any meaningful discussion of capitalism

(having refuted such critiques in the process of building his own conclusion) and focuses on the plight of moral agency in the age of globalization. His thesis turns out to be an inquiry into the limits of sentience and of moral engagements within increasingly deterritorialized sensibilities. Never does he wonder whether such morality requires any sustained knowledge of the economic and political forces undermining the world's cultures and peoples, nor whether globalization is in effect recalibrating human morality to bring the capitalist project to its apocalyptic conclusions.

Terry Eagleton has a different approach to the notion of culture as he tries to wrestle with its meaning and to reinvest it with radical content to confront the culture of globalization.[25] In a book dedicated to Edward Said, Eagleton begins by tracing the origin of the term (one of the most complex in the English language) to its etymological origins in nature and husbandry. Over time, "culture" came to mean several things at once, including mere self-cultivation when the process is individualized, and *Bildung* when the state participates (the common idea from Friedrich Schiller to Matthew Arnold). In the eighteenth century, it acquired its French sense and became "more or less synonymous with the [Enlightenment concept of] 'civilization.'" But the Germans, France's rivals, kept its meaning within narrower bounds. For them, civilization "played down national differences, whereas 'culture' highlighted them." Those differences would be heightened throughout the nineteenth century, especially as "civilization" came to be associated with industrial capitalism and imperialism. So the Germans used a Romantic notion of *Kultur* to criticize the ominous effects of capitalist and Eurocentric cosmopolitan values. "Born at the heart of the Enlightenment, the concept of culture now struck with Oedipal ferocity against its progenitors. Civilization was abstract, alienated, fragmented, mechanistic, utilitarian, in thrall to a crass faith in material progress; culture was holistic, organic, sensuous, autotelic, recollective. The conflict between culture and civilization thus belonged to a full-blown quarrel between tradition and modernity." Patrician, populist, and somewhat aristrocratic, *Kultur* expressed "a heartfelt sympathy for the Volk and a supercilious distaste for the Burgher." Herder best exemplifies the deployment and relativizing of culture to counter European hegemony in his statement: "What one nations holds indispensable to the circle of its thought has never entered into the mind of a second, and by a third has been deemed injurious." Marxism itself, according to Eagleton, was part of this Romantic tradition.[26]

In this sense, culture can turn into a "good utopia" and "become a form of immanent critique, judging the present to be lacking by measuring it against norms which it has generated itself." Situated simultaneously within civilization and its outside, it becomes a "set of potentials bred by history and subversively at work within it." But Eagleton adds: "The trick is to know how to unlock these capacities," since, as he states later, "no culture can be entirely negative." In any case, the clash between capitalism and cultures is real enough for Eagleton, as it is not for Tomlinson, and it cannot be theorized away. "Transnational capitalism weakens national cultures, just as it does economies, by cosmopolitanizing them." Cultures and religions are endowed with a strength and resiliency that are unmatched by their secular opponents. The bureaucratic alliances and ideologies of capitalist states fare poorly when dealing with religions such as Islam, for instance. Arguing over canons and embracing high culture or postmodernist attitudes won't thicken the commodified, pseudocultural experiences described by Tomlinson.[27] As Eagleton puts it:

If high culture is too rarefied to be an effective political force, much postmodern culture is too brittle, rootless and depoliticized. Neither shows up especially well when compared to Islam, for which culture is historically rooted and inescapably political. It is also a form of life for which considerable numbers of people are prepared to die, which may not be wise policy, but which is more than can be said for Mozart and Madonna. The wonders of satellite communication do not shape up well against sacred scripture.[28]

Eagleton clarifies for those who have not yet made the distinction that it is capitalist secularization, not the atheistic Left, that undermines religion. "Capitalism is naturally anti-foundational, melting all that is solid into air, and this provokes its fundamentalist reactions within the West as well as beyond it."[29]

By reembedding the meaning of culture in nature, Eagleton can then contemplate a common culture (since humans have the same bodies), one that allows for different people to enter into relationships born out of this common heritage.[30] But the question remains: How does one retrieve the world's culture from the onslaught of capitalism without equally highlighting religious and cultural differences or deploying a religion like Islam for that purpose? On the face of it, Slavoj Žižek has tried to answer that question when he seeks to defend Christianity as an alternative to the anticultural tendencies of capitalism.

He opens *The Fragile Absolute, or Why Is the Christian Legacy Worth*

Fighting For? with the promising salvo that Christianity and Marxism should fight together against "the onslaught of new spiritualism."[31] Instead of being caught up in the false consciousness of multiculturalism, which advocates ethnic and cultural tolerance,[32] Žižek advocates "*even more hatred*," not less, of the "common political enemy." Reasserting the validity of the spectral powers of the *Communist Manifesto* to fight the "monstrous ghosts" of capitalism, Žižek wants a new Marxist project without "the utopian-ideological notion of Communism as its inherent standard." He wants to break out of "the capitalist horizon *without* falling into the trap of returning to the eminently premodern notion of a balanced, (self-)restrained society (the 'pre-Cartesian' temptation to which most of today's ecology succumbs)." Instead of sorting out the cultural from the capitalist, Žižek is more interested in the "culturalization of the market economy."[33]

Refusing to go back to an older version of socialism or communism, Žižek reinterprets the Christian legacy by defining it as the explosive intrusion into the ordered, hierarchical, wise world of paganism and Jewish literalism and the promotion of Paul's notion of *agape* as the foundation of a community of outcasts who, in their utter devotion, glimpse the fragility of the Absolute. Christian love thus implies constant "unplugging" or "uncoupling" from one's object of desire. Through elaborate, Lacanian reflections on truth, language, several films, and several philosophers, Žižek reaches the conclusion, already hinted at in the beginning of the book, that "the subject is actually 'in' (caught in the web of) power only and precisely in so far as he does not fully identify with it but maintains a kind of distance towards it; on the other hand, the system (of public Law) is actually undermined by unreserved identification with it." In other words, "when we abandon the fantasmatic Otherness which makes life in constrained social reality bearable, we catch a glimpse of Another Space which can no longer be dismissed as a fantasmatic supplement to social reality." This is the "magic moment when *the Absolute appears* in all is fragility."[34]

If I understand this correctly, the claim here seems to be that— through some analogy with the Christian principle of *agape*—total, unconflicted surrender to capitalism produces utopian apparitions. Does this mean that in order to defeat capitalism one has to embrace it wholeheartedly and that the best way to accelerate the demise of capitalism is not to challenge it? And what action would one take after seeing those hopeful apparitions—start a new movement and thus enter the forbidden zone of utopia?

Although Žižek offers interesting insights on a variety of topics, his argument and thesis say nothing at all to people seriously interested in change, certainly nothing comparable to the heroic work conducted by liberation theologians within Christianity. If there is any ghost in the book, it is the "post-al," postmodernist ghost of the 1980s and 1990s that appears, with its highly reified discourse, clever analysis of various art forms, the whole sublimated into a theory whose goal is to rescue humanity (or at least Christians, I presume) from the deadly and apocalyptic horrors of capitalism.

For one of the most promising Western/liberal efforts to reexamine the Enlightenment legacy of universalism critically we must go back to John Gray. Noting the contradictory legacy of liberalism in *The Two Faces of Liberalism*,[35] Gray quickly announces that "if liberalism has a future, it is in giving up the search for a rational consensus on the best way of life." He agrees with the Hobbesian view that conflict—at every level of life— is unavoidable and that it is far better (and more rational) to seek coexistence than to aim for a global liberal regime that enfranchises all humans because, to begin with, there will never be a consensus on what constitutes the good life. Humans, he reminds us, have thrived in "forms of life that are different from one another" and "ancient societies were more hospitable to differences than ours . . . partly because the idea of human equality was weak or absent. Modernity begins not with the recognition of difference but with a demand for uniformity." Any attempt to categorize a different way of life or rival freedom as an error is "illiberal" and a "species of fundamentalism." Thus, instead of seeing liberalism as a system of universal principles, we can think of it as the enterprise of pursuing terms of coexistence among different ways of life. Because the "human good is shown in rival ways of living," because "self-creation is never *ex nihilo*," and because "even our most radical choices are not the expression of purely subjective preferences,"[36] we must conclude that there can't be one solution for all humanity and that cultural transcendence—even when sought through rigorous self-critique and a total repudiation of one's tradition— is impossible.

The incommensurability of ways of lives, both within and outside a particular community, is what troubles many liberals to the point of seeking to erase differences in the name of promoting them. It would be much better to "face this intellectually uncomfortable fact than to ignore it, or automatically attribute it to some deficiency on our part which could be eliminated by an increase in skill or knowledge; or, what is worse still, suppress one of the competing values altogether by pretending it is identical with its rival—and so end by distorting both," as Isaiah Berlin suggested.[37]

Gray doesn't abandon hybridity as a condition of life in the present global environment and thinks that, although regimes "need to reflect the ways of life and common identities of their citizens," they cannot assume any homogeneity (as communitarians, who are often astute critics of "liberal individualism," tend to do) and must conceive citizenship in the plural. But no single regime or philosophy fits all societies, not even the much heralded (but sometimes inconsistent and irrelevant) doctrine of human rights, partly because social needs are unstable, culturally specific, and historical. Again, to say as much is not to give up all judgment (societies still need to have basic protections against arbitrary violence), but to advocate an ethic of "value-pluralism" in a world with a "*modus vivendi*" outlook that "relinquishes the project of a universal regime" and explicitly affirms the plurality of rival values.[38]

This *modus vivendi* approach is certainly difficult to undertake, given that the West's long history of universalisms has left a strong imprint on every facet of social and political life. Yet it is the only solution that approximates (or, perhaps, even supersedes) the culture of *convivencia* that sustained the coexistence of religions in Muslim Spain. The approach requires the ability to share the same physical space with those who may be radically different and yet accept them as one would accept one's own. It also means accepting that there is no one truth and that all truths are contingent and cultural, a point that Stanley Fish has made even after 9/11. Responding to columnists such as Edward Rothstein and Andrew Sullivan, who seized the occasion to discredit postmodernist relativism and its refusal to concede the existence of transhistorical truths and to reassert a universal dichotomy of good and evil, Fish repeated that there are no universal truths. This philosophical quandary, however, doesn't prevent people from making decisions or render judgments about all kinds of things and justifying their decisions through recourse to some text, authority, discipline, tradition, or moral code. But these validating factors cannot be universals, or people would never disagree.

Fish challenges liberals and conservatives alike by expressing cynicism over the rush to absolve Islam after 9/11 in order to avoid alienating other nations and even an important U.S. constituency. But to say that Is-

lam has nothing to do with this is, as Fish puts it, "an amazing line of argument," for to say this, one would have to presume that someone or some
authority can decide what is the true religion, just as someone would have
to explain to what extent the defiance of al-Qaʿeda mirrors those of Christian denominations such as Protestants, Baptists, or Mormons. In matters
of religion, "there is no public space," since belief is an irreducible act not
open to philosophical negotiations or suspensions. Fish argues that to say
al-Qaʿeda members should act like Americans is to offend them further,
for, to them, America has lost its soul precisely because it has not adopted
religion as its foundational creed. Similarly, to imply that Islam must follow in the footprints of the history of Christianity (the Reformation) and
adopt secular principles is to heap more insult on such Muslims. "Privatization and secularization are not goals that Islam has yet to achieve; they
are specters that Islam (or some versions of it) pushes away as one would
push away death."

By contrast, Sullivan's article, which appeared in the 7 October 2001
issue of the *New York Times Magazine*, declares that Islam is a great religion, but one that is undermined by its lack of experience in tolerating
other great faiths. The problem with fundamentalism, in Sullivan's view, is
that it is against "freedom and modernity," vague terms that Sullivan does-
n't examine too closely. But, as Fish points out, one could easily argue that
Muslim extremists are, in fact, fighting for freedom and thus implicitly
challenge the presumed universality of the concept. One person's freedom
is another person's unfreedom. What Sullivan wants is a vacuous religion
("empty, insipid, and safe") that is no religion at all.

There is not much we can do about these fundamental differences,
Fish insists. "We have to live with the knowledge of two things: that we are
absolutely right and that there is no generally accepted measure by which
our rightness can be independently validated. That's just the way it is, and
we should get on with it."[39] Fish's unsettling conclusion—that al-Qaʿeda is
waging a religious war and that there are no universals—is, however, at
once true and somewhat simplistic, for it is not religion that wages war, but
the people who claim that religion. Islam, like American patriotism, remains a contested faith.

No matter how nuanced such critiques of universalist convictions
are, its proponents are often dismissed as politically correct, as if to deny
the superiority of the West is somehow to be disloyal to one's nation, class,
or race. That is the tenor in Keith Windschuttle's long commentary on the

work of Clifford Geertz. After affirming that the "universalizing principle has been one of the great strengths of Western culture and has been central to the self-assurance and development of Western civilization," Windschuttle faults Geertz (and, indirectly, Stanley Fish) for championing a multicultural agenda, with its irresponsibly relativist approach, although Windschuttle does mention that Geertz no longer believes in the value of cultural "imprisonment" because we live in a different world. "It is not that we must love one another or die," states Geertz, but "that we must know one another, and live with that knowledge, or end marooned in a Beckett-world of colliding soliloquy." That sounds nice, but Windschuttle would argue that such a position obscures the benefits of Western universalism, for the cultures still mired in the barbaric practices of suttee or cockfighting are cultures that have condemned themselves to even more generalized barbarism.[40]

Such polemical debates about the nature of truth have the effect occluding the diabolical effects of capitalism, just like those who blame Islam for not developing secular institutions that allow for multiple beliefs and tolerance. They obscure the ways in which its dividing structures bring people together in relations of intense antagonism. This is not to say that Muslims are to be exculpated from any responsibility or that they have not produced structures of oppression throughout their history. Islam's power may have been great during the Middle Ages, but Muslim history is as messy and prone to contradictions as any other history. Not only that, but given the complexities of the global condition, the practice of Islam must move from the narrowly legislative domain (based on an arguably outdated Shari'a) to a philosophical one, a proposition that was recently made in the case of Judaism by Douglas Rushkoff.

As the U.S. Jewish communities were wrestling over the charged issue of releasing the number of Jews in the United States—a figure that measures the rise or decline of the Jewish community—Rushkoff, a proud Jew who is deeply attached to his religion, wrote to suggest that Jews have embraced a racial concept of their religion (one that has been fostered on them by their enemies) and have thus lost sight of the fundamental ethical concepts of Judaism, which are based on "radical pluralism" (since God remains nameless), social justice, and making the world a better place. Rushkoff thus redefines monotheism to preserve its universalist dimensions without eradicating his faith's particularity. This is, admittedly, not an easy thing to do, but there is no solution outside this formula.[41]

Despite all the recriminations against Muslims for not challenging Islam from within after 9/11, a few scholars of Muslim jurisprudence had been doing just that, although, for some inexplicable reason, they never get the exposure that novelists such as Salman Rushdie or columnists like Thomas Friedman enjoy in the U.S. media. (On one occasion, both Rushdie and Friedman published similar arguments on the same Op-Ed page of the *New York Times*.)[42] The Egyptian Muhammad Sa'id al-'Ashmawy has, in fact, charted out a path for Muslims and non-Muslims, one that shows that Islam could be articulated through a philosophical outlook that could detribalize the religion without doing injury to its spirit and the faith of Muslims. Yet the author of *Against Islamic Extremism*, a former chief justice who lives under permanent protection in Cairo, is, according to his translator, practically unknown in the West.[43] Al-'Ashmawy has shown that Islam was meant to address all humans and is part of a much older legacy that started in ancient Egypt. The human-god of ancient Egypt, Osiris (probably Idriss in the Qur'an), Lord of Ma'at ("righteousness, justice, good conduct, and order"), is the prototype of much of the monotheistic Jewish religion in the Old Testament. The mention of "Amen" (which means "God" in ancient Egyptian), circumcision, and the prohibition of pork are three of the many striking similarities between the two. Although historians look for Mesopotamian influences, such influences came later, when Judaism confined itself in legal rules and the ethno-tribal concept of a "chosen people." As the Torah was expanded to include the Talmud (rabbinical rules), it became narrower and closed.[44]

By rebelling against the heavily legalistic Jewish tradition, Christianity, whose symbol of the cross long existed in ancient Egypt as the "ankh," was reverting back to the old, conscious-based practice of the Egyptians. "Jesus Christ," writes al-'Ashmawy in a claim that is remarkably Emersonian, "was against formal institutions. From history it is quite clear that institutions were, and are, always dependent on texts, enslaving people and monopolizing the right of knowing the truth, explaining it and applying it." Islam, for example, began as a universal message, but was eventually reduced to the legalistic, narrow range of the Shari'a, an institution that is wrongly sanctified. For al-'Ashmawy, all humans share in the common ancestry of ancient Egypt, and it is, therefore, wrong to assume that one's ethics are exclusive, since "all the faithful are one community and that humanity is one and always one." All good people, the Qur'an states in 2:62 and 3:84, have a good place in heaven, and each religion preaches its own

Shari'a, its own path or method. Therefore, "As history is one chain with many links, religion is one vision with many paths."[45]

However, according to al-'Ashamawy, Judaism, Christianity, and Islam grew into "closed systems" that excluded others from their sphere of salvation and thus made the quest of "creative coexistence among these juridical systems" more difficult. But because salvation is never an individualistic venture and must include all, it can only happen if we accept the principle of "one religion, many paths, several interpretations, changeable law and flexible jurisprudence" to allow for the miraculous individual to live in harmony with his or her environment. "The true and only way to realize salvation is to feel, understand and live as one in all, and all in one."[46]

For this reason, both bringing religion into of politics and bringing politics into religion are bound to produce violence and oppression, in al-'Ashmawy's view. Religion and politics are both set up to control human behavior and activities, and although the two may have been fused in ancient Egypt, then by Alexander the Great in the Hellenistic period, and in the reign of Julius Caesar after that, all the way to the divine right of kings throughout the Middle Ages, the concept of the infallible caliph is contrary to the precepts of Islam, since, according to Islam, no human, including the Prophet, is infallible. Because it was established during Islam's phase of expansion, the tribally defined caliphate has been mostly a despotic institution, treating people as herds and wrongly dividing the world into the abodes of peace and war. Religion and politics must thus be separated to demarcate their respective spheres more properly, for "when religion is meshed with politics it becomes an ideology, not a religion, and its followers become politicians or party members."[47]

There are several reasons why this separation must be maintained, al-'Ashmawy believes, not least of which is the violence involved in creating a "religio-political" institution with narrow, tribal ethics that exclude others as wrong. "The result is that each sect finds, in their relative ethical code, justifications for the murder, injury or extermination of others." Moreover, neither the Qur'an nor the prophetic tradition provides any guidelines for the right political system. The most cited verse in favor of Islamic government ("Whosoever judges not by that which Allah has revealed, such are the Kafirun [unbelievers]" [5: 55]) was revealed in the context of a "specific incident" involving a Jewish dispute.[48] Thus, al-'Ashmawy concludes that Islam "is absolutely against religious government" since it is "concerned with people, not with systems; with the conscience, not with legal rules;

with the spirit, not with the letter of the law." A good government must be one that provides justice and includes all humans, regardless of belief, and a true Shari'a is one that upholds the principle of mercy, which includes, among other things, looking "for what is human, not for the text, to look for the spirit of the text, not the letter of the text" and to "spread prosperity, liberty, equality, justice and love" everywhere and with everyone.[49]

Al-'Ashmawy still tries to answer the question of "why is there a call for an Islamic government?" and provides a list of reasons, ranging from corruption and the rule of dictatorships to colonialism, Western cultural hegemony, and the marginalization of Third World people by dominant international systems increasingly characterized by disorder. To deal with their economic, political, and cultural displacement, Muslim "militants have created movements of terror" across the world, "distorted the image of Islam, and isolated Muslims from history."

Al-'Ashmawy knows very well that without the reform of Islam, the future of Islam and humanity looks quite grim,[50] but I don't think that his vague call for integration into an ill-defined global culture is the answer. If the goal of Muslims is to catch up with the West's levels of development, Muslim frustration will not abate, because the global economic structure is built to ensure the continued control of an elite capitalist class over the world's resources, as the eminent scholar Marshall G. S. Hodgson knew.[51] Globalization, as James Wolfenshon, director of the World Bank (a post reserved for Americans), once admitted, "is not working at the level of the people." And because of this economic fundamentalism, all other freedoms take a back seat, and as Noreena Hertz puts it, "those disenfranchised by the Silent Takeover or those who choose to speak for the disenfranchised will keep on trying to batter down the doors of power, in whatever ways they see most fit."[52]

It is against and within this global economic background that Islam appears in the form that it does today. This is not to say that the strong tribal culture that both bonds Muslims and, in many ways, oppresses them is the exclusive result of world conditions. As much as its manifestations mirror Western ideological fundamentalisms, it still retains its own worldview. Islam, as Bruce Lawrence has argued, "cannot be understood except as a major and complex religious system, shaped as much by its own metaphysical postulates and ethical demands as by the circumstances of Muslim polities in the modern world."[53] To see Islam as a self-contained religion divorced from history is to replicate the Muslim extremists' view of their religion, and this kind of thinking only delays the solution to an urgent problem. Not only must economic reality be taken into account when any analysis or study of Islam is undertaken, but those who want Islam to reform cannot hope for this outcome without, at the same time, willing to consider major reforms within their own traditions.

Of course, as Lawrence explains, one doesn't have to be "a Marxist or a capitalist to apply the standard of distributive justice, nor does one have to accept the judgment of modernization theorists, that Muslims must accommodate to the values as well as the structures of modernity," for there is simply no solution outside the larger Islamic consciousness (however vaguely defined). Tariq al-Bishri, the Egyptian theorist, was right to postulate that Islam must be part of any liberatory movement in the Arab world, for the religion is so closely associated with Muslim identity and resistance in the modern period not to be invoked in its long-overdue venture of self-reexamination.

Writing from Jerusalem on the eve of the U.S. war on Iraq in March 2003, Avishai Margalit warned the West not to conflate the war on terror or on Saddam with the predicament of Arabs and Muslims in the contemporary era. Ruled by what he called "mukhabart regimes" (police states), torn away from their traditional safety nets, and besieged by extremists, Arabs and Muslims cannot hope to confront this triple challenge without having recourse to some version of Islam. "I find it hard to believe," concluded Margalit, "that any ideology, except some benign version of Islam, can successfully compete both against the mukhabart regimes and against the menacing Islamism of bin Laden. The ideology that will address both the prospects and the dreams of the people in these countries cannot be imposed or manipulated from the outside; but it can and should be helped from the outside."[54]

The challenge for Muslims is how to reconceptualize their faith and keep their "difference" (as Lawrence emphasizes) in a world that hasn't tolerated significant differences in the last half millennium. To think that the only way for Islam to get better is to adopt Western ways is to revert back to the very Eurocentric prejudices (shared by both Left and Right) that have led to the crippling global impasse.[55] The attempts at synthesizing democratic principles and capitalist modernization with Islam currently taking place in Turkey, Malaysia, and, to some extent, Iran, could lead the way out.[56] Most Iranian reformers challenging clerical rule in their country do not want to do away with Islam as a paradigmatic principle, but want to give substance to their constitutional provisions stressing freedom and equality. Even in Iraq, the influential Shi'ite cleric Ayatollah Mohammed Bakr al-Hakim espoused a liberal form of Islam, before he was killed in a bomb explosion outside the Imam Ali mosque in Najaf on 29 August 2003.[57] These are promising initiatives, but without an overhaul of the global economic structure, they may not amount to much and, in the long run, may very well lead to more of the same frustrations that have radicalized Islam elsewhere.

To champion "globalization" as a solution to Muslims' problems, as the influential columnist Thomas Friedman often does, is to miss the crucial connection between ideology and economics, and, inadvertently, to reduce the differences between West and Islam to an ahistorical "clash of civilizations" thesis. In a column written in the guise of a letter or memo addressed by President George W. Bush to the leaders of the Muslim world in the fall of 2002, Friedman makes Bush challenge his addressees to allow the "Muslim center" to fight the "harsh fundamentalism" that has infected Muslim societies— basically to open up a war within Islam in order to prevent a war against the United States, which is only another 9/11 away. Although who Friedman's Muslim leadership might be remains unexamined, the idea is a good one, and is, in fact, badly needed. But to exculpate the United States by saying that Bush has distanced himself from the "Christians who smear Islam with a broad brush" and that intolerance in the United States was defeated by the Civil War does not address a variety of other more insidious forms of intolerance that are aggravating the fundamentalism that Friedman very rightly deplores. To be sure, Friedman is aware of U.S. blindness to others people's concerns, but, earlier that year, when he wrote as a teacher to extol the United States as a beacon of freedom and democracy, he assigned the Constitution and the Declaration of Independence to those who transgress their own nation's ideals.[58] Thus, somewhat like Negri and Hardt and Tomlinson, the United States Constitution reemerges as the solution to a world in disarray.

The American Revolution, as I argued earlier, did initiate a radical break with history and endowed the United States with a great deal of strength and confidence to influence world affairs. But even if we choose not to examine the darker side of this legacy (the fate of women, blacks, Indians, the working classes, and nonwhite people in general), the ideals of the Revolution and the Constitution that Friedman and others want to revive have long been undermined by the triumph of capitalism and its ongoing legacy of conquest. And it is this legacy that has produced the religious extremism that has intensified the West's fear in a world where safety has become the main goal of politics. Ironically, the month before Friedman had President Bush address Muslim leaders, his colleague, the columnist Paul Krugman, wrote a devastating article showing how the "tectonic shifts that have taken place in the distribution of income and wealth" in the United States have destroyed American equality, polarized American politics, and moved the country to the Right.[59] Because the wealthy must be protected from the ever-threatening masses, law and order issues have become a staple of political campaigns, sowing even more fear and panic in an already emotionally frayed citizenry. And what applies to the United States also applies worldwide—the gates of the rich are forever fortified against a tide of human misery and cultural difference beating incessantly against their walls. As one member of the Italian parliament commented on the North African desperadoes washing up on Italy's long, uncontrollable shores, such immigration cannot be stopped. "It's like stopping a thunderstorm or the tides."[60]

Susan Dunn, who has done a remarkable job of comparing the effects and legacies of both the American and French Revolutions, has shown that the farsighted French Declaration of Rights of 1792 linked economic justice with the pursuit of happiness. But neither France nor the United States have been able to live up to the lofty principles of their revolutions. In both countries, consumers replaced citizens. "Politically apathetic citizens and political parties mired in intellectual stagnation lounge at the threshold of the new millennium," notes Dunn. With so much deadlock in government—a legacy of Madison's government of too many checks and balances—the United States, like France, has to renew its traditions by restoring ideological conflict and contestation—the very recipe Friedman recommends for Muslims in these uncertain times.

Every nation, not just emerging democracies or poor countries, needs a revolution, a view that would have been approved by Woodrow Wilson, who, as a senior in Princeton in 1879, argued against the system of checks and balances. Thomas Jefferson himself had expected every generation to produce its own constitution. This is all the more urgent now that the American empire rests on a profoundly unstable financial system, one that, as Kevin Phillips noted in his masterly history of wealth and democracy in the United States, produces mammoth class divisions and, in effect, disenfranchises most Americans from their democratic rights, an outcome that was never envisioned by the Founding Fathers. Because such a republic, in Phillips's concluding assessment, cannot stand, what the United States needs, in Dunn's view, is (Jeffersonian) audacity, not the meaningless valorizing of "the buzzwords 'moderate,' 'mainstream.' and 'middle of the road'" that "accompany the scramble to the insipid center."[61] The same applies on a global scale. Without understanding and confronting the colossal powers of a world dominated by multinational corporations and their interests, democracy becomes, in the opinion of José Saramago, the Portuguese Nobel laureate in literature, an empty ritual.[62]

For Muslims to think that catching up with an economic model that has failed the ideals of the American Revolution would lead them to a better future is dangerous daydreaming, if only because the habits of the rich are already seriously compromising the global habitat necessary for human survival. Daniel B. Botkin, a biologist, leading environmentalist, and author of the seminal *Discordant Harmonies: A New Ecology for the 21st Century*, answered the question of whether a global American lifestyle—the measure of ultimate success for all nations—is possible by replying that facts clearly indicate that "there aren't enough resources to go around for everybody to live at the level we in America live at" and that "somebody's going to have to give up something." In fact, Botkin thinks that "one of the big questions of our time is" how to "have a good quality of human life, physically and spiritually, that uses fewer resources per person?" His answer is remarkable in that it proposes a spiritual program. "My belief," he said, "is that we will not attain sustainability until we learn to love both nature and people. To love nature, you have to find a way to make a deep connection with it."[63]

After having detailed the "terrors" of globalization and the trail of corpses and detritus it leaves behind in its march of folly, Teresa Brennan sees the hope for what she calls a "policy of reversal" only in small-scale production systems sustained by a "spiritual authority" and "resistance," at least in the United States. "All the great religions of the West and the Book," she notes, "insist on restraining human free will in terms of how it *paces* itself."[64]

The ritual of consumerism has become so deep-seated in rich nations that citizens and even religious orders are deploying shopping to force progressive change. Noreena Hertz writes that the "Church of England-approved prayer for the millennium, *New Start Worship*, counsels the faithful that 'where we shop, how we shop, and what we buy is a living statement of what we believe.'" Thus, "Shopping which involves the shopper in making ethical and religious judgments may be nearer to the worship God requires than any number of pious prayers in church. . . . If we take our roles as God's stewards seriously, shoppers collectively are a very powerful group." The liturgy even enjoins the faithful to buy only the products that are not tainted by exploitation. Indeed, so at odds is the Church of England with the reigning dogma of globalization that a vocal champion of social justice and a critic of capitalism, the Most Reverend Rowan Williams, was elected and "enthroned" to head the church in late February 2003.[65] Similarly, the U.S.-based Interfaith Center on Corporate Responsibility, a shareholder organization with combined assets in excess of one hundred and ten billion dollars, aims at forcing change by promoting fair employment practices and condemning racism. But corporations are fighting back, of course, and are funding all sorts of organizations, including leaders of religious groups. Not long ago, the World Health Organization reported that tobacco companies are trying to influence Muslim scholars to challenge Qur'anic interpretations that prohibit the use of tobacco.[66]

By reclaiming what David Bollier has called in the U.S. context our global "commons" from unfair corporate takeovers and monopolies of public resources, agency will be restored to people and nations alike, people would feel more fully integrated in their natural habitats, and the impulse for encounters with others will grow out of sincere curiosity and genuine friendship, not economic compulsion or forced relocation.[67] Pope John Paul II, who once fought "godless" Communism, is now raising his dying voice against the threat of free markets. In August 2002, when he visited his native Poland, he warned millions of Poles about the perils of capitalism and called for "a spirit of mercy, of fraternal solidarity" in that country.[68] A similar message was voiced by South Africa's president, Thabo Mbeki, at the opening of the world summit for sustainable development in Johannesburg later that year when he reminded his audience of the need to regain "the noble concept of human solidarity" and "outgrow market fundamentalism."[69] Religions, including Islam, could play a vital role in this process if, as Theodore Von Laue once put it, "the ethnocentric stereotypes and preconceptions that have contributed to national unity—and even to religious belief—in the past" are "replaced by more capacious symbols."[70]

A world of multiple Shari'as must then be allowed to flourish, a testament to cultural diversity under the overarching principle of the indivisible oneness of human civilization. Not only does the literalist Shari'a preached by extremists obscure the historicity of Islam and the latter's creation of cosmopolitan cultures in the premodern period, but there is no alternative to historicizing Islam in order to help the Muslim community, or *ummah*, to wrestle with the material conditions of the present. The reassessment of the Shari'a and the *ummah*, the resolution of the tension between communalism and universalism, and the creation of a dialogue between the world's heritages without doing away with the bases of religion are undertakings that are long overdue, since these were exactly some of the recommendations contemplated by Hodgson in his epic survey of Islam in world history.[71] But because Islam needs to be defundamentalized away from the pressures that lead to extremism and violence, the world's social, economic, and political practices need to be critically examined, not merely for academic purposes, and certainly not for the promotion of one way of life or belief system over another, but because the alternative could condemn all humans to an intolerably hellish fate.

I believe that the solution must be conceived in the plural, allowing the world's nations to choose cultural directions that don't do violence to their traditions, for it is this violence that unleashes many into the perilous world of alienation and cripples progressive social agendas, with consequences that can be utterly devastating to the entire global community. Any philosophy that doesn't question its universalist tendencies often falls into a fundamentalist and sometimes imperialist stance, despite the best of intentions. This is not an easy undertaking, for it is nearly impossible for people not to project out of their familiar experience and assume their values to be natural. What further complicates this challenge is that universalism has a long history, particularly in the West, and most likely cannot be undone in the near term. In *The Sense of Reality*, Isaiah Berlin traced the universalism of Western philosophical concepts all the way back to classical Greece and concluded that such predispositions have serious implications for human understanding:

At some point I realized that what all these views have in common was a Platonic ideal: in the first place, that, as in the sciences, all genuine questions must have one true answer and one only, all the rest being necessarily errors; in the second place, that there must be a dependable path towards the discovery of these truths; in the third place, that the true answers, when found, must necessarily be compatible with one another and form a single whole.[72]

John Mohawk explains that the various "revitalization movements" that dot Western history are all attempts to achieve a sort of perfection, and that all eventually result in oppression and subjugation on a massive scale. Europeans' self-proclaimed right to decide what is best for others led to slavery, the genocide of the Indians, racism, the Holocaust, the bombing of Japan in 1945, and the constant demonization of nonwhite Others. Revitalization movements such as Marxism and Nazism (and, I would add, religious extremism) are marked by their intolerant idealism and unquestioned sense of truth. Capitalism falls squarely into this category, for its advocates are often blindly committed to eradicating and fighting any attempt to rethink the system. Yet Mohawk shows that global capitalism is "a formula for creating conditions that could easily heighten nationalism, increase pressure on already destitute populations, and provide fertile ground for future and unpredictable revitalization movements. Such movements may be unavoidable, but," Mohawk warns, "it is unwise to create conditions that have historically given them birth."[73] Those who champion Western culture may do well to remember that Plato's ideal republic, governed by enlightened rational philosophers, is a socialist one:

No one must have any private property whatsoever, except what is absolutely necessary. Secondly, no one must have lodging or storehouse at all which is not open to all comers. . . . They must live in common, attending in messes as if they were in the field. . . . [Philosophers] of all in the piety dare not have any dealings with gold or silver or even touch them or come under the same roof with them.[74]

For many Muslims, Islam is the solution, just as Christianity may be the best option for devout Christians, Judaism for Jews, Hinduism for Hindus, and even enlightened secularism for upholders of Enlightenment ideals and the best principles of the American Revolution. Islam, reinterpreted in light of present global realities, becomes one element in a larger, multifaceted struggle against the dehumanizing forces that endanger human civilization, including the violent forces of religious extremism. The Iranian Ayatollah Mortaza Motahhari, "the foremost Shi'ite theorist on jihad," according to Bruce Lawrence, had the right Muslim insight when in the 1960s, he restricted the notion of jihad by broadening its injunctions to include non-Muslims, other nations, and, in fact, all of humanity. "I do not think," wrote Motahhari, "that any one has any doubts that the holiest form of jihad and the holiest form of war is that which is fought in defense of humanity and of humanity's rights." If one adds the Singaporan Riduan Wu Chia Chung Ibn Abdullah's notion of an "elastic practice of Islam" that accommodates cultural differences in a world of plural traditions,[75] one can, in fact, begin to visualize a world of provincial cultures tied together by their common bond of humanity.

Reprovincializing cultures could thicken the human experience by reconnecting humans to their natural environment. The seductive ideology of technological efficiency and the maximization of profits and freedom that is promoted by capitalism is founded on the conception of a mediocre, conformist, and docile human, one whose life is segmented into the contradictory demands of being an efficient producer, a zealous consumer, a social animal (*"animal communicant"*), and a collection of organs that can be manipulated at will. Yet because economic systems, in the first instance, are reflections of cultural and religious traditions—a fact that, ironically, global investors carefully take into account—humanity cannot have a universal rationality, for human beings, with their complex existential needs, belong first and foremost to a culture and a religion. To create an economy geared to serve humans, it is, therefore, imperative to rule out the notion that a free-market economy is the only option to manage the material life of a society or that human solidarity can be measured by a new set of economic indicators.[76]

Restoring and preserving cultural singularities, therefore, are humanity's way out of its crisis. By the end of 2002, at a time when Islam appeared ever more atavistic in its antimodern fury, Jean Baudrillard accused the hegemonic, oppressive, and corrosive tendencies of modernity, progress, and globalization of being responsible for the world's tragedy and read the different forms of violence and retreat into identities as reactions against these forms of universalism. "It would be a mistake to condemn such upheavals as populist, archaic, even terroristic. Anything that makes the news today is reacting against this abstract universalism—including Islam's antagonism to Western values (and it is because Islam's contestation is the most vehement that it is considered enemy number one)." In fact, what the world is witnessing is not a "clash of civilizations," but a quasi-anthropological conflict pitting the West's abstract universalism against the world's irreducible singularities. And in a such a world, to be different is, in fact, to be heretical, even a terrorist.[77]

For cultures to regain their strength and resist the alienating effects of globalization, they must be embedded in place and speak from and for their provinces, not through some nebulous global identity. In his manifesto for Native Americans, Vine Deloria Jr. insists on this principle by associating cultural independence with land and the revival of native religions. Rejecting Western universalist ideologies, including Christianity, as violent and exploitative, he called for "a cultural leave-us-alone agreement, in spirit and in fact." For Deloria, there simply is no culture if a people has no place of its own. "No movement can sustain itself, no people can continue, no government can function, and no religion can become a reality except it be bound to a land area of its own. The Jews have managed to sustain themselves in the Diaspora for over two thousand years, but in the expectation of their homeland's restoration." (Rabbi Jonathan Sacks made the same argument when he observed that the long suffering of Jews in the Diaspora explains their "existential need . . . to have, somewhere on earth, [a] defensible space.") Global, digital humans produce a race of angels with their cult of Unknown Soldiers, as Alain Finkielkraut noted.[78] (It is the lack of a specific sacred place, not merely of an undefined continent, in African American mythology that makes African Americans' predicament extremely challenging, in my opinion.)

At a time when people are declaring themselves citizens of the world in an attempt to transcend the dark forces of nationalism and religious convictions, a call for cultural difference must surely evoke the specter of intolerance that a global cosmopolis is designed to prevent; yet it is globalism in all its expressions that has fundamentalized cultures and pushed them into the violent nativist stances that are now being condemned in the name of the Enlightenment. (I consider this a form of cultural "blowback," a vicious cycle through which the West manufactures its own Other with one set of practices and then seeks to eliminate him in the name of another.) Notions of hybridity and impurity could appear to complicate the belief in the uniqueness of cultures, yet (and I am not trying to define the elusive and catch-all term of "culture" here) both notions are the ironic and inevitable outcomes of history, not the manifestations of agency. It is modern (capitalist) civilization that produces the ghostliness that, in Geoffery Hartman's view, opens the way to the most extreme forms of nativism and which can only be alleviated through a re-embedding in culture. "In brief," says Hartman, "*the function of cultures remains the same throughout history: to convert longing into belonging.* Culture is always site specific in that respect. The site includes language in its density."[79] Jean Améry, born Hans Mayer in Vienna, meditated on his homelessness thus: "With twenty-seven years of exile behind me, my spiritual compatriots are Proust, Sartre,

Beckett. Yet, I am still convinced that the best way to commune with kindred souls of the spirit is to be with fellow countrymen on the streets of a village or in a city. Cultural internationalism can prosper only when one enjoys a secure sense of national belonging."[80]

Deloria's despair of the cancerous white culture is such that he expects America to "return to the red man" because whites have never been transplanted. To him, "white" Americans engaged in destructive exploitation, but developed no culture or people, only a "violent conglomerate of individuals." Deloria prophesies that, unified by their humanity, Indians will "wear down the white man and finally outlast him." Thus, Deloria sees hope in a culturally rooted and place-bound "peoplehood," rather than in Marx's working classes or Negri's and Hardt's multitude, for by "accepting ourselves and defining the values within which we can be most comfortable we can find peace. In essence, we must all create social isolates which have economic bases that support creative and innovative efforts to customize values we need."[81] About thirty years after Deloria's manifesto was initially published, Taiaiake Alfred wrote an updated version expanding Deloria's concept of tribalism into a broader "indigenous" movement, but otherwise reiterating the same rejection of "models of government rooted in European cultural values" while offering a more detailed philosophy of governance and leadership based on the revitalization or "requickening" of traditional values without exoticizing the past or surrendering to annihilation.[82]

The world's non-Western peoples cannot prosper without reconnecting with their mutilated traditions, which, in most cases, means their religions. The insistence on secular solutions in profoundly religious cultures is yet another sign of Eurocentrism, since, as Braudel explained, only in the West and a few other minor instances have people chosen to turn away from religion. "Almost all civilizations are pervaded or submerged by religion, by the supernatural, and by magic: they have always been steeped in it, they draw from it the most powerful motives in their particular psychology."[83]

Secular univeralism is not the answer the world's people, as Jonathan Sacks has so cogently articulated when outlining his "theology of difference," one that is not narrowly tribal, or dangerously universal, or vacuously cosmopolitan, but "based on the deep understanding that passes between people who, knowing how important attachments are to them, understand how deeply someone else's different attachments matter to them." An orthodox Jew who has been called fundamentalist, Rabbi Sacks nevertheless condemns all sorts of fundamentalism, whether religious, scientific, or economic. He is against any attempt to force a diverse world into a single outlook or ideology and thus to resurrect the Tower of Babel, the ultimate symbol of homogeneity. From a Hebrew biblical perspective, Judaism would have to be against Eurocentrism, imperialism, and capitalism, for, as Sacks emphasizes, *"Judaism was born as a protest against empires, because imperialism and its latter-day successors, totalitarianism and fundamentalism, are attempts to impose a single truth on a plural world."* Like Mohawk, Sacks traces the West's penchant for universalist thought to Plato, whose logic proceeds from the particular to the universal, and contrasts it with the Hebrew Bible's "anti-Platonic narrative," which proceeds from the universal to the particular. It is the particular that is the ultimate goal of the moral quest. "There is no road to human solidarity," writes Sacks, "that does not begin with moral particularity." Indeed, the biblical narrative establishes the diversity of faiths as humanity's fate, each faith with its own language and syntax under one God, who, in Sacks's view, is larger and more encompassing than religion.

Such diversity, however, should not entail intolerance and hatred. On the contrary, Sacks notes: Even as God made the Jews a separate people, he commanded them, in no fewer than thirty-six instances, to love the stranger. And although Judaism is world-oriented and values market economies, the biblical mandates of the sabbath, together with sabbatical and jubilee years, place limits on economic practices by reminding people of the larger imperative of social justice and human solidarity, for the market, left to its own devices, would create what amounts to an ungodly order.[84] Despairing of the amoral rules of Western liberal democracies and condemning the present global economic system with its intolerable inequities, Sacks calls for "covenantal relationships," not "contractual" ones, since the former are "acts or moral engagement" based on the assumption of equality (before God) and are thus global and multigenerational, whereas contracts are contingent and assume power differentials. Only such a covenant could allow for global conversation to take place between different faiths and cultures.[85]

The year that had been designated by the United Nations as the International Year of Dialogue between Civilizations, 2001,[86] brought secular and Islamic fundamentalisms to an apocalyptic clash that continues to steer the world into ever more perilous directions. In such an unpromising situation, Sacks's "theology of difference," with its ethic of conversation, must now be espoused by peace-loving people as the only way out of an even bleaker future. This means that Muslims, despite the strong pressures on them to conform, must speak out about the need to rethink religious practice in a world that is full, as Zygmunt Bauman put it.[87] Religion binds, but it must now bind around a new set of principles and ethics. There is no going back to a golden age of the Prophet and the Righteous Caliphs, just as there is no need whatsoever to convert the world to Islam or to keep assuming that non-Muslims are somehow fallen and not as deserving of paradise. No one knows what God thinks of others or how non-Muslim monotheists will be judged. The Qur'anic injunction to state *lakum deenukum wa liya deen* (you have your religion and I have mine) must be the guiding principle of every Muslim from now on, both within Muslim societies and across the world. God is experienced differently across cultures—that is His will, expressed in the Qur'an and the Bible. An even greater burden falls on a West whose imperial universalist doctrines have produced the Islam that haunts its imagination.

In his 1999 BBC Reith Lectures, Anthony Giddens, the prominent sociologist of modernity, affirmed that the current process of globalization is "highly uneven in its consequences" and predicted that the twenty-first century will be marked by a clash between fundamentalism and "cosmopolitan tolerance," two polar tendencies that are born out of the same global capitalist process: If globalization produces "shell institutions" that fail to address fundamental human needs, how, then, are the traditions that have sustained human communities to be preserved and sustained? Can people bear to live in a world of emptiness, a world where nothing is sacred? Giddens refuses such a bleak prospect, for a life without passion is not worth living. Thus, for Giddens, traditions must be defended in nontraditional ways, and democracies must be further democratized. Since fundamentalism, in Giddens's view, is about how people go about protecting and defending their traditions, about the methods they use, not the content of their beliefs,[88] one cannot stress enough the urgency of relieving the pressure on non-Western, noncapitalist cultures by fashioning a way of life that does no violence to their senses of self and their identities. Not to do so is to perpetuate the post-Andalusian legacy of discord and tragedy that has befallen *all* the world's cultures.

The West, within its secular, capitalist model is now wrestling ghosts of its own making, ghosts that appear here and there, in the mountainous terrain of Afghanistan and the slums of major Western cities, among evangelical Christians and Muslim extremists, in Arabian deserts and glaciers, in Asia and Latin America, at work and at home, in the Other and in the West itself. We have all become ghosts under a global system that affects everything it touches, makes a few obscenely wealthy, impoverishes cultures, and enriches no one. Not to rethink our individual heritages, question our supremacist values—whatever shape they take—and restore humans to their natural habitats is to condemn the future to a fate more even hellish than ours. Given the world's record in the last half millennium, there doesn't seem much choice left. A well-thought-out philosophy of provincialism could give more substance to the process of global peace by replenishing the multiple traditions that make up our embattled human civilization.

Notes

PREFACE

1. See, for instance, Emily Eakin, "An Old Amour, More Off than On," *New York Times*, 6 July 2002.

2. The transcript of the inaugural address was published in the *New York Times*, 21 January 2001. For the text of the State of the Union Address, see *New York Times*, 29 January 2003. The text of the president's remarks to his troops aboard the *Abraham Lincoln* was published in the *New York Times*, 2 May 2003. For an account of the U.S. military might and why it is impossible for any other nation to match it, see Gregg Easterbrook, "American Power Moves beyond the Mere Super," *New York Times*, 27 April 2003. James Atlas argued that the neoconservative elements in the Bush administration are all connected through their affiliation to the ideas of the European-born Leo Strauss, a political philosopher who believed that spreading freedom and reading the classics are essential to preserving Western civilization, although, as early as 1964, Strauss acknowledged Islam's rivalry with Christianity's universalist claims and how both cultures had to settle for a tense coexistence. See James Atlas, "A Classicist's Legacy: New Empire Builders," *New York Times*, 4 May 2003. For more on the effect of Leo Strauss's views on influential policymakers in the Bush administration, see Seymour M. Hirsh, "Selective Intelligence," *New Yorker*, 7 April 2003, 43–45. In one of his columns, William Pfaff noted that Strauss's "bleak and anti-utopian philosophy [with its insistence on "moral clarity" and justification for elite rule] goes against practically everything Americans want to believe" and "contradicts the neoconservatives' own declared policy ambitions to make the Muslim world democratic." Yet Strauss didn't approve of hegemonic rule. See William Pfaff, "The Long Reach of Leo Strauss," *International Herald Tribune*, 15 May 2003. Jenny Strauss Clay, the daughter of Leo Strauss, wrote to exculpate her father from any association with neoconservative policies. She described her father—a small man with a great passion for reading Plato, teaching the Great Books, an admirer of Churchill and Lincoln, who at one time wanted to raise rabbits—as a defender if "liberal democracy and "an enemy of any regime that aspired to global domination." See Jenny Strauss Clay, "The Real Leo Strauss," *New York Times*, 7 June 2003.

3. Yahya Sadowski, "Vérités et mensonges sur l'enjeu pétrolier," *Le Monde diplomatique*, April 2003, 18–19.

4. Hubert Védrine, "Comment nier le choc Islam-Occident?" *Le Monde*, 27 February 2003. The statistical figures are taken from Régis Debray's "Letter from America," composed in the tradition of St. Jean de Crèvecoeur, and adapted Debray's book, *L'Édit de Caracalla ou plaidoyer pour les États-Unis d'Occident* (Paris: Librairie Arthème Fayard, 2002). The letter is addressed to Debray by a certain Xavier de C***, a recently naturalized U.S. citizen, who makes the case for the enfranchisement of all Europe into the American empire (as in the Roman model), thus, in one stroke, eliminating the so-called transatlantic rift by renaming the new entity the United States of the West. This is one of the wittiest and most enlightening pieces I have read on the subject of the undisputed U.S. hegemony in global affairs and the role of Europe in this unipolar world. See Régis Debray, "Letter from America," trans. John Howe, *New Left Review* 19 (January–February 2003): 29–40. France is concerned about the eventual retreat of Europe in world affairs and commerce as the United States maintains its demographic advantage (Europe's fertility rates are too low) and as China, despite its aging population, is fast catching up. In a report titled "Chronique d'un déclin annoncé," the Institut français de relations internationals " projected a sure decline of Europe's economic powers if the continent doesn't expand eastward toward Russia and Turkey and southward to include North African countries." It is interesting to note that Islam will thus be, more than ever, an inextricable part of Europe's landscape. For a commentary on this report, see Eric le Boucher, "Le déclin assuré de l'Europe au XXIe siècle, sauf si . . . " *Le Monde*, 3 May 2003.

5. François Burgat, "De l'islamisme au postislamise, vie et mort d'un concept," *Esprit* (August–September 2001): 92.

6. Suzanne Daley, "More Vehemently than Ever, Europe Is Scorning the U.S." *New York Times*, 9 April 2000.

7. Marc Ferro, *Le Choc de l' Islam: XVIIIe-XXIe Siècle* (Paris: Éditions Odile Jacob, 2002), 248.

CHAPTER I

1. In *Race Experts: How Racial Etiquette, Sensitivity Training, and New Age Therapy Hijacked the Civil Rights Revolution* (New York: Norton, 2001), Elizabeth Quinn Lasch believes the way out of this impasse is through a reactivated sense of citizenship and commitment to a democratic project. In the prologue, she mentions the African-American economist Glenn Loury as one of many who had gone beyond the narrow framework within which race issues are processed in the United States. Yet this example turned out to be ironic. After years of opposing much of the classic liberal view and remedy for blacks in the United States, Loury, long the voice of the U.S. conservative movement, eventually found himself caught in the same social web afflicting most African Americans (one he had earlier ascribed to mere irresponsibility) and, through an initial process of Christian conversion, found his way back to his social identity and the liberal agenda that undergirds it. See Adam Shatz, "About Face," *New York Times Magazine*, 20 January 2002, 18–23.

2. The question of representation continues to challenge scholarship. As an anthropologist, Clifford surely knows that this is a haunting and enigmatic question, for silence—the only unpolemical option—is itself a no option, not only because silence can speak volumes, but also because it has real material effects on anthropologists working out of a bourgeois academic institution. Clifford's choice to maintain cultural differences without reducing such differences to essences is unavoidable on both practical and ontological counts: Not doing anthropology would mean no longer being an academic, and erasing cultural differences would give the false and premature impression of a global sameness that is nowhere on the horizon of human civilization. Clifford does his best to separate cultural differences from essences and states that "identity is conjunctural, not essential" and that "authenticity is relational," but without essences, identity becomes a set of strategic political and creative practices. (Clifford, *The Predicament of Culture*, 11–12.) Without the substance of some essence, such a definition, stretched to its limit, reduces all cultures to an essential sameness that is reminiscent of the very Nietzscehan cosmopolitanism that Clifford rejects in Said's thesis. Indeed, Clifford's use of the Bakhtinian concept of heteroglossia to describe the "bewildering diversity of idioms" in our "multivocal world" and his rejection of the insularity of cultures and essences does bring him—inadvertently—closer to Said's critique of Orientalism, for the conception of a sealed, unchanging culture is the "essence" of the Orientalist discourse that Said questions. Other (non-Western) cultures probably have always believed themselves living in a polyphonous world and may not need such reminders.

3. Bernard Lewis, "The Question of Orientalism," *New York Review of Books*, 24 June 1982, 55–56.

4. Ross Chambers, "Representation and Authority," *Comparative Studies in History and Society* 22, no. 4 (1980): 509; Amal Rassam, "Representation and Aggression," *Comparative Studies in History and Society* 22, no. 4 (1980): 508.

5. See, for instance, Bill Ashcroft and Pal Ahluwalia, *Edward Said: The Paradox of Identity* (London: Routledge, 1999); Valerie Kennedy, *Edward Said: A Critical Introduction* (Cambridge,: Polity, 2000); *The Edward Said Reader*, ed. Mustafa Bayoumi and Andrew Rubin (New York: Vintage, 2000).

6. James Clifford, *The Predicament of Culture: Twentieth-Century Ethnography, Literature, and Art* (Cambridge, Mass.: Harvard University Press, 1988), 261, 274–75.

7. Edward Said, *Orientalism* (New York: Vintage, 1979), 67.

8. Ibid., 67, 70, 60.

9. Ibid., 50, 55, 32–33, 35, 85.

10. Quoted in ibid., 172.

11. H. A. R. Gibb, *Modern Trends in Islam*; quoted in ibid., 105–6.

12. See Mohamed 'Abid al-Jabri, *Naqdh al-'aql al-'arabi* (Critique of the Arab mind), vol. 1, *Takween al-'aql al-'arabi* (Formation of the Arab mind) (Casablanca: Al-markaz athaqafi al-'arabi, 1991).

13. Said, *Orientalism*, 172.

14. Marx's rhetorical intentions, in my view, are exactly what he states. Such views would have been consistent with his view of history.

15. Karl Marx, *Surveys from Exile*, ed. David Fernbach (London: Pelican Books, 1973), 306–7; quoted in Said, *Orientalism*, 153.

16. Said, *Orientalism*, 221.

17. Part of this unavoidable ambivalence in Said's work may be caused by his appeal to and critique of Western humanist ideals, with their universalist tendencies and hierarchical worldview. See Kennedy, *Edward Said*, 31–33.

18. Said, *Orientalism*, 211.

19. Bernard Lewis, *The Muslim Discovery of Europe* (New York: Norton, 1982). The consequences, however, were not the same, and one must be wary of the tendency of these relativist acts to level down major historical differences into a similar moral equivalence. The Euro-American imagination, driven by capitalist expansion and profit, prevented the West from turning its colonialism into a more humane venture.

20. See Kennedy, *Edward Said*, 15.

21. Eric Hobsbawm, *The Age of Revolution: Europe 1789–1848* (1962; New York: Barnes & Noble Books, 1996), ix; Susan Dunn, *Sister Revolutions: French Lightning, American Light* (New York: Faber and Faber, 1999).

22. Michel Maffesoli, "The Social Ambiance," *Current Sociology* 41 (autumn 1993): 7–8.

23. Quoted in ibid., 1.

24. Gilbert Durand, "The Implication of the Imaginary and Societies," *Current Sociology* 41 (autumn 1993): 23, 13–14.

25. Cornelius Castoriadis, *The Imaginary Institution of Society*, trans. Kathleen Blamey (Cambridge, Mass.: MIT Press, 1988).

26. Ibid., 36, 54.

27. Ibid., 56.

28. Ibid., 56, 60.

29. Ibid., 67.

30. Ibid., 178, 180, 182, 343, 359, 369.

31. Ibid. 364.

32. Ibid., 362–63, 364, 365.

33. Hobsbawm, *Age of Revolution*, ix.

34. Ibid., 1, 3.

35. Ibid., *Age of Revolution*, 21.

36. Ibid., 26.

37. Ibid., 65.

38. Ibid., 78–79, 90–92.

39. See the chapter on land in ibid., 149–67.

40. Ibid., 181.

41. Ibid., 183, 185, 189, 217, 220, 220 n. 242, 222, 225. Hobsbawm says that

"what we now know as Arab nationalism—a product of the twentieth century—has come out of the cities, not the nomadic encampments" (139).

42. Quoted in Dunn, *Sister Revolutions*, 11.

43. Quoted in ibid., 4.

44. Ibid., 9.

45. Ibid., 175–84.

46. Ibid., 190.

47. Mohammed Sharafuddin, *Islam and Romantic Orientalism: Literary Encounters with the Orient* (London: I.B. Tauris, 1994), ix, xvii, xviii.

48. Quoted in ibid., xxii.

49. Ibid., xxiii, xxiv-xxix.

CHAPTER 2

1. Andrew Curry, "The Crusades: The Truth about the Epic Clash between Christianity and Islam," *U.S. News and World Report*, 8 April 2002, 36–42.

2. David E. Stannard, *American Holocaust: The Conquest of the New World* (New York: Oxford University Press, 1992), 61.

3. María Rosa Menocal, "A Golden Reign of Tolerance," *New York Times*, 28 March 2002. For detailed examples of how that Andalusian culture was lived and experienced by the three monotheistic religions, see her *Ornament of the World: How Muslims, Jews, and Christians Created a Culture of Tolerance in Medieval Spain* (Boston: Back Bay Books, 2002). Because the book was completed on the eve of 9/11, Menocal added a postscript, but resisted the temptation to revise the book in light of that tragic event.

4. Charles C. Mann, "1491," *Atlantic*, March 2002, 41–53. Mann wrote that, "worldwide, more than half the crops grown today were initially developed in the Americas" (48). And when such crops were exported back to the Old World, the result was, ironically, a population boom. What applied in Mexico and Peru was also true of New England. When John Smith visited Massachusetts in 1614, he found the land "so planted with Gardens and Corne fields, and so well inhabited with a goodly, strong and well proportioned people" that he preferred to live there than any other place on earth (49). The Indians, meanwhile, found Europeans dirty and uncouth.

5. Bernard Lewis, "What Went Wrong?" *Atlantic*, January 2002, 43–45.

6. The term *conviviencia* seems to have originated with Ramón Menéndez Pidal, author of *Orígenes del español*, but it was his disciple, Américo Castro, who first gave it its current meaning. See Thomas F. Glick, "Convivencia: An Introductory Note," in *Convivencia: Jews, Muslims, and Christians in Medieval Spain*, ed. Vivian B. Mann et al. (New York: George Braziller, 1992), 1.

7. Richard Fletcher, *Moorish Spain* (New York: Henry Holt, 1992), 5.

8. Edward Gibbon famously said that had the Muslims not been defeated at Tours and Poitiers by Charles Martel in 732, all of Europe would have become

Muslim, a claim that Philip Hitti contested by saying that "the Arab-Berber wave, already almost a thousand miles from its starting place in Gibraltar, had reached a natural standstill. It had lost its momentum and spent itself." Quoted in López-Baralt, *Islam in Spanish Literature: From the Middle Ages to the Present*, trans. Andrew Hurley (Leiden: E.J. Brill, 1992), 5.

9. Stanley Lane-Poole, *The Story of the Moors in Spain*. (1886; Baltimore, Md.: Black Classic Press, 1990), 50.

10. Although 'Isa or Ice de Gebir, a fifteenth-century imam of Segovia, enunciated a "thirteen-article creed" for the Mudejar community in the Arabized Spanish literary vernacular known as *aljamîa*, his *Brevario sunnî* or Sunni Breviary, reaffirmed many of Islam's orthodox teachings, including, paradoxically, the obligation to migrate away from the land of unbelievers. See L. P. Harvey, *Islamic Spain, 1250 to 1500* (Chicago: University of Chicago Press, 1990), 78–97; Abraham Leon Sachar, *A History of the Jews* (1964; New York: Knopf, 1968), 169. While their coreligionists suffered in Christian Europe, "the happy union of Hebrew and Moslem culture produced a renaissance in literature and philosophy, in science and religion. Even architecture flourished and some of the most beautiful churches in Spain speak to the modern pilgrim of their glory in a day when they served as synagogues and received the prayers of a proud and wealthy Jewish community" (169).

11. Fletcher, *Moorish Spain*, 144.

12. See J. H. Elliott, *Imperial Spain, 1469–1716* (London: Penguin, 1963), 31–32.

13. Ibid., 45–49.

14. Bernard Vincent, "La chrétienté à l'assaut de Grenade," *Manière de voir 64* (*Le Monde diplomatique*), July-August, 2002, 15–17.

15. Lane-Poole, *The Story of the Moors in Spain*, 266.

16. Anwar G. Chejne, *Islam and the West: The Moriscos* (Albany, N.Y.: State University of New York Press, 1983), 6.

17. Harvey, *Islamic Spain*, 330–39.

18. Kirkpatrick Sale, *The Conquest of Paradise: Christopher Columbus and the Columbian Legacy* (New York: Alfred Knopf, 1990), 16.

19. Alexander's predecessor, Pope Nicholas V, had issued a brief (known as Brief Dom Diversas) to Portugal on 16 June 1452 stating: "We grant to you by these present documents, with our Apostolic Authority, full and free permission to invade, search out, capture and subjugate the Saracens and pagans and any other unbelievers and enemies of Christ wherever they may be, as well as their kingdoms, duchies, counties, principalities, and other property . . . and to reduce their persons into perpetual slavery." Quoted in John C. Mohawk, *Utopian Legacies: A History of Conquest and Oppression in the Western World* (Santa Fe, N. Mex.: Clear Lights Publishers, 2000, 101.

20. Harvey, *Islamic Spain*, 325. Part of the failure of the capitulations to "provide lasting protection for the Muslims of Granada" may be due to the fact that the treaty was mainly a deal struck between Boabdil and Ferdinand. See Harvey,

Islamic Spain, 313. Unlike Moors, unconverted Jews were given three years to leave the country. See Harvey, *Islamic Spain,* 321.

21. Elliott, *Imperial Spain,* 53.

22. Muslims began to live under Christian rule in Spain beginning in 1085, when Toledo fell to Alfonso VI. Such Muslims became known as Mudejars. But after the fall of Granada and the forced conversions of the Moors, Muslims became Moriscos. See Chejne, *Islam and the West,* 2–3.

23. Harvey, *Islamic Spain,* 55–67. Generally, the case of pagans and Jews wasn't useful, but given later practices and the Alfonso X's views, the Mudejar case approximated that of the Jews more than anyone else in Spanish history. In his legal code *Las Siete Partidas,* Alfonso X wrote:

> Moors are a sort of people who believe that Mahomat was the prophet or messenger of God. Because the works or actions he performed do not demonstrate any great holiness on his part, such as might justify according to him such holy status, their law is like an insult to God. . . . And so we say that the Moors should live among the Christians in the same manner as . . . the Jews, observing their own law and causing no offense to ours.

Quoted in Harvery, *Islamic Spain,* 66. The Capitulations of November 1491 would be less lenient to Jews.

24. Harvey uses the term "Mudejar" in the sense of "a Muslim who, after the surrender of a territory to a Christian ruler, remained there without changing religion, and entered into a relationship of vassalage under a Christian king" (3).

25. Harvey, *Islamic Spain,* x.

26. Stannard, *American Holocaust,* 181. The Lateran Council of 1215 stated:

> Whereas in certain provinces the divers forms of dress serve to distinguish Christians from Jews and Saracens, in others there is such confusion that no difference is apparent, and thus it can occur that the Christians by mistake may mingle with the womenfolk of the Jews and Saracens, or the Jews and Saracens with the Christian women. In order to prevent the continuation, under the cloak of ignorance, of such damnable mixing, and so there can be henceforward be no shadow of an excuse, we hereby decree that such people of both sexes through all Christendom at all times shall be distinguishable by the nature of their clothing.

Quoted in Harvey, *Islamic Spain,* 65–66. The anxiety over women reveals the long-standing fear of genetic dilution or miscegenation in the West.

27. Deborah Root, "Speaking Christian: Orthodoxy and Difference in Sixteenth-Century Spain," *Representations* 23 (summer 1988): 118, 126–27.

28. López-Baralt, *Islam in Spanish Literature,* 34.

29. Quoted in Stannard, *American Holocaust,* 161.

30. Lane-Poole, *The Story of the Moors in Spain,* 270–79.

31. Quoted in Root, "Speaking Christian," 120.

32. Barbara Fuchs, *Mimesis and Empire: The New World, Islam, and European Identities* (Cambridge: Cambridge University Press, 2001), 99; see Root, "Speaking Christian," 119.

33. Root, "Speaking Christian," 130.

34. Fuchs, *Mimesis and Empire*, 113.

35. Elliott, *Imperial Spain*, 223–24.

36. López-Baralt, *Islam in Spanish Literature*, 27. Spain was too genetically mixed to seriously believe in its new genealogical myth.

37. Tzvetan Todorov, *The Conquest of America: The Question of the Other*, trans. Richard Howard (1984; Norman: University of Oklahoma Press, 1999), 5, 10–12.

38. Quoted in Harvey, *Islamic Spain*, 324.

39. Thus was Arabic introduced to the New World upon initial contact. Samuel Eliot Morison, *The European Discovery of America: The Southern Voyages, 1492–1616* (New York: Oxford University Press, 1974); cited in López-Baralt, *Islam in Spanish Literature*, 9–10.

40. Elliott, *Imperial Spain*, 60–61.

41. The Calabrian political theorist Tommaso Campanella (1568–1639) wrote that the name Christophorus "should be interpreted to mean 'he who carries Christ' . . . and as Columbus. Columba, the Church. And in another place: all the world shall serve you." Quoted in Anthony Pagden, *Lords of All the World: Ideologies of Empire in Spain, Britiain, and France c. 1500–c. 1800* (New Haven: Yale University Press, 1995), 40. The whole name of Columbus could also be a fiction that lends itself wonderfully to the myths woven around him. Hans Koning remarks that Columbus's name is the Latinized version penned down by Petrus Martyr, the "great chronicler of the discoveries." Otherwise, the French know him as "Colomb," the Portuguese as "Colom," and the Spaniards as "Colón." Hans Koning, *Columbus: His Enterprise. Exploding the Myth* (1976; New York: Monthly Review Press, 1991), 21.

42. Elliott, *Imperial Spain*, 44; 60–61.

43. Todorov, *The Conquest of America*, 5. The term "genocide" was coined by Raphael Lemkin, a Jewish linguist from Poland who waged a long and exhausting battle to draw the world's attention to the evil of annihilating entire peoples, beginning with the Armenians. After fleeing Nazi-controlled Poland, he was invited to the United States by a Duke University professor and used his appointment to convince U.S. leaders and world opinion that the extermination of entire peoples can never be justified. Knowing that words such as "barbarity," "vandalism," or even "extermination," can't do justice to this very specific crime, he settled on "genocide" (the strategy of coining a new term was inspired by George Eastman's invention of the catchy term "Kodak" for his new cameras), a term that was accepted by the UN Steering Committee (with the crucial support of the Saudi judge Abdul Monim Bey Riad) and later incorporated in the 1948 Convention on the Prevention and Punishment of the Crime of Genocide. Lemkin died soon af-

ter his victory. See Samantha Power, *"A Problem from Hell": America and the Age of Genocide* (New York: Basic Books, 2002), chaps. 2–3 (17–60).

44. Sale, *The Conquest of Paradise*, 13.

45. In Fuchs, *Mimesis and Empire*, 7.

46. See Sale, *The Conquest of Paradise*. Francisco López de Gómara is quoted on 3, Adam Smith on 225.

47. Pagden, *Lords of All the World*, 2.

48. Sale, *The Conquest of Paradise*, 31–33.

49. Stannard, *American Holocaust*, 58, 62.

50. Sale, *The Conquest of Paradise*, 40.

51. Ibid., 18. Koning also establishes the rise of the "modern" nation-state in 1492. See his *Columbus*, 17.

52. Sale, *The Conquest of Paradise*, 45.

53. Friedell, *A Cultural History of the Modern Age*, vol. 1 (1930; New York: Knopf, 1964), chap. 5; quoted in Sale, *The Conquest of Paradise*, 46.

54. Sale, *The Conquest of Paradise*, 112.

55. Stannard, *American Holocaust*, 11. In his *Stolen Continents: The "New World" Through Indian Eyes* (Boston: Houghton Mifflin, 1992), Ronald Wright estimated the number to be around 100 million (4).

56. Stannard, *American Holocaust*, 3–4.

57. Ibid., *American Holocaust*, 5, 7–8.

58. Wright, *Stolen Continents*, 50. Only the Moorish city of Cordova could have rivaled such splendor. Under the caliphate of 'Abd al-Rahman III, it was home to half a million inhabitants, three hundred public baths, paved illuminated streets, seven hundred mosques, seventy libraries and truly mesmerizing palatial architecture. The ruler al-Hakam II established twenty-seven schools in the city and endowed the University of Cordova with more than found hundred thousand volumes, purchased from all over the East and personally annotated by him. See López-Baralt, *Islam in Spanish Literature*, 13–14.

59. Wright, *Stolen Continents*, 84–85, 91, 93.

60. Mohawk, *Utopian Legacies*, 111–12.

61. Stannard, *American Holocaust*, 95.

62. As is common in Spanish America, Cristóbal Colón's bones presumably were dug up in Valladolid, where he died anonymously in 1514, and shipped around before settling either in Santo Domingo or Seville. See *The Conquest of Paradise*, 216.

63. Sale, *The Conquest of Paradise*, 123–25, 164, 155–56, 177, 235.

64. Ibid., 241–57.

65. Ibid., 258.

66. Quoted in ibid., 264.

67. Ibid., 267–95, 296–324.

68. *The Broken Spears: The Aztec Account of the Conquest of Mexico*, expanded

and updated edition, ed. and introduction by Miguel Leon-Portilla (1962; Boston: Beacon Press, 1992), 51–52.

69. Ibid., 67–68.

70. Ibid., 146.

71. Bartolomé de Las Casas, *The Devastation of the Indies: A Brief Account*, trans. Herma Briffault (Baltimore: The Johns Hopkins University Press, 1992), 27, 28, 29, 41, 104, 101–8, 128.

72. Wright, *Stolen Continents*, 150, 151, 157–58, 159–60.

73. Ibid., 181.

74. Quoted in ibid., 165–66.

75. Quoted in ibid., 187.

76. Ibid., 185.

77. Quoted in Wright, *Stolen Continents*, 204

78. Ibid., 230.

79. Ibid., 233–38.

80. Quoted in ibid., 303.

81. Ibid., 304.

82. Anthony Pagden's preface in Todorov, *The Conquest of America*, xii–xiii.

83. Todorov, *The Conquest of America*, 42–43, 56–47, 49

84. Ibid., 77–80.

85. Ibid., 82–83.

86. Ibid., 97.

87. Ibid., 107–8.

88. Ibid., *The Conquest of America*, 106.

89. Stannard, *American Holocaust*, 233.

90. Todorov, *The Conquest of America*, 107.

91. In *The German Ideology*, Marx writes that "we do not set out from what men say, imagine, conceive, nor from men as narrated, thought of, imagined, conceived, in order to arrive at men in the flesh. We set out from real, active men, and on the basis of their real life-process we demonstrate the development of the ideological reflexes and echoes of this life-process." Excerpt in Erich Fromm, *Marx's Concept of Man* (New York: Continuum, 1961), 198.

92. Elliott, *Imperial Spain*, 65.

93. Todorov, *The Conquest of America*, 123.

94. Ibid., 127.

95. Ibid., 129, 131, 132, 133.

96. Ibid., 145.

97. Pagden, *Lords of All the World*, 91.

98. Patricia Seed, *Ceremonies of Possession in Europe's Conquest of the New World, 1492–1640* (Cambridge: Cambridge University Press, 1995), 69–99. The recourse to Islamic precedent in the conquest of America is yet another ironic layer to Spain's impossible attempt to cleanse itself of Islam.

99. Quoted in Mohawk, *Utopian Legacies*, 107–110.

100. Mohawk, *Utopian Legacies,* 111.

101. Peter Martyr 4, 4; quoted in Todorov, *The Conquest of America,* 150–5.

102. Quoted in Todorov, *The Conquest of America,* 151.

103. Lewis Hanke, *The Spanish Struggle for Justice in the Conquest of America* (Philadelphia: University of Pennsylvania Press, 1949), 123; Mohawk, *Utopian Legacies,* 137–138.

104. Pagden, *Lords of All the World,* 100.

105. Quoted in Hanke, *The Spanish Struggle for Justice,* 122.

106. Seed, *Ceremonies of Possession,* 92–93.

107. Todorov, *The Conquest of America,* 165, 166, 168, 176.

108. Ibid., 190, 189.

109. Las Casas, *Apologética historia* 3, 254; quoted in Todorov, *The Conquest of America,* 190–91.

110. Todorov, *The Conquest of America,* 192.

111. Quoted in Seed, *Ceremonies of Possession,* 77.

112. Ibid., 203, 209.

113. Quoted in ibid., 237–38.

114. Elliott, *Imperial Spain,* 72.

115. Todorov, *The Conquest of America,* 238–39.

116. Fletcher, *Moorish Spain,* 7; Elliott, *Imperial Spain,* 67, 70.

117. Fletcher, *Moorish Spain,* 7.

118. Hanke, *The Spanish Struggle for Justice,* 164.

119. Fuchs, *Mimesis and Empire,* 1.

120. Pagden, *Lords of All the World,* 74.

121. Todorov, *The Conquest of America,* 108.

122. Wright, *Stolen Continents,* 21, 36; Fuchs, *Mimesis and Empire,* 74, 75.

123. Fuchs, *Mimesis and Empire,* 2–3.

124. Ramón Eduardo Ruiz, *Triumphs and Tragedy: A History of the Mexican People* (New York: Norton, 1992), 39, 93–95.

125. Sale, *The Conquest of Paradise,* 51–55.

126. Quoted in ibid., 91.

127. Sale, *The Conquest of Paradise,* 370.

128. Todorov, *The Conquest of America,* 245.

129. Harvey, *Islamic Spain,* ix.

130. Pagden, *Lords of All the World,* 8–9.

131. Anthony Pagden, *The Fall of Natural Man: The American Indian and the Origins of Comparative Ethnology,* corrected and expanded edition (Cambridge: Cambridge University Press, 1986), 4–5.

132. Ibid., 10.

133. Chejne, *Islam and the West,* 13–14, 4.

CHAPTER 3

1. Nabil Matar, *Turks, Moors, and Englishmen in the Age of Discovery* (New York: Columbia University Press, 1999), 9, ix.

2. Ibid., 14–15.

3. Ibid., 39, 40.

4. Ibid., 63, 72.

5. Ibid., 76, 78, 81–82.

6. Ibid., 92, 98, 104.

7. Ibid., 98–99, 136, 135, 137, 107.

8. Ibid., 151–53. In 1633, Henry Marsh wrote the clearest call for holy war, although, a few years later (in 1639) Thomas Fuller wrote against it. See Matar, *Turks, Moors, and Englishmen in the Age of Discovery*, 155–57, 160–62.

9. Ibid., 153, 166.

10. Ibid., 170–72.

11. Quoted in ibid., 171.

12. Ibid., 179.

13. See Sylvanie A. Diouf's definitive work to date on the subject, *Servants of Allah: African Muslims Enslaved in the Americas* (New York: New York University Press, 1998), 17.

14. The number of Muslims—considered the fastest-growing religion in the United States in the last ffiteen years or so—was estimated to be between five and six million before the 9/11 attacks. Such estimates now appear to have been highly exaggerated, and that the number, according to two studies, probably doesn't exceed two million. See Gustav Niebuhr, "Studies Suggest Lower Count For Number of U.S. Muslims," *New York Times*, 25 October 2001.

15. See Michael A. Gomez, *Exchanging Our Country Marks: The Transformation of African Identities in the Colonial and Antebellum South* (Chapel Hill: University of North Carolina Press, 1998), chap. 4 (59–87).

16. See Allan D. Austin, *African Muslims in Antebellum America* (New York: Routledge, 1997), 5–6. The fifty-four-page document titled *Some Memoirs of the Life of Job Ben Solomon* was published in 1734.

17. Theodore Dwight, "Condition and Character of Negroes in Africa," *Methodist Quarterly Review* 46 (January 1864), 77–78. Dwight also said that pagans lived in a high state of culture.

18. Most of the preceding information can be found in Diouf's *Servants of Allah*. Also see Richard Brent Turner, *Islam in the African-American Experience* (Bloomington: University of Indiana Press, 1997), particularly chap. 1, "Muslims in a Strange Land: African Muslim Slaves in America," 11–46; and C. Eric Lincoln, "The American Muslim Mission in the Context of American Social History," in *The Muslim Community in North America*, ed. Earle H. Waugh et al. (Edmonton: University of Alberta Press, 1983), 215–33,

19. Paul Baepler, "The Barbary Captivity Narrative in Early America," *Early*

American Literature 30, no. 2 (1995), 95–120. Baepler suspects that Gee's narrative may have even influenced the Indian captivity narrative. Because Gee's narrative appeared more or less contemporaneously with Mary Rowlandson's account, published in 1682, Baepler ventures:

> we should reconsider a long-held belief about American literature: that the Indian captivity narrative, often considered the first indigenous American genre, had, if not precedents, then at least influences as far away as Africa. Cotton Mather would most likely have recognized the cross- influence himself, for his father not only wrote the introduction to Mary Rowlandson's famous narrative but he himself preached two sermons on colonials enduring African slavery, and in those sermons, he included short Barbary captivity narratives (95).

Gee's narrative structure and his rather fair treatment of his captors also anticipates one of the salient features of Barbary captivity narratives discussed later in this chapter.

20. Cited in Matar, *Turks, Moors, and Englishmen*, 94.

21. See Cotton Mather, *An Epistle to the Christian Indians* (Boston: Bartholomew Green and John Allen, 1700) and *A Pastoral Letter to the English Captives, in Africa* (Boston: B. Green and J. Allen, 1698).

22. Robert J. Allison, *The Crescent Obscured: The United States and the Muslim World, 1776–1815* (New York: Oxford University Press, 1995), 47.

23. Ibid., 47, 49, 35, 59.

24. Ibid., 50–51.

25. Ibid., 45, 53, 57, 62.

26. Fuad Sha'ban, *Islam and Arabs in Early American Thought: The Roots of Orientalism in America* (Durham, N.C.: The Acorn Press, in association with Duke University Islamic and Arabian Development Studies, 1991), vii–xii.

27. See Page Smith, *The Rise of Industrial America* (New York: McGraw-Hill, 1984), 554; quoted in ibid., xvi.

28. Sacvan Bercovitch, *The Puritan Origins of the American Self* (New Haven: Yale University Press, 1975), 136, 139.

29. Ibid., 18. President Dwight D. Eisenhower, like Congress, was responding to the Communist threat and wanted to differentiate his God-loving society from the godless Soviets. In 1954, Congress amended the Pledge of Allegiance—ironically authored by Francis Bellamy, a Christian socialist, and published on 8 September 1892 as a tribute to Americanism and its ideals—to include the words "under God" after "nation indivisible." By doing so, Congress added what the Constitution had deliberately left out, for the word "God" doesn't appear once in that document. See Arthur Schlesinger, Jr., "When Patriotism Wasn't Religious," *New York Times*, 7 July 2002. In 1955, a Florida democrat, Charles E. Bennett, introduced legislation to inscribe "In God We Trust" on U.S. currency. Coins had been stamped with this motto since the 1860s, but Congressman Bennett's legisla-

tion covered bills, as well. It was unanimously approved in both chambers and signed into law by President Eisenhower. The following year, Congress turned the phrase "In God We Trust" into the U.S. national motto. See John Files, "Charles E. Bennett Dies at 92: Put 'In God We Trust' on Bills," *New York Times*, 10 September 2003.

30. See Bercovitch, *The Puritan Origins of the American Self*, 157.

31. Thomas J. Schlereth, *The Cosmopolitan Ideal in Enlightenment Thought: Its Form and Function in the Ideas of Franklin, Hume, and Voltaire, 1694–1790* (Notre Dame, Ind.: The University of Notre Dame Press, 1977), xii–xiii.

32. Ibid., 17–18. Benjamin Franklin wrote: "Prose Writing has been of great Use to me in the Course of my Life, and was a principal means of my Advancement."

33. Ibid.

34. David Hume, "Of the Standard of Taste," *Essays* I: 266; quoted in ibid., 22.

35. Ibid., 31, 36, 44, 57, 62, 66, 72.

36. Ibid., 73–75, 88–91.

37. Ibid., 97–103.

38. Ibid., 106–7, 111–12, 124–25.

39. Ibid., 126–36.

40. Sha ban, *Islam and Arabs in Early American Thought* 23.

41. Allison, *The Crescent Obscured*, xiv.

42. Ibid., xvii.

43. Ibid., 13.

44. Ibid., 25, 26. Jefferson assumed office on 4 March 1801. See Tyrone G. Martin, *Most Fortunate Ship: A Narrative History of Old Ironsides*, revised ed. (Annapolis, Md.: Naval Institute Press, 1997), 83.

45. Ibid., 33

46. Ibid., xvi.

47. Ibid., 187, 201, 204.

48. "The parallels between this song and the one [Key] wrote after watching the British bombard Fort McHenry in September 1814 are striking. The tune is the same, as is the rhyme scheme of the chorus. In the more famous later version, the fate of the 'star-spangled flag of our nation' is in doubt throughout the perilous fight. In this song, however, it obscures the Muslim crescent, whose hollow splendor is cast in shadow by the true glory of the American flag and the republic it symbolizes." Allison, *The Crescent Obscured*, 205–6. A Baltimore actor later sang Key's "Defence of Fort McHenry" in a public performance and called it "The Star-Spangled Banner." Following a twenty-year effort during which more than forty bills and joint resolutions were introduced in Congress, it was finally adopted as national anthem on 3 March 1931. But the actual words were not included in the legal documents. Key himself had written several versions with slight variations, so discrepancies in the exact wording still occur. See http://www.usflag.org/francis.scott.key.html.

49. Malini Johar Schueller, *U.S. Orientalisms: Race, Nation, and Gender in Literature, 1790–1890* (Ann Arbor: University of Michigan Press, 1998), viii. Schueller uses the more accurate expression "USAmerican" to differentiate the United States from other American nations, but I have kept the adjective "American" for the sake of discursive consistency and since it is clear that I am referring to the United States, not to Canada or any Latin America country.

50. Ibid., 3, 10, 12, 66, 65.

51. Ibid., 19, 20, 40–42.

52. Gordon S. Wood, *The Radicalism of the American Revolution* (New York: Knopf, 1992); Joyce Appleby, *Inheriting the Revolution: The First Generation of Americans* (Cambridge, Mass.: The Belknap Press of Harvard University Press, 2000).

53. Wood, *The Radicalism of the American Revolution*, 38, 55. Wood shows that despite the later reading of his autobiography as the parable of the self-made, frugal, and economizing man, Franklin's retirement at the age of 42 shows that he was very much an integral part of this culture.

54. Ibid., 92, 123, 184, 186–87, 222–25.

55. Ibid., 152, 278.

56. Quoted in ibid., 338.

57. Ibid., 347, 357.

58. Appleby, *Inheriting the Revolution*, 3, 7, 8, 11–13, 17.

59. Ibid., 29, 33, 34, 41–45. The German traveler is quoted on 35.

60. Ibid., 45, 55.

61. Ibid., 57, 88–89.

62. Ibid., 95, 96–100, 128.

63. Ibid., 133, 137, 139, 141, 152, 155–56, 160, 195.

64. Ibid., 174, 182, 183–84, 193.

65. Ibid., 179–99, 202, 203, 204, 206, 214–15.

66. Ibid., 227–31.

67. Ibid., 248, 249.

68. Ibid., 252–53.

69. Quoted in ibid., 258.

70. Ibid., 265.

71. Ibid., 266.

72. Cited in Jack P. Greene, "Search for Identity: An Interpretation of the Meaning of Selected Patterns of Social Response in Eighteenth-Century America," *Journal of Social History* 3 (1970): 191 n. 5.

73. Greene, "Search for Identity," 189–224.

74. Quoted in Andrew J. Bacevich, "New Rome, New Jerusalem," *Wilson Quarterly* 26 (summer 2002): 51.

75. John Phillip Reid, *The Concept of Liberty in the Age of the American Revolution* (Chicago: The University of Chicago Press, 1988), 1.

76. Edmund S. Morgan, "Slavery and Freedom: The American Paradox," *Journal of American History* 59 (June 1972): 5–29.

77. Reid, *The Concept of Liberty*, 46, 47–48, 50–52.

78. Joseph Towers, *A Letter to Dr. Samuel Johnson: Occasioned by His Late Political Publications. With an Appendix. Containing Some Observations on a Pamphlet Lately Published by Dr. Shebbeare* (London, 1775); quoted in Reid, *The Concept of Liberty*, 58.

79. Quoted in ibid., 66–67.

80. Ibid., 68–73.

81. Anonymous. *A Discourse, Addressed to the Sons of Liberty, at a Solemn Assembly, near Liberty-Tree, in Boston, February 14, 1766*; quoted. in ibid., 91.

82. Ibid., 92.

83. Ibid., 98, 105.

84. Quoted in ibid., 107.

85. Ibid., 120.

86. Quoted in ibid., 122.

87. Quoted in Gary B. Nash, *Race and Revolution* (Madison, Wisc.: Madison House, 1990), 19.

88. Nash, *Race and Revolution*, 48–49.

89. Ibid., 57–59, 77, 79, 83.

90. Quoted in ibid., 190.

91. Nash, *Race and Revolution*, 189.

92. Quoted in Paul Baepler, "The Barbary Captivity Narrative in Early America," *Early American Literature* 30, no. 2 (1995): 113; 95–120.

93. Lotfi Ben Rejeb, "America's Captive Freemen in North Africa: The Comparative Method in Abolitionist Persuasion," *Slavery and Abolition* 9, no. 1 (1988): 61.

94. Ibid., 62.

95. Lotfi Ben Rejeb, "Barbary's Character in European Letters, 1514–1830: An Ideological Prelude to Colonization," *Dialectical Anthroplogy* 6, no. 4 (June 1982): 349.

96. See, for instance, David Brion Davis, *The Problem of Slavery in Western Culture* (New York: Oxford University Press, 1966), 182, 447.

97. The significance of Islam in shaping American consciousness and establishing a sense of national identity has been masterfully elaborated in Allison's *The Crescent Obscured*.

98. *A Journal of the Captivity and Sufferings of John Foss; Several Years a Prisoner in Algiers*, 2d ed. (Newburyport: A. March, 1798). Page references in the text are from this edition.

99. Royall Tyler, *The Algerine Captive; or, The Life and Adventures of Doctor Updike Underhill, Six Years a Prisoner Among the Algerines*, a facsimile reproduction of the London edition of 1802, with an introduction by Jack B. Moore (1797; Gainesville, Fla.: Scholars' Facsimiles and Reprints, 1967). Page references in the text are from this edition.

100. See Don L. Cook's introduction to his edition for the "Modern Reader" (New Haven, Conn.: College and University Press, 1970), 26. Cook's modernized edition is based on the 1797 edition. A New Library paperback edition is now available.

101. Ada Lou Carson and Herbert L. Carson, *Royall Tyler* (Boston: Twayne, 1979), 28–33.

102. Quoted in ibid., 67.

103. Quoted in ibid., 67.

104. Ibid., 67. Also see G. Thomas Tanselle, *Royall Tyler* (Cambridge, Mass.: Harvard University Press, 1967), 268 n. 29.

105. Tanselle, *Royall Tyler*, 142.

106. Quoted in ibid., 141.

107. Cooper opens his 1822 review of Maria Sedgwick's *A New England Tale*, published in the *Repository*, by lamenting the paucity of literature that truly reflects American society:

> We have seen but two attempts of this sort which merit any praise, a story called Salem Witchcraft, and Mr. Tyler's forgotten, and we fear, lost narrative of the Algerine Captive, both of which relate to times long past. Any future collector of our national tales, would do well to snatch these from oblivion, and to give them that place among the memorials of other days, which is due to the early and authentic historians of a country.

See James Fenimore Cooper, *Early Critical Essays*, facsimile reproductions from *The Literary and Scientific Repository, and Critical Review*, introduction by James F. Beard, Jr. (Gainesville, Fla.: Scholars' Facsimiles and Reprints, 1955), 97–98.

108. Quoted in ibid., 146.

109. Ibid., 180, 149, 167, 179.

110. James Riley, *An Authentic Narrative of the Loss of the American Brig Commerce, Wrecked on the Western Coast of Africa, in the Month of August, 1815 . . .* (New York: Riley, 1817). Page references in the text are from this edition.

111. Ben Rejeb, "Barbary's Character in European Letters," 348.

112. In John L. Scripp's authorized biography of Lincoln (which was read by Lincoln before publication), Riley's *Narrative* is mentioned sixth in a list of books including the Bible. "Riley's *Narrative* was without a doubt one of the greatest forces in developing Lincoln's unfavorable reaction to slavery." See R. Gerald McMurty, "The Influence of Riley's *Narrative* upon Abraham Lincoln," *Indiana Magazine of History*, June 1934, 133–38.

113. Gerald R. Ford, "Inclusive America, Under Attack," *New York Times*, 8 August 1999.

114. See William S. McFeely, *Frederick Douglass* (New York: Norton, 1991), 5, 36; Allison, *The Crescent Obscured*, 101

115. Cited in Chris Mooney, "The Barbary Analogy," *The American Prospect Online*, 16 October 2001.

116. *The American Literary Revolution, 1783–1837,* ed. Robert E. Spiller (New York: New York University Press, 1967), 282–83.

CHAPTER 4

1. Eric Hobsbawm, *The Age of Capital: 1848–1875* (1975; New York: Barnes and Noble, 1996), 3, 1, 4, 9–26, 47.
2. Ibid., 116–34, 135, 139, 193–206, 275, 276.
3. Ibid., 303–8.
4. Quoted in Theodore Von Laue, *The World Revolution of Westernization: The Twentieth Century in Global Perspective* (New York: Oxford University Press, 1987), 161.
5. E. J. Hobsbawm, *The Age of Empire: 1875–1914* (New York: Pantheon, 1987), 2, 10, 9.
6. Ibid., 26–32.
7. Ibid., 60, 64, 69, 70–72, 76, 77–79.
8. Ibid., 88, 102–3, 105–6, 110.
9. Ibid., 231, 253–56, 263–66, 271–75.
10. Ibid., 277, 284–85, 286–92, 301.
11. Von Laue, *World Revolution of Westernization,* 3–8.
12. Quoted in ibid., 16.
13. Ibid., 25–26.
14. Quoted in ibid., 30.
15. Quoted in ibid.
16. Quoted in ibid., 83.
17. Quoted in ibid., 105–6.
18. Ibid., 125.
19. Eric Hobsbawm, *The Age of Extremes: A History of the World, 1914–1991* (New York: Pantheon Books, 1994), 6–8, 15, 208.
20. Ibid., 292, 320–34.
21. Ibid., 334, 339, 342.
22. Ibid., 349, 347, 431.
23. Herman Melville, *Journal of a Visit to Europe and the Levant* (1837); quoted in Fuad Sha'ban, *Islam and Arabs in Early American Thought: The Roots of Orientalism in America* (Durham, N.C.: The Acorn Press, in association with Duke University Islamic and Arabian Development Studies, 1991), 94–95.
24. Sha'ban, *Islam and Arabs in Early American Thought,* 95–96.
25. Ibid., 106, 111.
26. Quoted in ibid., 142.
27. Ibid., 143, 172–73.
28. Quoted. in ibid., 189–90.
29. *Virginia Pamphlets,* I (1–20); quoted in ibid., 195.
30. "Orientalism." *The Knickerbocker* 41 (June 1853).

31. See Elizabeth Ammons, *Edith Wharton's Argument with America* (Athens: University of Georgia Press, 1980), 142; Mary Suzanne Schirber, "*Fighting France*: Travel Writing in the Grotesque," in *A Forward Glance: New Essays on Edith Wharton*, ed. Clare Colquitt, Susan Goodman, and Candace Waid (Newark: University of Delaware Press, 1999), 139–48; ; Mary Suzanne Schirber, "Edith Wharton and the Dog-Eared Travel Book," in *Wretched Exotic: Essays on Edith Wharton in Europe*, ed. Katherine Joslin and Alan Price (New York: Peter Lang, 1993), 147–64; Judith L. Sensibar, "Edith Wharton as Propagandist and Novelist: Competing Visions of 'The Great War,'" in *A Forward Glance*, 149–71; Stephanie Batcos, "A 'Fairy tale every minute': The Autobiographical Journey and Edith Wharton's *In Morocco*," in *A Forward Glance*, 173–87; Roger Asselineau, "Edith Wharton—She Thought in French and Wrote in English," in *Wretched Exotic*, 355–63; Frederick Wegener, "Edith Wharton on French Colonial Charities for Women: An Unknown Travel Essay," *Tulsa Studies in Women's Literature* 1 (spring 1998): 11–36 (including original and footnoted translation).

32. See William A. Hoisington, Jr., *Lyautey and the French Conquest of Morocco* (New York: St. Martin's Press, 1995); Alan Scham, *Lyautey in Morocco: Protectorate Administration, 1912–1925* (Berkeley: University of California Press, 1970). Daniel Rivet, *Le Maroc de Lyautey à Mohammed V: Le double visage du protectorat* (Paris: Denoel, 1999). D. Lloyd George's assessment of Lyautey is in his foreword to Vice Admiral C. V. Usborne's *The Conquest of Morocco* (London: Stanley Paul and Co., 1936), 14.

33. John Maier, *Desert Songs: Western Images of Morocco and Moroccan Images of the West* (Albany: State Uuniversity of New York Press, 1996), 63–87, 95–97; Alison Baker, *Voices of Resistance: Oral Histories of Moroccan Women* (Albany: State University of New York Press, 1998). In 1909, a Spanish journalist attributed the defeat of Spanish forces in the Rif to "the decisive role played by Moroccan women" (18). In 1913, the women of Khmisset rose up in rebellion against the French and had to be subdued by French military power. In the Middle Atlas, women did the same, urging their men to war with ululations and shaming them if they retreated (19).

34. Alfred Kazin wrote that Wharton "could hate and hate hard, but the object of her hatred was the emerging new class of brokers and industrialists, the makers and promoters of the industrial era who were beginning to expropriate and supplant her own class. She disliked them no less fiercely than did the rebellious novelists of the muckrake era." She was affronted by such parvenus. The Midwest was America's hinterland, but unlike Morocco's, this was a bland and provincial land. Alfred Kazin, "Edith Wharton," in *Edith Wharton: A Collection of Critical Essays*, ed. Irving Howe (Englewood Cliffs, N.J.: Prentice-Hall, 1962), 89–94.

35. Edith Wharton, *In Morocco* (1919; New York: Ecco, 1996), 222–23. Page numbers in the text are from this edition.

36. Gregorio Lopez y Fuentes, *El Indio*, trans. Anita Brenner (New York: Continuum, 1996). Page numbers in the text are from this edition.

37. *Native American Testimony: A Chronicle of Indian-White Relations from Prophecy to the Present, 1492–2000,* rev. and updated, ed. Peter Nabokov, foreword by Vine Deloria, Jr. (New York: Penguin, 1999). Page numbers in the text are from this edition.

38. John C. Mohawk, *Utopian Legacies: A History of Conquest and Oppression in the Western World* (Santa Fe, N.Mex.: Clear Lights Publishers, 2000), 8.

39. N. Scott Momaday, *House Made of Dawn* (1968; New York: Perennial Classics, 1999). Page references in the text are from this edition.

40. Leslie Marmon Silko, *Ceremony* (1977; New York: Penguin, 1986). Page numbers in the text are from this edition.

41. Leslie Marmon Silko, *Almanac of the Dead* (New York: Penguin, 1992). First published by Simon and Schuster 1991. Page numbers in the text are from this edition.

42. Quoted in *Native American Testimony,* 438–40.

43. Quoted in *Native American Testimony,* 447.

44. *Native American Testimony,* 469–70.

45. See George Collier, with Elizabeth Lowery Quaratiello, *Basta! Land and the Zapatista Rebellion in Chiapas,* foreword by Peter Rosset (Oakland, Ca.: The Institute for Food and Development Policy, 1994), 1. This book was one of the earliest to provide a full background to the Zapatista rebellion.

46. Ibid., 16, 78, 81–87.

47. Alan Riding, *Distant Neighbors: A Portrait of the Mexicans* (1984; New York: Vintage, 1989), 4, 364, 370–71.

48. Driss Chriabi, *The Butts,* trans. Hugh A. Carter (Washington D.C.: Three Continents Press, 1983). Page numbers in the text are from this edition.

49. Abdelrahman Munif, *Variations on Night and Day,* trans. Peter Theroux (New York: Pantheon Books, 1993). Page references in the text are from this edition.

50. Abdelrahman Munif, *Cities of Salt,* trans. Peter Theroux (New York: Vintage International, 1989). Page references in the text are from this edition.

51. Abdelrahman Munif, *The Trench,* trans. Peter Theroux (New York: Vintage International, 1993). Page references in the text are from this edition.

52. Daniel Yergin, *The Prize: The Epic Quest for Oil, Money, and Power* (New York: Simon and Schuster, 1991), 14–15. "Hydrocarbon Man" emerged as a particularly full-blown species in the postwar period, when cheap oil fuelled rapid industrialization in war-torn Europe and Japan and forever changed American culture. Suburbanization (as a form of anti-Communism) made cars indispensable. Shopping centers, motels, Holiday Inns, McDonalds, and Howard Johnsons were all conceived to cater to the hurried and exhausted motorist. America became a "drive-in society" as the automobile became associated with rites of passage, romance, and even marriage. "One survey in the late 1960s found that almost 40 percent of all marriages in America were proposed in a car." See chap. 27 (541–61).

53. Sandra Mackey, *The Saudis: Inside the Desert Kingdom* (Boston: Houghton Mifflin, 1987), 368.

54. Noureddine Afaya, *L'Occident dans l'imaginaire arabo-musulman* (Casablanca, Morocco: Éditions Toubkal, 1997).

55. Ibid., 11, 12–13, 14, 15.

56. Ibid., 43.

57. Of him, Jacque Berque said: "To endow Egypt with the modern classics, make it a friend to Greek reason, integrate it into the world without taking away from the country's luminous identity, make it a beacon of historical reason among the Arabs . . . the man, as a man and an artist, was qualified to undertake such a project." Quoted in ibid., 45. My translation.

58. Ibid., 37–40.

59. Ibid., 47–57.

60. Ibid., 58, 67.

61. Ibid., 67–68, 81.

62. Ibid., 82–86.

63. Ibid., 86–105.

64. Ibid., 107–32.

65. Ibid., 133–34.

CHAPTER 5

1. In its January 2002 meeting, the American Dialect Society voted the expression "9/11" as "most likely to last." Terms such as "burka," "weaponize," and "hawala" were added to the fourth edition of the *American Heritage Dictionary*. "Madrassah" and "Wahhabism" were already included. A new category of people has been identified: "Osamaniacs" (women infatuated with Osama) and "Osamaphiles." See Janny Scott, "Words of 9/11 Go from Coffee Shops to the Dictionaries," *New York Times*, 24 February 2002.

2. For a interesting cultural studies analysis of Osama bin Laden's face, see Bill Wasik, "American Lucifer," *Harper's*, December 2001, 52–53.

3. Even ardent pro-American middle-class Kuwaitis were more likely to believe Osama bin Laden and distrust the United States. Some even named their sons after the Saudi renegade. See Douglas Jehl, "For Some Kuwaitis, the Ardor for America Cools," *New York Times*, 16 November 2001.

4. Steven Erlanger, "Italy's Premier Calls Western Civilization Superior to Islamic World," *New York Times*, 27 September 2001. Berlusconi's statement was followed by a flood of denunciations and commentary, although the prime minister didn't recant his views or what *Le Monde* called in its editorial, his "gaffe." "La 'gaffe' de Berlusconi," *Le Monde*, 28 September 2001. Melinda Henneberger, "Berlusconi Stands by Remarks on Islam," *New York Times*, 29 September 2001. At odds with national (i.e., anti-American) sentiments, Berlusconi considers himself a Bush admirer and ally of the United States. See Melinda Henneberger, "A Bush Admirer Longs to Join America's A-List," *New York Times*, 20 October 2001.

5. Bernard Lewis, "What Went Wrong?" *Atlantic*, January 2002, 43–45.

6. Fareed Zakaria, "Why Do They Hate Us?" Special Report. *Newsweek*, 15 October 2001, 22–40; Fareed Zakaria, "How to Save the Arab World," *Newsweek*, 24 December 2001, 22–28; Margaret Thatcher, "Advice to a Superpower," *New*

York Times, 11 February 2002.; Thomas L. Friedman, "The 2 Domes of Belgium," *New York Times*, 27 January 2002. Friedman called Muslims in Europe "perennial outsiders" who are humiliated by their low social status.

7. See excerpts from his testimony to the Senate Select Intelligence Committee on 6 February 2002 in "Words of the C.I.A. Chief on Terror," *New York Times*, 7 February 2002.

8. Sachs is quoted in Joseph Kahn, "A Business Plan for Islam Inc.," *New York Times*, 30 December 2001. The idea of a "new Marshall Plan" was proposed by Richard Sokolsky and Joseph McMillan in an Op-Ed article: "Foreign Aid in Our Own Defense," *New York Times*, 12 February 2002.

9. Peter Steinfels, "Amid Islam's Complexity, Scholars Are Challenged to Influence Change without Compromising," *New York Times*, 29 September 2001. Jay Tolson, of the *U.S. News and World Report* wrote to say that the real struggle is within Islam and that the United States would be wise to support the right Muslim groups. See Jay Tolson, "Fight to the Finish," *U.S. News and World Report*, 1 October 2001, 36–39.

10. Lamin Sanneh, "Faith and the Secular State," *New York Times*, 23 September 200; Thomas Cahill, "The One and True Faith: Is It Tolerance?" *New York Times*, 3 February 2002; Douglas Frantz, "Turkey, Well Along Road to Secularism, Fears Detour to Islamism," *New York Times*, 8 January 2002. The Frantz article chronicles the fate of Recep Tayyip Erdogan, the popular Islamist ex-mayor of Istanbul, in conflicted Turkey. In late 2002, Erdogan's Islamist party won a landslide victory in Turkey's elections, but Erdogan, who had been convicted for reading subversive poetry, was barred from serving as a lawmaker or prime minister. In March 2003, as the United States prepared to attack Iraq, and after the Turkish parliament had turned down a U.S. request to use Turkish territory to stage an attack from the North, Erdogan overcame the legal barrier to become prime minister.

11. Pierre Bourdieu called globalization a deliberate political process often taking place outside of public view. He thereby contests the view that globalization is a "natural" event. See his "Pour un savoir engagé," *Le Monde diplomatique*, February 2002, 3. Amartya Sen, the Nobel Prize economist, separates globalization from Westernization by showing that ideas and technologies have always traveled through trade. The problem for him is "the inequity in the overall balance of institutional arrangements—which produces very unequal sharing of the benefits of globalization." See Amartya Sen, "How to Judge Globalism," *The American Prospect*, 14 January 2002.

12. Linda Tuhiwai Smith, *Decolonizing Methodologies: Research and Indigenous Peoples* (London: Zed, 1999), 1.

13. Gaddis Smith, "The U.S. vs. International Terrorists: A Chapter From Our Past," *American Heritage*, August 1977, 37–43.

14. Ibid.

15. Program heard on 13 September 2001 around 3: 43 P.M. in Portland, Maine.

16. Richard Leiby, "Terrorists by Another Name: The Barbary Pirates," *Washington Post*, 15 October 2001.

17. Stephen Wrage, "Pirates and Parasites," *Washington Post*, 20 October 2001.

18. Paul Johnson, "The Answer to Terrorism? Colonialism," *Wall Street Journal*, 9 October 2001; "Colonialism's Back—and Not a Moment Too Soon," *New York Times Magazine*, 18 April 1993, 22, 43–44.

19. T. Kendall, "Two Hundred Years Ago Islam Bullied U.S.," *Boston Globe*, 28 October 2001.

20. Paul Baepler, "Rewriting the Barbary Captivity Narratiuve: The Perdicaris Affair and the Last Barbary Pirate," *Prospects: An Annual of American Cultural Studies* 24 (1999): 177–211.

21. Avishai Margalit and Ian Buruma, "Occidentalism," *New York Review of Books*, 17 January 2002, 4–7. The authors describe many of the modern "isms"—Nazism, fascism, communism, Islamism, and so on—as "heroic creeds" rejecting the mediocrity of bourgeois values.

22. David H. Bennett, *The Party of Fear: From Nativist Movements to the New Right in American History* (Chapel Hill: The University of North Carolina Press, 1988).

23. Nicholas D. Kristoff, "Terrorism beyond Islam," *New York Times*, 8 January 2002. Of course, Kristoff predictably says that these attitudes were tempered by successful modernization and that Islam would do well to note that modernization doesn't necessarily undermine national honor, as the Meiji reforms in Japan illustrate.

24. Jean Ziegler, "Décalages nord-sud à l'internationale socialiste," *Le Monde diplomatique*, November 1992, 9.

25. Somini Sengupta, "Child Traffickers Prey on Bangladesh," *New York Times*, 29 April 2002.

26. Rachel L. Swarns, "Unthinkable Attack Jolts a Crime-Weary Country," *New York Times*, 16 November 2001.

27. Elisabeth Rosenthal, "Blinded by Poverty: The Dark Side of Capitalism," *New York Times*, 21 November 2000; Michael Wines, "An Ailing Russia Lives a Tough Life That's Getting Shorter," *New York Times*, 3 December 2000. The *New York Times* reported that these numbers have began to stabilize as the rich have stopped feasting on boar and are now eating sushi, exercising, and breathing flavored oxygen. They want to look slim, tan, and beautiful. Sabrina Tavernise, "Waiter, Forget the Boar. I'd Rather Have Oxygen," *New York Times*, 24 September 2002.

28. "Study Finds Poverty Deepening in Former Communist Countries," *New York Times*, 12 October 2000.

29. Barbara Crossette, "U.N. Warns that Trafficking in Human Beings Is Growing," *New York Times*, 25 June 2000; David Binder, "In Europe, Sex Slavery Is Thriving Despite Raids," *New York Times*, 20 October 2002; Joel Brinkley, "Vast Trade in Forced Labor Portrayed in C.I. A. Report," *New York Times*, 2 April 2000.

30. Roger Cohen, "The Oldest Profession Seeks New Market in West Europe," *New York Times*, 19 April 2000; Alison Smale, "The Dark Side of the Global Economy," *New York Times*, 26 August 2001; Leslie Wayne, "America's For-Profit Secret Army," *New York Times*, 13 October 2002.

31. See Françoise Loncle, "L'Europe de l'Ouest, proxénète des femmes de l'Est," *Le Monde diplomatique*, Novermber 2001, 8–9.

32. See Timothy Egan, "Technology Sent Wall Street into Market for Pornography," *New York Times*, 23 October 2000; Frank Rich, "Naked Capitalists," *New York Times Magazine*, 20 May 2001, 51–56, 80–82, 92. Eric Scholsser, *Reefer Madness: Sex, Drugs, and Cheap Labor in the American Black Market* (Boston: Houghton Mifflin, 2003), 114, 220.

33. Matthew Brzezinski, "Re-engineering the Drug Business," *New York Times Magazine*, 23 June 2002, 24–29, 46, 54–55; Scholsser, *Reefer Madness*, 14.

34. Jack Hitt, "Bandits in the Global Shipping Lanes," *New York Times Magazine*, 20 August 2000, 37–41, 52, 68–69. Scholsser, *Reefer Madness*, 216, 6.

35. World Health Organization, "First Ever Global Report on Violence and Health Released" (http://www.who.int/mediacentre/releases/pr73/en/).

36. Ford Fessenden, "They Threaten, Seethe and Unhinge, Then Kill in Quantity," *New York Times*, 9 April 2000; *New York Times*, "Two Million Inmates, and Counting," *New York Times*, 9 April 2003; in 1997, 49.4 percent of the U.S. prison population was black, while only 47.9 percent was white. See Teresa Brennan, *Globalization and Its Terrors: Daily Life in the West* (New York: Routledge, 2003), 83, and 215 n. 29.

37. William Pfaff, "Scaring America Half to Death," *International Herald Tribune*, 8 May 2003; Elaine Sciolino, "A Crime-Weary France Plans a Crackdown," *New York Times*, 24 October 2002. On cars and SUVs, see Keith Bradsher, "The Latest Fashion: Fear-of-Crime Design," *New York Times*, 25 July 2000. *New York Times*, "U.S. Traffic Deaths Set a 12–Year High; Alcohol is Big Factor," *New York Times*, 24 April 2003.

38. Barbara Crossette, "U.N. Board Says Legal Drug Increases in Rich Countries," *New York Times*, 21 February 2001; Robert Pear, "New Study Finds 60 Million Uninsured during a Year," *New York Times*, 13 May 2003; Scholsser, *Reefer Madness*, 220; *New York Times*, "Agency Puts Hunger No. 1 on List of World's Top Health Risks," *New York Times*, 31 October 2002; Seth Mydans, "Clustering in Cities, Asians Are Becoming Obese," *New York Times*, 13 March 2003; Jonathan Amos, "Obesity Is Changing Human Shape," *BBC News Online*, 9 September 2002; Denise Grady, "Exchanging Obesity Risks for Surgery's," *New York Times*, 12 October 2000. Bariatric surgeries have gone up since then, reaching sixty thousand in 2002. See Raymond Hernandez, "Politician, as Last Resort, Sheds Weight by Surgery," *New York Times*, 16 November 2002.

39. Greg Winter, "States Attempt to Curb Sales of Soda and Candy in Schools," *New York Times*, 9 September 2001; Greg Winter, "America Rubs Its

Stomach, and Says Bring It On," *New York Times*, 7 July 2002; Don Peck, "The Weight of the World," *Atlantic*, June 2003, 38–39.

40. Sara Rimer, "Parents of Troubled Youths Are Seeking Help at Any Cost," *New York Times*, 10 September 2001. In fact, a new market specializing in the modification of American teenagers' behavior is flourishing overseas. See Tim Weiner, "Parents, Shopping for Discipline, Turn to Tough Schools Abroad," *New York Times*, 9 May 2003.

41. Raymond Hernandez, "Children's Sexual Exploitation Underestimated, Study Finds," *New York Times*, 10 September 2001.

42. Jeff Madrick, "Economic Scene," *New York Times*, 13 June 2002. On drug abuse in the United States, see the press release "Annual Household Survey Finds Millions of Americans in Denial About Drug Abuse" at http://www.samhsa.gov/news/content/2001nhsda.htm. For the whole report, see http://www.samhsa.gov/oas/nhsda/2k1nhsda/vol1/toc.htm. Robert Pear, "Number of People Living in Poverty Increases in U.S.," *New York Times*, 25 September 2002; Sam Dillon, "Report Finds Deep Poverty Is on the Rise," *New York Times*, 30 April 2003; Brennan, *Globalization and Its Terrors*, 83. Haya El Nasser, "Sinking Feeling Confirmed by Economic Date," *USA Today*, 25 September 2002; Sheryl Gay Stolberg, "Children's Use of Prescription Drugs Is Surging, Study Shows," *New York Times*, 19 September 2002.

43. Brennan, *Globalization and Its Terrors*, 10, 19–95.

44. "Des entreprises plus riches que des pays, selon le classement onusien des entités économiques," *Yahoo! Actualités*, 12 August 2002.

45. Kate Jennings, "The Hypocrisy of Wall Street Culture," *New York Times*, 14 July 2002; Andrew Ross Sorkin, "Murdoch Adds to His Empire by Agreeing to Buy DirecTV," *New York Times*, 10 April 2003.

46. Ted C. Fishman, "Making a Killing," *Harper's*, August 2002, 33–41.

47. For a list of billionaires, see http://www.forbes.com/2002/02/28/billion-aires_print.html. For an analysis of the *Forbes* list, see John Cavanagh and Sarah Anderson, "World's Billionaires Take a Hit, But Still Soar," Institute for Policy Studies at http://www.ips-dc.org/projects/global_econ/billionaires.htm.

48. Stanely Hoffman, "Clash of Globalizations," *Foreign Affairs* 81, July–August 2002, 104–15.

49. Edward S. Herman, "The Threat of Globalization," *Global Policy Forum*, April 1999; http://www.globalpolicy.org/globaliz/define/hermantk.htm.

50. Interview with Lucy Komisar, *The Progressive*, June 2000, 34–38. In a separate article, Joseph Stiglitz showed that by 2003, Russia's gross domestic product was less than a third of what it had been in 1990 and that, even expecting an annual growth rate of 4 percent, "it will take Russia's economy another decade to get back to where it was when communism collapsed." Joseph Stiglitz, "The Ruin of Russia," *Guardian*, 9 April 2003.

51. John Gray, "The Era of Globalization Is Over," *New Statesman*, 24 September 2001.

52. Tina Rosenberg, "The Free-Trade Fix," *New York Times Magazine*, 18 August 2002, 28–33, 50, 74–75.

53. Edmund L. Andrews, "Rich Nations Criticized for Barriers to Trade," *New York Times*, 30 September 2002.

54. Mark Weisbrot, "Why Globalisation Fails to Deliver," *Observer*, 28 July 2002.

55. Mark Townsend and Jason Burke, "Earth 'will expire by 2050,'" *Observer*, 7 July 2002.

56. Andrew C. Revkin, "Large Ice Shelf Disintegrates at Great Speed," *New York Times*, 20 March 2002; Andrew C. Revkin, "Study of Antarctic Points to Rising Sea Levels," *New York Times*, 7 March 2003. In 2000, when the United Nations convened the world's religious leaders for a summit in New York, an Eskimo leader from Greenland told the audience that his people had reported that the glacier was melting. See Jonathan Sacks, *The Dignity of Difference: How to Avoid the Clash of Civilizations* (New York: Continuum, 2002), 6.

57. See Douglas Jehl, "In Race to Tap the Euphrates, the Upper Hand is Mainstream," *New York Times*, 25 August 2002; John Tagliabue, "As Multinationals Run the Taps, Anger Rises over Water for Profit," *New York Times*, 26 August 2002; Maude Barlow and Tony Clarke, "Who Owns Water?" *The Nation*, 2 September 2002; Maude Barlow and Tony Clarke, "Fight-Back in Bolivia," *The Nation*, 2 September 2002.

58. Juan Forero, "Still Poor, Latin Americans Protest Push for Open Markets," *New York Times*, 19 July 2002. See "L'Amérique latine en chiffres," *Le Monde diplomatique*, September 2002; Juan Forero, "Latin America's Political Compass Veers Toward the Left," *New York Times*, 19 January 2003; William Finnegan, "The Economics of Empire," *Harper's*, May 2003, 45. A profile of Evo Morales appears in Juan Forero, "From Llama Trails to the Corridors of Power," *New York Times*, 6 July 2002.

59. See Romilly Greenhill's and Ann Pettifor's report for the Jubilee Research at the New Economics Foundation's "The United States as a H[eavily] I[ndebted] P[rosperous] C[ountry]," April 2002 http://www.jubilee2000uk.org/analysis. Click on reports and on j+usa7.htm.

60. See Edmund L. Andrews, "Sluggish U.S. Economy a Global Concern," *New York Times*, 27 September 2002. As the United States embarked on shaping the Middle East in 2003 and establishing a foothold in the region, foreign investors controlled "about $8 trillion" of the country's "financial assets." "This," historian Niall Ferguson commented, "could make for a fragile Pax Americana if [these] foreign investors decide to reduce their stakes in the American economy, possibly trading their dollars for the increasingly vigorous Euro." See Niall Ferguson, "True Cost of Hegemony: Huge Debt," *New York Times*, 20 April 2003; Frédéric F. Clairmont, "Vivre à crédit ou le credo de la première puissance du monde," *Le Monde diplomatique*, April 2003, 20–21. Clairmont states that foreign investors control 42 percent of U.S. Treasury bonds.

61. Martin Walker has shown that as of 2000, the U.S. military had at least 646 bases overseas and 182,000 troops around the world. The United States also dominates the world financially, politically, and culturally. Most of the "world's intellectual talent" is trained in American universities, which gives the United States unparalleled influence. "Never before has there been anything quite like this American domination of the world." See Martin Walker, "What Kind of Empire?" *Wilson Quarterly* 26 (summer 2002): 36–49. In his first inaugural address in 1789, George Washington stated that "the preservation of the sacred fire of liberty" had been entrusted to the "American people." (52). But if the United States was the New Jerusalem, in Philip Freneau's expression, it has become the New Rome after the fall of the Berlin Wall in 1989. In this new order, the notion of freedom seems to have been radically configured to mean "maximizing opportunities for the creation of wealth and removing whatever impediments remain to confine the sovereign self. Freedom has come to mean treating the market and market values as sacrosanct." See Andrew J. Bacevich, "New Rome, New Jerusalem," *Wilson Quarterly* 26 (summer 2002): 50–58. On "postmodern liberalism" see Robert Cooper, "The New Liberal Imperialism," *Observer*, 7 April 2002. For a general assessment on the rehabilitation of imperialism, see John Bellamy Foster, "The Rediscovery of Imperialism," *Monthly Review* 54 (November 2002): 1–16.

62. Elaine Sciolino, "2015 Outlook: Enough Food, Scarce Water, Porous Borders," *New York Times*, 18 December 2000. President Bush himself warns against the growing ranks of poverty. In "The National Security Strategy of the United States," he stated: "A world where some live in comfort and plenty, while half of the human race lives on less than $2 a day, is neither just nor stable. Including all of the world's poor in an expanding circle of development—and opportunity—is a moral imperative and one of the top priorities of U.S. international policy." President Bush's full text, released on September 20, 2002, was published by the *New York Times* at http://www.nytimes.com/2002/09/20/politics/20STEXT_FULL.html. (A free membership in nytimes.com is necessary to view this URL.)

63. See, for example, Constantin von Barloewen, "La culture, facteur de la *Realpolitik*," *Le Monde diplomatique*, November 2001, 22–23.

64. Janet Wasko, "The Magical-Market World of Disney," *Monthly Review* 52, April 2001, 71.

65. Seth Mydans, "Thais with a Different Look, Flaunt Your Genes," *New York Times*, 29 August 2002. Norimitsu Onishi, "Globalization of Beauty Makes Slimness Trendy," *New York Times*, 3 October 2002; Elaine Sciolino, "Iran's Well-Covered Women Remodel a Part that Shows," *New York Times*, 22 September 2000.

66. Edward Rothstein, "Damning (Yet Desiring) Mickey and the Big Mac," *New York Times*, 3 March 2002.

67. Antonio Negri and Michael Hardt, *Empire* (Cambridge, Mass.: Harvard University Press, 2000). Page references in the text are from this edition.

68. Edward Said, *Culture and Imperialism* (New York: Random House, 1994);

quoted in John Mowitt, "In the Wake of Eurocentrism," *Cultural Critique* 47 (winter 2001): 4.

69. See Mowitt's whole essay, "In the Wake of Eurocentrism," 3–15. George Yúdice made a similar observation in "We Are *Not* the World," *Social Text* nos. 31–32 (1992): 202–16.

70. Immanuel Wallerstein, "Eurocentrism and Its Avatars: The Dilemmas of Social Science," *New Left Review*, no. 226 (November–December 1997): 93–107. A view is emerging that Europe had no monopoly on modernity and that to claim otherwise is to be Eurocentric. Thus, in an attempt to rehabilitate or vindicate the "other," modernity has been extricated from the cultural and economic matrices that enabled it in the first place. To say that any country could have reached capitalism on its own is to suggest that capitalism is a benign economic system, not one unavoidably founded on genocidal violence.

71. Eric Wolf, *Europe and the People without History* (Berkeley: University of California Press, 1982).

72. More than decade ago, Ali Mazrui made this observation in *Cultural Forces in World Politics* (Portsmouth, N.H.: Heinemann, 1990).

73. In *The Holy Family* (1845), Marx explained: "The *slavery of civil society* is *in appearance* the greatest *freedom* because it is in appearance the fully developed *independence* of the individual, who considers as his *own* freedom the uncurbed movement, no longer bound by a common bond or by man, of the estranged elements of his life, such as property, industry, religion, etc., whereas actually this is his fully developed slavery and inhumanity." Quoted in Richard N. Hunt, *Political Ideas of Marx and Engels*, vol. 2, *Classical Marxism, 1850–1895* (Pittsburgh: University of Pittsburgh Press, 1984), 165.

74. Hardt and Negri, *Empire*, xv, 9, 15, 24, 36.

75. Ibid., 45, 65, 66.

76. Here the authors seem to recognize how difficult it is for Western progressives not to be Eurocentric by reminding us that even Las Casas and Marx were unavoidably Eurocentric (116–20).

77. Ibid., 73, 74–78, 85, 86, 88–89, 102–3, 106–9, 112–13, 134–36.

78. Ibid., 145.

79. Many have argued that the Zapatista rebellion in Chiapas is the first truly postmodern revolution.

80. Hardt and Negri, *Empire*, 149, 196.

81. Ibid., 200–1. A similar point was made by Eric Wolf in *Europe and the People without History*, 383.

82. This argument is followed by a long, sprawling part that includes an entire section of the United States Constitution and the four major phases of U.S. constitutional history (160–82) and that concludes with the portraits of two fictional antiheroes: Melville's Bartleby and J. M. Coetzee's Micahel K. as prototypes of the "politics of refusal," each being a homo tantum ("mere man and nothing more"). This humanism of refusal, this homo tantum, however, needs to move toward the

enriching homo homo eclipsed in the long (and bloody) centuries of modernity's crisis (203–4).

83. Ibid., 210–12.

84. Ibid., 221–39, 240–59, 307, 329–32, 335, 350.

85. The trauma caused by such crossings never seems to cross the authors' minds. These crossings are somehow stripped of the powerful pain and loss of life endured by workers and illegal aliens, who never inhabit their new positions elsewhere the same way postcolonial intellectuals do.

86. Ibid., 356–64, 385–86, 389–92.

87. Ibid., 396, 400, 402–3.

88. See Hobsbawm, *The Age of Revolution*; Susan Dunn, *Sister Revolutions: French Lightning, American Light* (New York: Faber and Faber, 1999). As indicated in Chapter 1, Dunn's study shows that the American Revolution was first celebrated in glowing terms before it gradually lost its luster. Hobsbawm totally dismisses the American Revolution and pays more attention to the "dual revolution" (industrial in Britain and political in France, both bourgeois). Howard Zinn sees the United States Constitution as a document that serves the interests of the rich and also of the petty bourgeoisie, since the latter provides the "broad base of support" that acts as a buffer "against the blacks, Indians, [and] the very poor whites." These bourgeois and farmers "enable the elite to keep control with a minimum of coercion, a maximum of law—all made palatable by the fanfare of patriotism and unity." Howard Zinn, *A People's History of the United States* (1980; New York: HarperPerennial, 1990), 98–99.

89. Comment on an exchange in *Dissent*.

90. Bobby Sayyid, *A Fundamental Fear: Eurocentrism and the Emergence of Islamism* (London: Zed, 1996).

91. Ibid., 8, 13, 14, 17.

92. Ibid., 40, 41, 42, 45.

93. Ibid., 57, 70, 86, 73, 77.

94. Ibid., 100, 103.

95. Ibid., 114.

96. Ibid., 128, 129, 150–51.

97. See her aptly titled *Enemy in the Mirror: Islamic Fundamentalism and the Limits of Modern Rationalism* (Princeton: Princeton University Press, 1999).

98. By 2003, Sayyid Qutb was described by scholars looking for the cultural roots of Islamic terrorism as al-Qa'eda's philosopher. See Paul Berman, "The Philosopher of Terror," *New York Times Magazine*, 23 March 2003, 24–29, 56, 59, 65–69.

99. Ibid., 121–22.

100. Quoted in ibid., 145.

101. Ibid., 152.

102. Margalit and Buruma, "Occidentalism." The authors conclude in their essay—in which they show that fascist, anti-Western movements are motivated by a deep contempt for the soulless, opportunistic, unheroic bourgeois—that anti-Westernism is not necessarily a religious or even Islamic phenomenon. Of course, "Occidentalism" demonizes these "isms" without seeing them as grotesque (but

natural) outgrowths of the system against which they wage holy war. Occidentalism, or anti-Westernism, naturally implies a unified Western civilization that ex-
ists only at the level of political rhetoric. Even after 9/11, U.S. periodicals occasionally reported incidents of anti-Americanism in Europe, both in France and
elsewhere. Salman Rushdie wrote in an Op-Ed piece for the *New York Times* (4
February 2002) describing the extent of anti-Americanism in Europe, even in
Britain, and urging the United States to work in consensus with its European al-
lies. Readers wrote back to the editor (10 February 2002) confirming their experiences with anti-Americanism and thus, unwittingly, undermining the existence of
a vast cultural unity called the "West." By 2003, on the eve of the U.S. attack on
Iraq, what many call "anti-Americanism" grew into such a global crescendo that
seasoned U.S. diplomats publicly resigned from office to protest their own government's policies.

103. Sophie Bessis, *L' Occident et les autres: Histoire d'une suprématie* (Paris:
Éditions La Découverte, 2001). Page references in the text are from this edition.

104. Ibid., 7.

105. Ibid., 41, 42, 52.

106. Ibid., 59–62, 63–69.

107. Ibid., 69–77, 80–81.

108. Ibid., 86.

109. Ibid., 88–89, 107, 108–9.

110. Ibid., 113–20.

111. Ibid., 126–27, 129, 131.

112. Ibid., 205, 211–21, 213, 222–32.

113. Ibid., 136–46, 158.

114. Ibid., 163, 159–75.

115. See Pierre Vermeren, *Le Maroc en transition* (Paris: La Découverte, 2001).

116. Bessis, *L' Occident et les autres,* 182–94.

117. Ibid., 237, 258.

118. Ibid., 262, 263, 267, 269.

119. By 2002, Moroccan Jews in Israel were still feeling that life in Morocco is
better. See Leslie Susser, "Israel: But What's the Cure?" *Jerusalem Report.com,* 18
November 2002.

120. Bessis, 272–74, 281–87.

121. Ibid., 295–307.

122. Ibid., 331–32, 329.

123. Thomas Lemahieu. "Nord-Sud: les inégalités explosives." Interview with
Sophie Bessis. *L'Humanité,* 14 September 2001.

124. Peter McLaren, *Revolutionary Multiculturalism: Pedagogies of Dissent for
the New Millennium* (Boulder, Colo.: Westview, 1997), 47, 68, 286–87.

CHAPTER 6

1. Stephen Toulmin, *Cosmopolis: The Hidden Agenda of Modernity* (New York:
The Free Press, 1990).

2. Ibid., 28, 41.

3. Fernand Braudel, *A History of Civilizations* (New York: Penguin, 1983),
327–28.

4. Toumlin, *Cosmopolis*, 77.

5. Ibid., 117.

6. See chap. 3 in ibid.

7. Max Horkheimer and Theodor W. Adorno, *Dialectic of Enlightenment*, trans. John Cumming (1944 in German; New York: Continuum, 2001).

8. Ibid., xi, xiii, xv, 3, 7, 13, 16, 25, 84, 91, 154–55, 166–68.

9. Isaiah Berlin, "Notes on Prejudice," *New York Review of Books*, 18 October 2001, 12.

10. John Gray, *False Dawn: The Delusions of Global Capitalism* (New York: The New Press, 1998). Terry Eagleton, "Humanity and Other Animals," review of *Straw Dogs*, by John Gray, *Guardian*, 7 September 2002. About a week later, Jason Cowley reviewed the same book in the *Observer* and was much more enthusiastic about it. Jason Cowley, "Life Is Meaningless. And Yet ... ," *Observer*, 15 September 2002.

11. Gray, *False Dawn*, 1, 2, 17, 117–18.

12. Ibid., 20.

13. Ibid., 36, 37, 38.

14. Ibid., 104, 105, 111, 129.

15. Charles A. Kupchan, "The End of the West," *Atlantic*, November 2002, 42–44. Several polls taken during this period confirmed the growing gap in sensibilities between Europeans and Americans.

16. Gray, *False Dawn*, 132, 163–65, 203.

17. V. I. Lenin, *Imperialism: The Highest Stage of Capitalism* (New York: International Publishers, 1939). Lenin shows again and again that capitalism inevitably leads to the conditions that Gray bemoans.

18. John Tomlinson, *Globalization and Culture* (Chicago: The University of Chicago Press, 1999), 2, 3.

19. Ibid., 9, 11–12. On how the West has been deterritorialized, see Serge Latouche, *L'Occidentalisation du monde: Essai sur la signification, la portée et les limites de l'uniformisation planétaire* (Paris: Éditions La Découverte, 1989).

20. Tomlinson, *Globalization and Culture*, 58–60, 30.

21. Ibid., 75, 85, 95.

22. Ibid., 106, 108–13, 120–28, 134, 138–41, 149, 180. For more on the concept on non-places, see Marc Augé, *Non-Places: Introduction to the Anthropology of Supermodernity*, trans. John Howe (London: Verso, 1995).

23. Ibid., 194–95.

24. Ibid., 196, 198–99, 200, 206.

25. Terry Eagleton, *The Idea of Culture* (Oxford: Blackwell, 2000).

26. Ibid., 9, 11, 12, 17.

27. Ibid., 22, 23, 24, 62, 68.

28. Ibid., 81

29. Ibid., 70–74.

30. Ibid., 111.

31. Slavoj Žižek, *The Fragile Absolute, or Why Is the Christian Legacy Worth Fighting For?* (New York: Verso, 2000).

32. Eagleton is also critical of the postcolonial mantras of hybridity.

33. Ibid., 2, 11–15, 19–20, 25.

34. Ibid., 128, 129–30, 148, 158, 159.

35. John Gray, *The Two Faces of Liberalism* (New York: New Press, 2000). I think of John Gray as this era's Las Casas, a scholar who once inspired the Thatcherite political economy but who has since come to see the dangers of laissez-faire capitalism, particularly its Anglo-American variety.

36. Ibid., 1, 4, 20–21, 33, 34, 65.

37. Quoted in Gray, *The Two Faces of Liberalism*, 82.

38. Ibid., 107, 122, 137.

39. Stanley Fish, "Postmodern Warfare," *Harper's*, July 2002, 33–40. Daniel Pipes, in a different context, and speaking from a very different position, made a similar point by arguing that the attempt to whitewash the concept of "jihad" in liberal academic circles takes away from the historicity and real meaning of the term. See his "Jihad and the Professors," *Commentary* (November 2002): 17–21.

40. Keith Windschuttle, "The Ethnocentrism of Clifford Geertz," *New Criterion*, October 2002, 5–12.

41. Douglass Rushkoff, "Don't Judge Judaism by the Numbers," *New York Times*, 20 November 2002. By November 30, the long-awaited and by now controversial report on the number of Jews in the United States was still not being released. See *New York Times*, "Delay of Report on U.S. Jews Touches Off Fight," *New York Times*, 30 November 2002.

42. Salman Rushdie, "No More Fanaticism as Usual," *New York Times*, 27 November 2002; Thomas L. Friedman, "Defusing the Holy Bomb," *New York Times*, 27 November 2002.

43. See *Against Islamic Extremism: The Writings of Muhammad Sa'id al-'Ashmawy*, ed. Carloyn Flueher-Lobban (Gainesville: University Press of Florida, 1998).

44. Ibid., 37, 55.   46. Ibid., 55–66.

45. Ibid., 18, 51–57.   47. Ibid., 68–69, 71, 73–78.

48. Ibid., 72, 78, 6. In an interview, Khaled Abou El Fadl, a professor of law at UCLA, reiterated al-'Ashmawy's claim that the Qur'an contains very few legal injunctions to serve as a thorough guide for an Islamic law. "The Koran is not a detailed code of law," wrote El Fadl. Actually, "it has very little law compared to the Old Testament" and mostly limits itself to "very general moral exhortations that would not qualify as a code of law by any stretch of the imagination." See Abou El Fadl, "A Dissident's Look at Islam and the Muslim World," *Chronicle of Higher Education*, 4 October 2002, B17

49. *Against Islamic Extremism*, 79, 90.

50. Ibid., 86, 127, 123.

51. Marshall G. S. Hodgson, *The Venture of Islam: Conscience and History in a World Civilization*, vol. 3, *The Gunpowder Empires and Modern Times* (Chicago: University of Chicago Press, 1974), 384.

52. Noreena Hertz, *The Silent Takeover: Global Capitalism and the Death of Democracy* (New York: The Free Press, 2001), 199, 12. For a good article on the effect of what the billionaire trader George Soros called "market fundamentalism," see William Finnegan, "The Economics of Empire," *Harper's*, May 2003, 41–54.

53. See Bruce Lawrence, *Shattering the Myth: Islam Beyond Violence* (Princeton, N.J.: Princeton University Press, 1998).

54. Ibid., 3, 35, 38, 25, 49. Avishai Margalit, "The Wrong War," *New York Review of Books*, 13 February 2003, 5.

55. Ibid., 18.

56. On Iran and Malaysia, see Lawrence, *Shattering the Myth*, 100–101, 160–71. Lawrence sheds an interesting light on the power struggles taking place in Iran. There, both the elected *majlis* (parliament) and the appointed Council of Guardians are members of the middle class and represent three factions within that class, with the conservative council more inclined to protect capitalist interests than the radical or even centrist-pragmatist faction. In Malaysia, meanwhile, Mahathir's widely discussed "Vision 2020," supported by the Institute of Islamic Understanding Malaysia or IKIM, seeks to find a synthesis between Islam and corporate culture.

57. Saeed Razavi-Faqih and Ian Urbina, "The Fight for Iran's Democratic Ideals," *New York Times*, 10 December 2002; Susan Sachs, "Cleric Calls for Pluralistic Government in Iraq," *New York Times*, 25 May 2003; Neil MacFarquhar and Richard A. Oppel, Jr., "Car Bomb in Iraq Kills 95 at Shiite Mosque," *New York Times*, 30 August 2003.

58. Thomas L. Friedman, "Defusing the Holy Bomb,"; "9/11 Lesson Plan," *New York Times*, 4 September 2002.

59. Paul Krugman, "For Richer," *New York Times Magazine*, 20 October 2002.

60. Frank Bruni, "Perilous Immigrant Crossings Frustrate Italy," *New York Times*, 3 December 2002.

61. Susan Dunn, *Sister Revolutions: French Lightning, American Light* (New York: Faber and Faber, 1999), 159–61, 198–99, 201–202, 208; Kevin Phillips, *Wealth and Democracy: A Political History of the American Rich* (New York: Broadway Books, 2002), 417–22.

62. José Saramago, "De la justice à la démocratie, en passant par les cloches," *Le Monde diplomatique*, March 2002, 3.

63. Claudia Dreifus, "Adjusting Attitudes on Energy to Keep Our Favorite Things," *New York Times*, 20 August 2002.

64. Brennan, *Globalization and its Terrors*, 154–68.

65. See Warren Hoge, "Archbishop of Canterbury Enthroned," *New York Times*, 28 March 2003.

66. Hertz, *The Silent Takeover*, 116, 124, 143.

67. David Bollier, "Reclaiming the Commons," *Boston Review* 27 (summer 2002): 4–11.

68. See Frank Bruni, ""Bidding Emotional Goodbye, Pope Ends Visit to His Past," *New York Times*, 20 August 2002.

69. For the text of Mbeki's full speech, see http://www.un.org/events/wssd/statements/openingsaE.htm.

70. Von Laue, *The Global Revolution of Westernization*, 366.

71. Hodgson, *The Venture of Islam*, 3: 433–38.

72. Quoted in John C. Mohawk, *Utopian Legacies: A History of Conquest and Oppression in the Western World* (Santa Fe, N. Mex.: Clear Lights Publishers, 2000), 9.

73. Ibid., 264–66.

74. Quoted in ibid., 40–41.

75. Lawrence, *Shattering the Myth*, 175–78, 183–84.

76. See Roger Lesgards, "Résister par la création culturelle," *Le Monde diplomatique*, 28 December 2001; Constantin von Barloewen, "La culture, facteur de la *Realpolitik*," *Le Monde diplomatique*, November 2001, 22–23; Jacques Robin, "Cette grande implosion de l'an 2002," *Le Monde diplomatque*, March 2002, 26.

77. Jean Baudrillard, "La violence de la mondialisation," *Le Monde diplomatique*, November 2002, 18–19.

78. Alain Finkielkraut, *In the Name of Humanity: Reflections on the Twentieth Century*, trans. Judith Friedlander (New York: Columbia University Press, 2000), 66, 105.

79. Geoffrey H. Hartman, *The Fateful Question of Culture* (New York: Columbia University Press, 1997), 180.

80. Jean Améry, *Par-delà le crime et le châtiment: Eassais pour surmonter l'insurmontable* (Paris: Actes Sud, 1995), 88; quoted in Finkielkraut, *In the Name of Humanity*, 103.

81. Vine Deloria, Jr., *Custer Died for Your Sins: An Indian Manifesto* (1969; Norman: University of Oklahoma Press, 1988), 27, 179, 188, 178, 185, 224,195; Jonathan Sacks, *The Dignity of Difference: How to Avoid the Clash of Civilizations* (New York: Continuum, 2002), 189.

82. Taiaiake Alfred, *Peace, Power, Righteousness: An Indigenous Manifesto* (New York: Oxford University Press, 1999). I am grateful to Steven Salaita for bringing this book to my attention.

83. Braudel, *A History of Civilizations*, 23.

84. In a lyrical defense of the Sabbath, Judith Shulevitz, a columnist for the *New York Times Book Review*, explains that among the personal and social benefits of the Sabbath is that it "provides two things essential to anyone who wishes to lift himself out of the banality of mercantile culture: time to contemplate and distance from everyday demands." Judith Shulevitz, "Bring Back the Sabbath," *New York Times Magazine*, 2 March 2003, 50–53.

85. Sacks, *The Dignity of Difference*, 21, 201–2, 175, 60, 51, 65, 58–59, 117–18, 167–68, 11, 17, chap. 8, 205–6, 2–3, 83–84.

86. Ibid., 5.

87. Zygmunt Bauman, "Global Solidarity," *Tikkun*, January–February 2002, 12–13.

88. Anthony Giddens, *Runaway World: How Globalization is Reshaping Our Lives* (New York: Routledge, 2000).

Index